THE NEW HELOTS

Research in Ethnic Relations Series

The aim of this series is to publish books based on research carried out at the Centre for Research in Ethnic Relations, University of Warwick. It will also publish works from external authors, and the editor welcomes manuscripts from other writers and researchers working in the field of race and ethnic relations. The main emphasis of the series will be on books based on original research, although theoretical and policy discussions will also be included when they provide a practical understanding of issues of social and political relevance for students of race and ethnic relations and for those implementing equal opportunity and anti-racist policies.

Editor: Dr John Wrench
Senior Research Fellow
Centre for Research in Ethnic Relations

The New Helots

Migrants in the International Division of Labour

ROBIN COHEN

Gower

First published in paperback in 1988 by
Gower Publishing Company Limited
Gower House
Croft Road
Aldershot
Hants GU11 3HR
England

Gower Publishing Company
Old Post Road
Brookfield
Vermont 05036
USA

British Library Cataloguing in Publication Data
Cohen, Robin
    The new helots: migrants in the
    international division of labour
    1.Migrant labour
    1.Title
    305.5′62   HD 5855

    ISBN 0 566 05720 4
    ISBN 0 566 00932 3 (Hbk)

Printed and bound in Great Britain by
Biddles Ltd., Guildford and King's Lynn

For Miranda and Jason

Sparta was surrounded by a number of surviving non-Dorian communities, which she gradually incorporated or reduced to something approaching servile status, so providing herself with a valuable, but potentially dangerous subject population, the so-called Helots, which she could exploit but which she had to protect herself against

(Forrest 1966: 127)

Contents

List of tables and figures

Tables

Figures

x

Acknowledgements

I have incurred an unusual number of debts in the writing of this book. The inclusion of data on the Caribbean and Mexico was only made possible by the support of the foreign area fellowship programme, administered by St Antony's, Oxford and the grant of study leave by the University of the West Indies. Small grants were also received from the British Academy, the Dame Lillian Penson Fund and the Sir Ernest Cassel Educational Trust.

My colleagues and students in Trinidad opened up my eyes to the Caribbean region; the Zapata family provided hospitality in Mexico; my students in the sociology of migration course at Warwick helped me to omit otiose detail, hopefully thereby making this book an easier read for students. Sections of the book also represent an opening salvo of some further research to be conducted at the Centre for Research in Ethnic Relations. Attachment to the Centre allowed me more writing time than I otherwise would have found.

I would also like to thank staunch friends who have reawakened an interest in international labour issues. These include: Clive Harris in Birmingham, Peter Gutkind and Rosalind Boyd in Montreal, Jeff Henderson in Hong Kong, Peter Waterman and Ken Post in the Hague, Hoby Spalding in New York, Ronnie Munck in Ulster, Roger Southall in

Ottawa and my co-editors on the *Review of African Political Economy*. As to the manuscript itself, John Mattausch provided incisive comments, while Lynda Hemsley did a neat repair job to my ragged typing. As in the past, my heartfelt gratitude goes to Selina Cohen who helped with background research for Chapters 2 and 4 and who has sustained the spirit by her companionship and humour.

A note on usage

Labour, labour-power, labourers

Though it has not proved possible to be absolutely consistent throughout the text, I have normally found it useful not to conflate the term 'labour' with 'labour-power'. 'Labour-power' signifies the *capacity* to work for a given time, a given remuneration at a particular level of output and skill. It is this commodity that the employer buys. In general, the word 'labour' has been used in two senses. The first as an abstract category—as in labour versus capital. The second as a collective noun, where qualified by an adjective. Thus by 'unfree labour' I mean a number of unfree labourers; 'migrant labour' denotes migrant labourers, etc. However, when quoting or summarising the views of conventional economists, 'labour' is sometimes used in the sense of 'labour-power'. The usage of 'labour market' (the market for labour-power) and 'labour supply' (the supply of labourers) has also been retained.

1 Unfree labourers and modern migrants

In fact the veiled slavery of the wage earners in Europe needed the unqualified slavery of the New World as its pedestal.

(Marx 1976: 925)

It is only with considerable difficulty that a wage labourer can be described as 'free'. Free to clock in, free to accept the foreman's orders, free to work a 40-hour week, free to take only a short annual holiday, free to work overtime? It's an odd kind of freedom and one that recalls Anatole France's oft-quoted remark that rich and poor are equally forbidden to sleep under bridges, beg in the streets or steal bread. In fact, the very concept of 'labour' evokes compulsion. As Womack (1979: 739) has pointed out, for about 2500 years Western cultures distinguished between 'labour' and 'work'. The Greeks separated *ponein* from *ergazesthai*, the Romans distinguished *laborare* from *facere*, the Germans contrasted *arbeiten* with *werken*, and so on. In every European language, he writes: 'labour meant pain, effort, pangs, penalty, strain, drudgery, struggle, battle, suffering, grief, distress, poverty, loneliness, abandonment, ordeal, adversity, trouble. Work meant making, building, providing, causing, accomplishment, completion, satisfaction.' The secular distinction was paralleled by a religious viewpoint. For the Benedictines, 'labour' was not seen as noble or rewarding, but as a penance designed to avoid the spiritual dangers of idleness.

To understand the concept of a free labourer under capitalism, it is necessary to start with Marx's central idea that the working class forms itself as the agricultural pro-

1

ducer, the peasant, becomes detached from the soil. In these moments, 'great masses of men are suddenly and forcibly torn from their means of subsistence, and hurled on to the labour-market as free, unprotected and rightless proletarians' (Marx 1976: 876). In earlier translations the expression *vogelfrei* was rendered as 'unattached', rather than 'rightless', which perhaps better captures Marx's meaning. For him, the freedom of wage labourers comprises two elements. First, labourers are no longer part of the means of production themselves, as would be the case with a slave or a serf; they are, therefore, free of any direct proprietorial rights exercised over them. Second, they no longer own their own means of production (and subsistence) and therefore are unencumbered by their own tools or land; they are free, but of necessity required, to sell their remaining possession, their labour-power, in the market.

In his formulation, Marx indubitably captures the central aspect of the transition from European feudalism to capitalism, the first major reorganisation of the division of labour for hundreds of years. But what is far more uncertain is whether it is part of the intrinsic and necessary definition of a capitalist mode of production that it relies exclusively on free wage labourers (in the senses Marx indicated). In general, Marx *does* hold this view and it is one that I shall seek to contest—advancing indeed a contrary thesis that capitalism has always survived and even thrived, by deploying substantial numbers of unfree or semi-free labourers. This mixture of workers of different statuses is sometimes concealed by a national definition of the boundaries of the political economy (ignoring, therefore, imperialist relations), or is sometimes all too evident, as when quasi-free workers from the countryside or peripheral zones of the political economy are driven or sucked into the vortex of capitalist production.

But before elaborating this thesis—one that underpins the book as a whole—it should at least be said that Marx, on at least three occasions, does show cognisance of the important relationship between free and unfree forms of labour. The first is in the quote that opens this chapter, a marvellously succinct summary of a more general proposition. Unfortunately, it is clear that Marx (1976: 925, 928) intends us to

2

nderstand the pedestal of New World slavery supporting
ee European labour as part of what he later calls 'the pre-
istory of capital'. Second, Marx raises the interesting
xample of the late 15th-century Italian case of deproletarian-
sation when a slump in northern Italy's commercial
uperiority sent workers scuttling back to the countryside,
hus giving 'a previously unheard of impulse to small-scale
ultivation'. This example follows a comment which decisi-
ely sets the empirical limits to Marx's description (1976:
76) of the history of the expropriation of the peasantry, for
only in England, which is therefore taken as the example, has
the classic form' [italic added]. Finally, Marx (1976:
94–802) indirectly indicates a relationship between free and
nfree forms of labour when he looks at what he terms the
oating, stagnant and latent sections of the relative surplus
opulation. But these concepts are more properly considered
s a contribution to a theory of migration and, as such, will
e discussed in Chapter 2.

Even if there are hints of my counter proposition in
Marx's references to New World slavery and in his limiting
eference to the classical case of England (1976: 452), Marx
atly and unequivocally states that 'the capitalist form
resupposes from the outset the free wage-labourer who
ells his labour-power to capital'. By contrast, I seek to
demonstrate that capitalism has historically coexisted with a
ombination of labour regimes. I propose to do so by citing
xamples from a wide range of countries and periods—an
xercise that is more than random, but less than comprehen-
ive: 'less than' because I seek to illustrate my argument,
ather than write a complete history of capitalist labour
egimes. The history of unfree labour, of course, pre-dates
apitalism—and many early societies operated through a
ombination of compelled and free labour. For example,
Finley's powerful writings (1980; 1981) on Ancient Greece
rovide ample documentation of the mix of slave and free
abourers and the intermediate forms of dependent labour
etween the two polarities. The title of this book itself
vokes the case of Sparta's use of a subject people for
gricultural work. Bearing in mind the helots and slaves, if
women are also excluded (they didn't count as citizens),

3

Hegel's observation that the Greeks only knew that some men were free, is even more powerfully understood nowadays than he intended. A number of other pre-capitalist societies deployed vast armies of compelled labourers to erect the pyramids, religious monuments, irrigation systems and public works—from China, Burma, Mexico, Peru, Egypt, Mesopotamia, Persia to Rome, workers were coerced by military force and closely supervised by taskmasters.

Imported plantation workers

But, despite these intriguing examples from which no doubt some continuities can be established, my primary examples must begin as European capitalism expanded into what Wallerstein (1974) calls 'the modern world system' during the late 15th and early 16th centuries. The first and most obvious discontinuity is that slavery in the modern period was set in a wholly different context from classical slavery. Vast numbers were commercially trans-shipped from the labour reserve of western Africa as European supplies decreased and as the indigenous populations of the New World declined under the impact of European diseases, from food shortages triggered by depredations of imported animals, or as a result of being worked to death. The figures of population decline are every bit as staggering as the number of slaves shipped. In New Spain (Mexico), the population fell from 11 million in 1519 to about 1.5 million in about 1650. Similar steep falls are recorded for Brazil and Peru (Wallerstein 1974: 88, 89). The different context of New World slavery integrated the phenomenon into a capitalist world economy in a number of concrete ways. The slave was a commodity—a unit of labour-power—*par excellence*: the only concern for a slave's welfare was whether handling or shipping conditions affected the price received. From being a family retainer, a domestic servant, or a small farm labourer often working alongside their masters, most New World slaves became field hands working on large plantations, normally under the supervision of an overseer. Next, the product (sugar, coffee, tobacco, etc.) was itself directly

4

integrated into the capitalist world market, and followed the rhythms of market demand, such as that established by the triangular trade between Europe, Africa and the Americas. In polemicising against the populariser of dependancy theory, A. G. Frank, Laclau (1971) has quite legitimately argued that integration into a world market is quite a different thing from capitalist 'relations of production'. So it is, but it is implausible to imagine that the first does not affect the second. The supervision of work tasks, the division of labour, the de-skilling of the labour force, the production rhythms (all that is now called 'the labour process') together with the overtly capitalist relations of production in the processing plants (the sugar mills, rum distilleries, cotton ginneries, etc.) all show the influence of the world market on the forms and relations of plantation production (see Fraginals 1976). If these relations are not capitalist, they are a passable fair imitation thereof. But where, Laclau would object, is the wage? Even here, the formal appearance of slavery concealed a 'hidden wage'. Payments 'in kind' were often in commodities that could be traded, or were, like tobacco, used directly as currency. Paternalist favouritism and sources of income and subsistence from provision plots, were both ways for the plantation owner to subsidise his reproduction costs *and* a means of accumulating some modest savings by plantation workers. The hiring of slave workers for cash has also been reported (Fraginals 1976: 131–53). Had such possibilities for acquiring income not existed, it is impossible to otherwise explain why so many slaves were able to purchase their freedom when that became legally possible, or why 'freedmen' constituted from 30 per cent of the total population in pre-emancipation slave societies like Curacão, Minas Gerais (Brazil) or Puerto Rico (Cohen and Greene 1972: 4).

Those who hold that slavery in the New World constituted a separate mode of production, also take no account of the real (as opposed to formal) boundaries of the contemporary political economy. Instead, anachronistic notions of geographical and political sovereignty are projected back to a period when such national distinctions did not exist. This point will be returned to later in the text, when the concept

5

of a 'regional political economy' is developed, but the argument is best made in the 19th century by John Stuart Mill:

> [Our West Indian colonies] are hardly to be looked upon as countries carrying on an exchange of commodities with other countries, but more properly as outlying agricultural or manufacturing establishments belonging to a larger community . . . If Manchester, instead of being where it is, were on a rock in the North Sea (its present industry nonetheless continuing); it would still be but a town of England, not a country trading with England; it would be merely, as now, a place where England finds it convenient to carry on her cotton manufacture. The West Indies, in like manner, are the places where England finds it convenient to carry on the production of sugar, coffee and a few tropical commodities. (Cited in Fraser 1981: 320.)

This idea of a 'class of trading and exporting communities' (as Mill called them) firmly integrated into a central economy can give rise to the situation where different forms of labour regime can coexist within this larger unit. As Wallerstein (1974: 127) has it, 'Free labour is the form of labour control used for skilled work in core countries, whereas coerced labour is used for less skilled work in peripheral areas. The combination thereof is the essence of capitalism.' This comment can stand as a useful tendential statement, though I would argue that the geographical demarcations suggested by Wallerstein are too rigid to encompass the variety of labour forms in the central and outer zones of a regional political economy alike. Wallerstein's argument also takes little account of the more detailed controversy started by Nieboer (1910) at the turn of the century as to whether the introduction of slavery as an industrial system (as Nieboer terms it) is a variant pattern related to land scarcity, or whether, as Kloosterboer (1960) argues, such a labour regime can be explained by more general factors.

Whatever the specific causes for utilising slave labourers in particular areas, the general point is clear. If capitalism is compatible with slavery, why not with other forms of coerced or involuntary labour? These can range as widely as *repartimiento* or *cuatequil* labour (Mexico), *mita* (Peru), serfdom, debt bondage, apprentice labour, child labour, indentured or contract labour, penal labour, various forms of domestic service, *chibaro* mine labour (Southern Rhodesia), 'political' labour (British colonies), concentration-camp labour, 'corrective labour' and so on. To provide a detailed account of all these different forms of labour control would be superfluous, but I would like to comment on a number of these variants, both to show some sense of how the international division of labour evolved and to indicate the senses in which post-war international migrant labour can be seen as exhibiting some characteristics associated with earlier generations of unfree labourers.

The plantation economies of the New World and of other colonial areas provide a rich source of labour regimes. With the abolition of slavery (1834 in most British colonies, 1863 in the Netherlands' colonies, 1865 in the southern United States), most plantation societies operated a system of 'apprentice' labour. Normally, only children under six were completely free. The rest of the former slaves were compelled to work without payment (except for those forms of 'hidden wage' indicated earlier) for four to six years. Their new status was distinguished from their former status by the fact that, while apprentices could not themselves be bought or sold, they could buy their own freedom and were compelled to work for a maximum of only 45 hours a week. In Antigua, the plantation owners instituted highly restrictive contracts, rather than an apprenticeship system. Absence for half a day or less was met with one day's wages docked. If the labourer was absent for two days in a row, or two days in any fourteen days, one week's imprisonment, with hard labour followed. For negligence of various kinds, imprisonment for up to three months was the legal consequence. Such was the rough class justice of the times, that a breach of contract by the employer only rendered him liable to a maximum fine of £5. Other forms of compulsion directed against apprentices and former slaves included a requirement that previously free shacks now had to be rented and the rent paid in labour-power. The movable shacks (chattels) still visible in Barbados today date from the period when former slaves tried to escape this obligation. Even more compelling were the comprehensive extensions of the vagrancy laws. In Jamaica

(1840), a vagrant became any man who migrated and left h
wife and children unprovided for. In Mauritius (1855), tl
Franco-Mauritian plantocracy exacted an even harsher del
nition. Any able-bodied woman or man under sixty unab
to prove that they followed a trade or possessed sufficie
means of subsistence was required to find employme
within a period fixed by the police. If the person defaulte
employment on public works was required. After a furth
three months, a defaulter could be sentenced to work on
plantation or in a factory for up to three years (Kloosterbo
1960: 3–16).

Such were the desperate measures deployed to keep fo
mer slaves dependent on the plantation owners. Th
received conventional historical account is that many
these measures were unsuccessful and that in all plantatio
economies, slaves fled to the towns in large numbers to evac
the brutality of plantation work. More recently, moder
West Indian historians have questioned the extent to which
'flight from the land' did indeed take place (Fraser 198
328–34; Green 1976; Mintz 1974; Adamson 1972). That th
experience is more general than in the West Indies, is
proposition that Cooper (1980: 1) advances in the introduc
tion to his authoritative study of plantation labour in Zanz
bar and coastal Kenya. He writes: 'In case after case,
particular class—under the hallowed ideals of private prop
erty—kept land from the eager hands of ex-slaves an
vigorously applied the instruments of the state and the law t
block ex-slaves' access to resources and markets, to restric
their ability to move about, bargain, or refuse wage labou
and to undermine their attempts to become independer
producers.' But whatever the difficulties former slaves had i
freeing themselves from their prior status in the post
emancipation period, the planters cried 'labour scarcity' lon
and loud.

All over the European tropical possessions, an appeal wen
out for more and more hands, another cohort of helots. Th
demand was strongest where 'sugar was king', but it was als
strongly heard where, as in the South African diamon
discoveries of 1870, new sources of mineral wealth wer
opened out for commercial exploitation. John X. Merrimar

8

Commissioner for Crown Lands in the Cape Colony, ote in 1876, with some asperity, of the pressure mounted farmers and mineowners to persuade the government to port foreign labour:

In the Cape, the government is called upon to survey mankind from China to Peru in the hope of creating and maintaining a class of cheap labourers who will thankfully accept the position of helots and not be troubled with the inconvenient ambition of bettering this condition. (Cited in Magubane 1979: 77, 78.)

In the event it was to Asia that the colonials, hungry for our-power turned. South Africa's experiment in using inese mine labourers ended in political recrimination in itain and South Africa and in a local strike (Richardson 76), but sugar plantations in Natal, British Guiana, Fiji, inidad, Ceylon, Malaya, Burma, Mauritius, and else- ere, successfully found agricultural labourers in India (for aterial on Natal see Meer 1980). Hugh Tinker's carefully cumented account of the indentures required of Indian ourers is a stunning indictment of what, quoting Lord hn Russell, he considers was a 'new system of slavery'. he period of indentured labour lasted from 1839 to 1920 d though figures are inexact, Tinker (1974: 115) estimates at in the 40 years before 1870 over a million Indian ourers went to tropical plantations, though the figure uld be as high as two million. The indentured workers aracteristically signed on for five years and were given in turn, a free passage, medical attention, housing and a odest wage. In many cases a free or subsidised passage ck to India was guaranteed after ten years. While a otector was often appointed to safeguard Indian interests, hat made this system close to slavery were the mortality tes on the ships (which, for example, averaged over 17 per nt on ships to the West Indies in 1856), the poor housing d health conditions, the miserable wages and, above all, e extensive use of penal sanctions (Tinker 1974: 116–235). one year (1892), over 40 per cent of the adult indentured pulation was convicted under the penal labour laws of Fiji. he ineffectiveness of the Protector was indicated by the fact at in the same year only one conviction of an employer was

9

obtained on a charge brought by his employees (Tink
1974: 194). Tinker (1974: 383) concludes his definiti
account with this statement:

> The Blacks on the West Indian plantations were known
> chattel slaves; the dictionary defines a chattel as a 'moveab
> possession', and such an ascription is also appropriate to tl
> condition of the Indian coolies, the successors to the chatt
> slaves. With the legal termination of slavery, there came no en
> to bondage upon the tropical plantations.

Colonial labour regimes

Where European powers had indigenous sources of labou
power unimpaired by 'pacification' or European disease
they tapped the local reservoir to feed the insatiable appetit
of the farmers, mine owners and industrialists, rather tha
importing labourers. As I have dealt mainly with Britis
colonies, provided here are four illustrations of the use c
local labour-power involving different colonial powers—th
French in Madagascar, the Belgians in the Congo, th
Portuguese in their African colonies and the Spanish i
Latin America.

When the French took over Madagascar in 1896, the
freed 500 000 slaves, but in December of that year pro
claimed a legal obligation to work. Interestingly enough,
special folder or card was issued to indicate which of th
various forms of compulsory labour a male aged 16 to 60 wa
engaged in. (Chapter 5 discusses the significance of the us
of internal or external passports.) Failure to produce such
card resulted in three to six months' imprisonment whil
after prison a further period of work on public works wa
prescribed, equal to three times the length of the priso
service. An outcry in France about the death rate on compul
sory labour and military projects led to the repeal of compul
sory labour (1900) and the setting aside of penal sanctions o
contract labourers. Yet, despite these attempts at libera
reform, Kloosterboer (1960: 107–12) convincingly demon
strates that the continuities between slavery, other forms c

10

unfree labour and the development of a modern labour market are still remarkably persistent.

It was only in 1946 that in their other colonies the French finally abolished conscript military labour and *prestation*, a labour 'tax' that permitted the administration to compel all adult males to work on public projects for a number of days each year (Echenberg 1975: 171–92). But enduring though these systems of compelled labour were, French overseas laws acted as some constraint—one that was notably absent in the areas like Oubangi-Shari where *concessionaires* were given free licence to levy labour-power. The most notorious example was not, however, in the French zones, but in the Congo where the Belgian King, Leopold, ran the area as if it were his private fiefdom. Millions of Congolese were compelled to collect rubber for the king who argued that the system could only be changed 'when the Negro has generally shaken off his idleness and becomes ready to work for the love of wages alone' (Davies 1966: 33–5). Any resistance proffered to the recruiters of labour-power was frequently met by brutal violence. The Congolese who died trying to resist habituation to the capitalist work ethic numbered in their millions. As one contemporary French journalist commented of the Congo at the time: 'We are tree fellers in a forest of human beings' (cited Nzula *et al.* 1979: 84). The *modus operandi* of the Congo Free State is best described in the words of E. D. Morel, one of the leading members of a contemporary liberal pressure group, the Congo Reform Movement:

> The aboriginal citizens of this strange creation [the Congo State] were by law called upon to provide recruits for the army, workmen for the construction of important public works, transport of stores, building up of houses and prisons, cutting and maintenance of roads and bridges, upkeep of plantations and creation and repairs of rest-houses . . . They were compelled to labour, *with no legal limitation either in regard to time or to quality*, in the collection, coagulation and transport of india rubber for the profit of their governors. (Cited in Louis and Stengers 1968: 44.)

Many of the areas marked out for agricultural production in the Portuguese colonies in Angola, Mozambique and in

11

the Portuguese possessions off the west coast of Africa, were also under the immediate control of leaseholders whose needs for labour-power were serviced by the Portuguese administrators. Failure to comply with the legal demand to fulfil a work contract in Angola (and from 1902) Mozambique, was met by expulsion to the islands of São Tomé and Príncipe. Round the turn of the century, these two small islands produced about one-fifth of the world's cocoa crop, a level of production that was only made possible by the import of about 4000 labourers each year from other parts of the Portuguese empire. The gruesome conditions on the two islands were exposed by the writings of Nevinson (1906) and Cadbury (1910) who likened the labour regime on the cocoa plantations to a system of 'modern slavery'. Under the impact of these and later exposes, the Salazar regime promulgated the 1928 *Código do Trabalho dos Indigenas nas Colónias Portugueses de Africa*, which boldly stated that:

> The Government of the Republic does not impose, nor does it permit that any form of obligatory or forced labour is demanded of the natives of its colonies for private ends, but it does insist that they fulfil the moral duty which necessarily falls on them of seeking through work the means of subsistence, thus contributing to the general interest of humanity. (Cited in Head 1980: 70.)

In a detailed study of the labour regime of the Sena Sugar Estates in Zambezia province, Mozambique, Head vividly documents how the provisions of the 1928 code were violated or twisted for the ends of the estates. Whenever Portugal was attacked in the international fora, the first rhetorical phrases were cited to deny that forced labour existed. But, on the ground, it was the second half of the code's preamble and the more detailed subsequent provisions, that ruled the lives of workers and peasants in the Portuguese territories. As Head (1980: 71) puts it:

> It was through enforcing the clauses of the law which established how Africans were to fulfil their duty to work that the Government made sure that forced labour, where voluntary labour was not available, continued to furnish the needs of private employers. Denials of forced labour practices notwith

12

standing, the whole thrust of the labour law and other laws which supplemented it, was to oblige men to take up regular wage work whether they wanted it or not.

Such was the bankrupt and underdeveloped nature of Portuguese colonial capitalism, that it is only a small exaggeration to suggest that the Administration barely had any other purpose but to act as a state-registered gang of labour-power recruiters supplying the needs of private sugar, copra, sisal and cocoa plantations, companies in the Portuguese possessions, and mineowners in Southern Rhodesia and South Africa. The desperate need for revenue propelled the Portuguese to negotiate a labour-supply contract for the South African mines, paid for in gold deposited in Lisbon. The number of labourers supplied was not to diminish significantly until 1976, when there was a fall in recruitment from 115 000 to 45 000 workers. The fluctuations in supply between 1890 and 1976 are to be explained not by sudden moral afflictions, but by competing demands from companies operating in Mozambique, nationalist pressures from white workers in South Africa, a changing of capital/labour ratio on the mines and finally, the initial success of FRELIMO, the national liberation movement in Mozambique, in seeking to reduce the export of labourers to the mines, even though their remittances constituted at the time of independence, some 35 per cent of all export earnings (First 1983).

The final colonial example I wish to mention, is the repartimiento system in Spanish America. Broadly speaking, this system followed the establishment of the ecomienda system prevalent during the first 50 years of Spanish rule. The encomendero was allotted from 30 to 300 'Indians' who had to fulfil work tasks allocated to them and/or deliver a share of their produce in exchange for the encomendero attending to what was defined as their material (housing, clothing, food) and spiritual (Catholicism) needs. As this system was to a large extent an attempt to recreate Castilian feudalism, strictly speaking it predates my concern with capitalist unfree labour systems. The repartimiento system was, however, firmly integrated into the capitalist mode of

13

production in that the state took direct control of the recruitment and supervision of labourers; wages were paid, and in addition to public works, *repartimiento* labour was assigned to the mines (and to a lesser extent the textile industry). Though the periods of work were theoretically limited to two weeks in Mexico and four months each year in Peru, work periods were frequently and arbitrarily lengthened. One report concerned a cohort of 7000 men, women and children, destined for the mines of Potosi. Such were the conditions of work and travel that only 2000 villagers returned to their homes (cited Kloosterboer 1960: 92). The *repartimiento* system collapsed with the movements of independence of the South American countries from the Spanish crown, but local capital, which now commanded the labour market, turned out to be no less exacting than the Spanish administration. As Kloosterboer (1960: 99) argues:

> *Repartimiento* and *mita* (Peru) were abolished but the Indian profited little. Debt bondage became the order of the day and persisted in spite of the fine sentiments expressed in the constitutions. Indeed there was a marked worsening in the position of the debt slaves. This can be mainly attributed to the fact that the place of the patriarchal Crown—which had at least tried to attain a certain degree of protection for the natives—was now taken by the *laissez-faire* ideas of the new era.

That this description is not exaggerated is testified by one commentator who estimated that by the beginning of this century one-third of the Mexican people, or 80 per cent of all agricultural labourers, were debt slaves (Turner 1911: 108, 110). *Laissez-faire* was a concept that applied to employers not workers. The bosses took care to combine low wages with high prices of essential commodities and tools, which then forced workers to pay off a lifelong (and even inherited) debt by their further work. In addition, the *obrajes* (textile mills and factories) were often locked shut, even on Sunday when the priest would be admitted to administer the sacrament. In an extensive collection of many articles, Mexican and North American labour historians have shown how Mexican capitalism combined under the same roof various forms of labour—black Caribbean slaves, indigenous slaves

14

naborias (indentured servants), contract labourers, penal labour, debt peons and free workers. The textile mills in Cojaocan, for example, employed side by side a mixture of free workers, slaves and prisoners who slept in the workshops and cleaned and carded the wool dressed only in singlets—to avoid the sweat, dirt and fleas that additional garments would attract. A contemporary observer could see nothing to distinguish free from unfree workers: 'Every workshop resembles a dark prison—all appear half naked, covered in rags, thin and deformed' (Frost *et al.* 1979: 211).

The cases of French Madagascar, the Belgian Congo, Portuguese Africa and Spanish America all share certain features in common. The colonial state (in the form of Leopold's company in the Congo) actively organised the local labour markets and set up extensive systems of involuntary labour, legitimised by religious, moral or legal arguments. The workers so compelled, sometimes coexisted with free workers at the points of production (as in Mexico). In other areas, involuntary labour in colonial capitalist states paralleled a simultaneous deployment of *predominantly* free labour systems in the metropolitan state. Although the anti-colonial movements after the Second World War were to challenge this definition, it was not a totally empty claim made by Portugal and France that what is now deemed their 'colonies' were overseas provinces and departments of a single polity, a unified international division of labour. The overseas areas were, to paraphrase Mill's comment on the West Indies (see p. 6), the places where it was found convenient to specialise in the production of tropical commodities. In the case of Portuguese Africa, one of the commodities produced (or, strictly, reproduced) was labour-power itself, which was sold as wage labour in regional labour markets in exchange for gold used in Lisbon to support the continuance of merchant and the beginnings of industrial, capitalism. Finally, I have indicated that unfree labour systems survived in the tropics well into the present century. Even when they were formally abandoned, other, more subtle, compelling factors ensured that many workers never fully escaped the proprietorial relationship capital commanded over labour. Nor, again, were most workers able to sell their labour-power freely, both in the sense that their bargaining power remained highly circumscribed (by their weak market situation and by extra economic coercion) and in the sense that their mobility was restricted (normally by political means).

Unfree labour in core zones

It has already been suggested that Wallerstein's argument that unfree labour is confined to peripheral zones, with free labour obtaining in core zones, can only be treated as a tendential statement. Where extractive, infrastructural (ports, railways, roads) and manufacturing capital was able to establish itself in colonial areas, a free wage labour force (again using Marx's definition) did emerge and even the beginnings of class formation, organisation and consciousness can be found (for examples, see Cohen *et al*. 1979). On the other hand, unfree labour is far more common in the history of metropolitan-based capital than Wallerstein would lead us to suppose. His description of a 'second serfdom' in eastern Europe during the 16th century, only fits the 'unfree periphery' model if it is accepted that the area was a peripheral zone at the time. The revival of serfdom in Eastern Europe has often been treated by other writers as a demonstration that the transition from feudalism to capitalism was far more prolonged and far more problematic than Marx supposed. Insofar as shortages of workers compelled large farmers to concede small holdings to their labour force, Kautsky, and others, saw the transformation of the peasantry as being considerably delayed—even though he believed Marx's analysis would ultimately be proved correct (Goodman and Redclift 1981: 9–10). While it is true that Wallerstein's 'trade-centred' approach often obscures questions of the relations of production, on this occasion his analysis is quite clearly 'productionist', not 'circulationist'. I concur with Wallerstein in not seeing the second serfdom as a delayed feudalism, largely because the system of 'coerced cash-crop labour' (as he calls it) involved a different set of relationships to that of feudalism. The state enforced a legal

16

process by which part of the period spent on a large domain was devoted to production for the world market. Moreover, quoting Stahl, Wallerstein (1974: 90–100) shows that the revival of feudal exactions on the peasantry served a wholly different purpose, namely providing the basis for the primitive accumulation of capital.

While Wallerstein's description of the relations of production in 16th-century Eastern Europe is correct, it is at least doubtful that the area can be described as a 'periphery'. Certainly, the same designation cannot be applied to the United States, let alone England, three centuries later. Yet as Moore (1966: 116) has shown, the whole edifice of plantation slavery in the southern United States and of the cotton crop, in particular, was both essential and totally compatible with the growth of manufacturing capitalism in the US and England:

> Though the importance of cotton for the South is familiar, its significance for capitalist development as a whole is less well known. Between 1815 and 1866 the cotton trade exercised a decisive influence upon the rate of growth in the American economy. Up until about 1830 it was the most important cause of the growth of manufacturing in this century . . . From 1840 to the time of the Civil War, Great Britain drew from the Southern states, four-fifths of all her cotton imports. Hence it is clear that the plantation operated by slavery was no anachronistic excrescence on industrial capitalism. It was an integral part of this system and one of its prime motors in the world at large.

As in the other areas surveyed above, the end of slavery did not produce a free labour force, but rather produced one that was tightly constrained by the need for workers to eat, or to comply with political and legal restrictions. The passionate denunciations of the studies of the cliometricians by black activists and scholars arguing that the quantitative measurement of conditions in slave and post-slave regimes are a 'whitewash' of slavery, do not address themselves to Engerman's central point (1973: 45–6):

> The choice between working and starving faced by a legally-free individual seems no more attractive than a similar choice faced by a slave: and the ruling class may be able to impose legislation

which can provide themselves with the same economic benefits under either system of labour.

Corrigan, who uses this quote from Engerman in his wide-ranging article on the sociology of unfree labour (1977), immediately spots the further implications of the argument. Engerman uses a conventional economic vocabulary to show that the economic pressures and legislative coercion in the post-emancipation period, forced workers 'off what would be their desired supply curve if choice were voluntary'. This high participation rate, combined with the reduced costs of reproduction to the employer (i.e. the cost of housing and food were now borne by the free labourer), meant that the level of exploitation in the US could be *increased*. The post-emancipation period in the US was also marked by the enormous growth in debt peonage, convict and contract (normally one year) labour. The latter has now been generally extended, as will be seen in Chapter 2, to Mexican, Puerto Rican and Jamaican labourers (Daniel 1972: 19, 82ff.). Corrigan (1977: 442–3) also cites Starobin's work (1970) on *industrial* slavery, which showed that slaves were used efficiently and effectively in mines and manufacturing establishments, to secure a higher rate of return than that which was possible using free labour. In short, the division of labour in a 'core' country like the US, contrary to Wallerstein's argument, combined a system of free and unfree labour throughout its history as an expanding and leading capitalist power. The contemporary US division of labour continues to combine labour of widely different statuses.

A further refutation of the argument that the capitalist form presupposes the free wage labourer (Marx) or is spatially distributed exclusively in its core zones (Wallerstein) can, additionally, be advanced by considering the case of England, indisputably at the centre of the 19th and early 20th centuries capitalist mode of production. While he insists on the ultimate triumph of wage labour, it is worth remarking that Marx was conscious of the links between the forms of labour control prevalent in the different sections of the regional political economy. He observes, for example that 'the cotton industry introduced child-slavery in England' (Marx 1976: 925). Again, he and Engels document the way in which Irish workers were used by English employers as an oppressed section of the reserve army, 'the cause of abasement to which the English worker is exposed, a cause permanently active in forcing the whole class downwards' (cited in Castles and Kosack 1973: 17). As is well established, the trigger for mass Irish migration was provided by the enclosure movement, the depredations of absentee landlords, the ruin of domestic industry by British capitalist interests in the period following 1800, and the famines of 1822 and 1846/7. The last famine occasioned the death of one million people and the emigration of an even greater number. By 1851, there were 727 326 Irish immigrants in Britain, making up 2.9 per cent of the population in England and Wales and 7.2 per cent of the Scottish population (Castles and Kosack 1973: 16–17; Jackson 1963: 11).

Child labour and Irish migrant labour were but two forms of involuntary labour in England in the 19th century. As Corrigan points out, the *de facto* and *de jure* status of most adult English workers continued to be defined as 'servants' until the 1875 Employer and Workman Act. Six years later, service relationships still accounted for about one-third of the paid employed population, about the same as manufacturing. Young workers, agricultural workers and domestic servants were not legally recognised as free workers until the 1920s and 1930s. Corrigan also cites the work of the feminist historian, Leonore Davidoff, who has highlighted the numerical significance of the category 'domestic servants'. The number of servants grew from 751 541 to a peak of 1 386 167 in 1891, never falling below one million until the 1930s. Other prevalent forms of compulsion included bonded miners, collier-serfs (Scotland), labourers and servants contracted at 'hiring fairs', the system of tied cottages and the provision of allotments by employers anxious to lower reproduction costs and habituate their workers (Corrigan 1977: 438–41).

In short, neither Britain nor the United States have ever exhibited or, as will be shown, continue to display, a pure form of free labour regime.

Labour-repressive systems and emergency regimes

The term 'labour-repressive system' was introduced by Moore in his famous account of the social origins of dictatorship and democracy. In its original form, the term was used by Moore (1966: 435) to argue that labour-repressive agricultural systems, such as those found in the southern United States, in Japan, in Prussia (and in Tzarist Russia, though this is not developed), provide an infertile soil for the growth of parliamentary democracy and, instead, form part of the 'institutional complex' leading to fascism. Subsequently, the notion of a labour-repressive or labour-coercive economic system was deployed by southern African writers in an attempt to expand the original concept to cover the situations they described (Trapido 1971; van Onselen 1976). It is easy to see the attractions of such an exercise, but it is important to recognise that these authors have elided Moore's stress on agriculture, in order to cover the case of mining labour in southern Africa, and have also significantly deflected the specific political trajectory of Moore's arguments. My earlier discussion about the coexistence of unfree labour systems with free systems in many parts of the globe also questions the extent to which such labour-repressive economies are *sui generis*. Nonetheless, what does unite the original and expanded versions of the concept and what also has decisive bearing on my wider arguments, is the insistence of the aforementioned writers on the 'political means' used to organise and perpetuate the supply of labour-power. Often this takes the form of intense political repression and severe restrictions on the mobility of labourers, normally the construction of worker barracks (as in South Africa), or labour camps (as in the Soviet Union).

Mention of the Soviet Union also raises the issue of whether that regime should also be considered a labour-repressive system. On the one hand, this problem can be resolved by arguing (with Trotsky) that the Soviet Union is a state capitalist society and therefore can be expected to exhibit features common to those of other early capitalist labour-repressive regimes. On the other hand, it is possible to concur with Swianiewicz's argument (1965) that the USSR represents but one notable example of a general tendency to deploy forced labour at the early stages of industrialisation. While I have some sympathy with both these positions, the first can easily degenerate into a sterile set of insults traded between different left-wing sects, while the second dilutes the specific ideological and political content of the Soviet treatment of its labour problems. It may be that the attempt to use the notion of a labour-repressive economy to cover the cases of Imperial Germany, the antebellum southern United States, Meiji Japan, South Africa, Tzarist Russia after the serf emancipation and the Soviet Union, obscures more than it illuminates. While it correctly places at the centre of the definition the political organisation of the labour supply, the category must remain a tenuous one, for the equally primary role of the state in the colonial and plantation regimes discussed earlier should not be overlooked. It would seem therefore that the mechanisms of labour control and the particular division of labour constructed by the Soviet State are best described separately, without pressing them too firmly into one or other shallow Procrustean bed.

The indictments of the Soviet labour system are now widely diffused in western political circles, supported as they are by the periodic revivals of the cold war. Yet, despite a natural scholarly caution in accepting evidence generated in such circumstances, there is no way that the extensive use of forced labour in the Soviet Union can be 'willed away'. Solzhenitsyn's bitter torrent of criticism in *The Gulag Archipelago* (1979: 25) effectively conveys how *déclassé* intellectuals, 'malingering' workers and numerous national and religious minorities were shunted along the pipes of the Soviet 'sewage disposal system' towards the prisons and labour camps:

> The prison sewers were never empty. The blood, the sweat, and the urine into which we were pulped pulsed through them continuously. The history of this sewage system is the history of an endless swallow and flow; flood alternating with ebb and ebb again with flood; waves pouring in, some big, some small; brooks and rivulets flowing in from all sides; trickles oozing in

through gutters; and then just plain individually scooped-up droplets.

In the end, however, Solzhenitsyn's account remains, as he calls it, 'an experiment in literary investigation', abstracted from the regime's own conception of its objectives. The very codicils of government incorporate a set of strong interventionist principles in labour organisation. The Labour Law Code, for example, *obliges* all people between 16 and 50 to work, unless sickness or disability prevents them from so doing. There is simply no recognition of the right not to work. It is this logic that leads to the regime's view that a corrective labour camp is a proper means for requiring workers to fulfil their obligations to the community, the Party and the state. The same logic led to the idea of an 'economic crime' punishable by corrective labour—until recently the Soviets regarded crime as essentially a social problem exclusive to capitalist society. The *dirigist* character of the regime is also evident in its embrace of the rationality of comprehensive planning, which in turn requires an absolute monopoly over the labour market. Where compulsion was needed to develop northern Russia and Siberia, dig the canal system, mine the gold, or cut the lumber, GULAG (the central body administering the labour camps) could find plenty of unwilling recruits. These recruits were drawn from the six million kulaks whose liquidation as a class was deemed necessary, from saboteurs, religious dissenters and nomads. According to Dallin and Nicolaevsky, two writers openly hostile to the Soviet Union, only 15 per cent of the population of the camps could be deemed 'criminals' in the conventional understanding of that label. The same two authors estimated that 75 per cent of gold production was produced by forced labour, while they rather loosely put the overall number of forced labourers in the 1940s at 8 or 10 or 12 million. So large, at any rate, that the authors consider that 'forced labour must be considered one of the main classes in Soviet Russia's social structure—a class more numerous and economically no less important than that of free workers in industry' (1948: 87). In an even more obvious product of the cold war, Roger Baldwin and his

22

associates (1953) extend Dallin and Nicolaevsky's study, which they describe as 'the standard work on slave labour', to the cases of Czechoslovakia, Hungary, Bulgaria, Romania, Albania, East Germany, Poland, Yugoslavia and China.

In so far as it has been possible to proffer a moral excuse or rational explanation for the Soviet labour camps, their existence has been related to Stalin's particular excesses, the need to fracture or eliminate classes hostile to the revolution or to a particular emergency necessitated by the failures of the National Economic Planning period, and the consequent need to compel infrastructure developments, heavy industry and the rapid collectivisation of agriculture. The concept of an 'emergency' labour regime implies a sudden deviation from a normally more liberal set of arrangements. Certainly there were peaks in the utilisation of forced labour, in 1929/30, 1937/8 and 1944–6, which far exceeded the normal flow (Solzhenitsyn 1979: 24–5). But for a system which continued for nearly half a century, until Khruschev destroyed its worst features in the period after 1956, the notion that the Soviets were confronting an 'emergency' does seem a little disingenuous.

However, the concept of an 'emergency labour regime' does seem apposite when considering the very different use of concentration camp and foreign labour by the Nazis during the Second World War. The stunning horror of the Holocaust of the Jews, Gypsies and other *Untermenshen* has obscured the fact that the Nazi division of labour deployed millions of foreign labourers, in varying conditions of deprivation, in order to service the war machine. By 1943, the numbers of *Zwangsarbeitar* (compulsory workers) had reached 5.2 million. Some would argue that the Nazis' wild expansionist lunges across Europe reflected the need to find further sources of subjugated labour as much as the desire for raw material, stategic advantage or the assuagement of Hitler's megalomania (Homse 1967). Detailed studies of the German companies involved in the use of forced labour demonstrate how vital such labour was, both for war reproduction and for the super-profits realised by companies like I. G. Farben (Borkin 1978). In a review of Ferencz's book (1979) on Jewish forced labour, T. D. Noakes summarises the principal features of the system. Men and women, selected for their physical fitness, were set to work in 1634 forced-labour camps under the direction of the SS. Auschwitz and its 42 branch camps alone contained 144 000 forced workers. Himmler, whose control of the Party machine through the SS was absolute, was fully aware of the precious commodity he had under his control. An elaborate accounting system ensured that the companies that requested forced labour (they were not obliged to use such workers) paid the SS for every hour of skilled or unskilled labour-power they utilised. As Noakes (1980) explains:

> Over 200 companies availed themselves of the opportunity, employing over 250 000 inmates. They included many of the most prestigious firms in Germany: I. G. Farben, Krupp and Siemans, for example, all established works within the Auschwitz complex. The conditions in which these slave labourers worked were for the most part appalling and for the Jews they were worst of all. Over 30 000 Jews perished in three years working for the I. G. Farben Buna rubber factory in Auschwitz.

More recently, an account from the horse's mouth (the expression, I fear, insults a noble creature), in the person of Albert Speer, the Minister of Armaments from February 1942, makes clear that there were divisions of opinion on the question of forced labour within the Nazi hierarchy. According to his account, a debate took place as to whether Jews should be killed immediately as Aryan doctrine decreed, used first as slave labour, or worked to death. Speer's principal complaint (1981) is that Himmler used his access and control of forced labour to further his political ambitions rather than (as Speer advocated) use up the labour-power *first*, in a rational style based on 'American management'.

In so far as several million internees were worked to death or worked before they were put to death, this aspect of the Nazi labour regime demonstrates an extreme example of a case where the employer or the state become so obsessed with immediate production goals that the reproduction of labour-power, which alone can ensure the long-term viability of the division of labour, is relegated to a second place. There is obviously a theoretical limit beyond which the cos of acquiring fresh labour supplies will outstrip the benefits derived from the economics of death—a macabre calculation that will not be elaborated on here.

Unfree labourers and modern migrants

Stepping back and reviewing the argument so far—contrary to Marx, it has been argued that, historically, the international division of labour wrought by the capitalist mode of production has not been characterised by the exclusive use of free labour but by a combination of free and unfree labour regimes. This has applied throughout the history as much as the 'pre-history' of capital and has taken a variety of forms in different areas. The very diversity of forms of unfree labour allows me to put my counter-proposition in a simple way: capitalism successfully combines labour of differing statuses. Contrary to Wallerstein, I have argued that the spatial distribution of free and unfree labours is scattered at the outlying and central zones of a regional political economy, though I concur that there is a relative concentration of free workers in the metropole and unfree workers in the colonial areas. Unless one adopts the position that the Soviet Union is a state capitalist society (in which case the first counter-proposition holds), the mix of free and unfree labour is a feature that also appears in state socialist divisions of labour, certainly in the early phases of labour-intensive industrialisation. The final example showed how, for extreme ends, the Nazi state engineered a division of labour to mitigate a war production crisis by turning millions of conquered peoples into expendable helots.

Three more general theoretical positions have also been hinted at throughout the account, all of which will gain further expression later in the text. First, contrary to world systems theory, I believe that the particular international mix of free and involuntary labour is best set within the context of a more restricted definition of a 'regional political economy', the historical examples cited including Britain and the West Indies, Portugal and its colonies, and Nazi Germany and its conquered territories in eastern Europe.

25

The term 'regional political economy' itself should be regarded as an attempt to find a superior unit of analysis distinct from the global determinism and abstractions of world systems' theorists on the one hand and from the now clearly inadequate use of legally-defined states on the other.

Second, unlike the modes of production theorists, I believe that so determinant is the capitalist mode of production after initial settlement and conquest of the peripheral zones, that what is generally observed is not the articulation of two modes, but the subordination and encapsulation of a pre-capitalist *form* of production/reproduction. The word 'form' is used precisely to indicate the weakness and lack of autarky of the pre-capitalist area. This process of subordination in turn generates the commoditisation of agriculture and the production of unfree labourers destined to be deployed either at the core or the edge of the regional political economy. In other words, there is here the heart of an economic theory of migration.

Third, I insist on regional *political* economy, as it is my view that the state plays a central and directing role in the structuring of a division of labour, in the legitimation of an involuntary labour regime through legal and ideological means, in defining the relationship between free and unfree workers, in the recruitment and regulation of coerced labourers and, finally, in the policing of the frontiers of the metropolitan area of the regional political economy. The centrality of the state is indeed a theme running through successive labour regimes from plantation and colonial economics, the *de facto* and *de jure* status of workers in core countries, through to the so-called labour repressive economies and the cases of the Soviet Union and Nazi Germany.

It is this last theme, of political control, that provides one of the most important reasons for seeing the bulk of modern international migrants as, in some respects, involuntary labourers. Their existence in advanced capitalist political economies should be interpreted as the contemporary version of the demonstrated historic capacity for capitalism to combine different forms of labour. The range of political restrictions directed against post-1945 international migrants also distinguishes them from the huge hordes o migrants from Europe to North America in the 19th century and the first 30 years of the 20th century and from other similar migrations.

This last argument needs some demonstration by stepping back for a moment to provide a few background statistics of some modern migrations. These have been conveniently assembled by Power (1979). He points out that in the years between 1820 and 1927 there were about 37 million migrants to the USA, about 32 million coming directly from Europe. From the UK alone, some 10 million people left to settle overseas during the period 1820 to 1914, though of course many of them were going to areas other than the US, like the white Commonwealth (New Zealand, Australia, Canada). Although Britain was never a major net immigration country, offsetting her losses of emigrants were large immigrant streams of Irish (700 000 in 1851), Italians and eastern European Jews (120 000 between 1875 and 1914). Modest as the last streams were by post-1945 standards, they were sufficient to arouse anti-alien propaganda in England, thus leading to the establishment of a Royal Commission on the Aliens Question. Its findings were instructive. Only 0.69 per cent of the British population were aliens, compared with 1.38 per cent in Germany, 2.68 per cent in France and 9.58 per cent in Switzerland. During the First World War and up to 1930, the annual average increase of aliens entering the UK was less than 1000 a year (Power 1979: 10–13).

What can be inferred from these statistics? First, that where the numbers were small, as in Britain and Germany, there were no major efforts made to isolate aliens from the indigenous population through political means. Where they were larger, as in France and Switzerland, there were the beginnings of a policy of civic restriction. (In 1888 and 1893 the French Government obliged workers to register in their residential locality; the Swiss always refused to grant civic rights for foreigners.) But, even where they developed in the pre-Second World War period, the systems of internal political control were generally weak and in the labour-hungry countries of the Commonwealth and the United States internal controls were non-existent. That is not to say that no restrictions existed: on the contrary, Australia and

New Zealand operated official and non-official blocks to non-white *entry*, while in the US discriminating immigration legislation and quotas started against the Chinese in 1882, were extended to many other peoples in subsequent years (Miller 1974). Once, however, they were *in* the charmed circle, say that geographical space called the United States, immigrants were not only welcomed (and treated infinitely better than native Aztlan and American peoples), they constituted the raw material of the society itself. In songs and plays, in adult education classes and schools, the virtues of citizenship and loyalty to the American flag were drummed into the immigrant. Henry Ford was especially zealous in insisting on language and citizenship training for his immigrant car workers (Korman 1967). Many American scholars now argue that prior ethnic identities never fully disappeared in this melting pot. Glazer and Moynihan, the most vigorous defenders of this thesis, make the nice point that Israel Zangwill, the author of the 1908 hit Broadway play *The Melting Pot*, from which the phrase became popular, was himself increasingly drawn to Zionism and, eight years after the play opened, wrote that, 'it was vain for Paul to declare that there should be neither Jew nor Greek. Nature will return even if driven out with a pitch fork, still more if driven out by a dogma.' Yet, despite Zangwill's personal disillusionment, who can doubt that the pogrom orphan of the play, David Quixano, expressed both the mood and aspirations of the immigrants and the official ideology of Americanisation in his monologue:

> America is God's crucible, the great Melting Pot where all the races of Europe are melting and reforming! Here you stand, good folk, think I, when I see them at Ellis Island, here you stand in your fifty groups with your fifty languages and histories, and your fifty blood hatreds and rivalries, but you won't be long like that brothers, for these are the fires of Gods you've come to—these are the fires of God. A fig for your feuds and vendettas! German and Frenchmen, Irishmen and Englishmen, Jews and Russians—into the Crucible with you all. God is making the American. (Cited in Glazer and Moynihan 1963: 289–90.)

Another frequently-cited account, Oscar Handlin's sensitive portrait (1953: 204–6) of *The Uprooted*, lays great emphasis on the traumas of settlement. But, he says, the immigrant's conception of power was altered by one difference in the New World:

> Having settled and survived the five years, the newcomer was expected to become a citizen. Docile, he did what was expected of him. One day he took an oath, received a certificate, was naturalised. You might say, 'well that was one paper more? In his lifetime, many had been given him.' This one, carefully hidden in the bottom of the trunk was unique. It made the foreigner an American, equal in rights with every other man.

There is perhaps no need to press the point much further at this stage. Whatever the psychological barriers to adjustment to a new environment, whatever the continuance of ethnic sentiments, the pre-war migrant was a (usually) willing victim of the ideology and practice of Americanisation. By contrast, in the period after 1945, the US, like other advanced capitalist countries, has invented a plethora of categories, other than 'immigrant', to describe those who wish to cross their borders. The words tourist, visitor, student, guestworker, contract worker, illegal foreign worker, citizen of dependent territories, undocumented worker, section 10 worker (South Africa) all express the increasing hostility by the richer capitalist states (or more strictly their ruling classes) to international worker mobility. Post-1945 international migrants are generally distinguished by their exclusion from, or restricted opportunities to acquire, the full rights of citizenship in core countries. To the extent that migrants are prevented from becoming citizens and settlers they share characteristics of earlier generations of unfree workers and can be seen as their historical descendants.

In the subsequent chapters of this book, this thesis is developed with respect to three regional political economies: the US and its Caribbean and Mexican periphery (Chapter 2); white South Africa and its internal and surrounding periphery (Chapter 3); northern Europe and its labour reserves in the Mediterranean countries and in former colonial territories (Chapter 4). In rough orders of magnitude we are dealing with 11 to 12 million unfree workers in the US, 15 million migrants of differentiated, but often unfree, status in Europe, and perhaps 4 to 5 million unfree workers in South Africa.

The central industrial and agribusiness areas of white South Africa, northern Europe and the United States are without doubt the three major importers of labour-power during the period from 1945 to the mid-seventies. In this respect, the empirical material is properly concentrated on these countries. However, it is important to recognise that from the mid-seventies onwards, there are drastic official restrictions (sometimes evaded by illegal migrations) on the movement of migrants to these zones. This means that a full account of modern migrants would have to take into account migrations not only to advanced capitalist countries but also to alternative destinations in the newly-industrialising countries (NICs) as well as to 'city-states' like Hong Kong and Singapore. This issue gains further exposition in Chapter 7. All that needs to be noted here is that the extent of this migration points to structural shifts in the international division of labour (i.e. from my point of view how the mixes of free and involuntary labour become spatially redistributed). Looking at newer migrations also helps to indicate how the latent sections of the relative surplus population of labour-exporting zones have to find new destination points once they have been prevented from entering particular advanced capitalist countries.

A more complete picture of the spread of modern migrants can also be drawn from examining migration patterns from *sending*, rather than receiving, countries. Some remarkable findings of the extent of labour export emerge. Although Greece imports some migrants from Egypt and Pakistan, two million Greeks (out of a population of 10 million) work abroad. Portugal has lost 1.5 million people (out of 8.7 million) in the post-1945 period. Some 44 per cent of the North Yemeni adult labour force works abroad, a similar measure being 21 per cent for Lesotho and 11 to 12 per cent for Algeria and Tunisia. In some dramatic cases, like the island of Montserrat in the Caribbean, a process of depopulation has occurred as the emigration rate outstripped the live birth rate (Harris 1980: 38–9; Philpott 1973). The phrase 'the flight to work' for the most part summarises the reasons for the migrations described above (though a more adequate theory of migration is presented in Chapter 2). These migrations are largely distinct from the movements of political refugees or those caught up in the misfortunes of war—Ugandans, Somalis, Argentinians, Chileans, Bolivians, Cubans, Cambodians, Vietnamese, Bengalis, Afghanis, Poles and others have all fled from the rigours of their regimes in recent years. Although saying that these kinds of 'unscheduled' migrations are 'largely distinct' from more economically-rooted migrations, the distinction can break down in some cases. For example, it is impossible to separate brutal political repression from sheer grinding poverty in trying to account for the desperate attempts by Haitians to leave their island for the United States or Canada.

So while this book concentrates on economically-rooted migration to three core zones (the US, northern Europe and white South Africa), the extent of migration to other destinations should not be underestimated or the fact that many migrations are impelled by political oppression be discounted. Concentration on the three major selected zones, does, however, give an opportunity to investigate three major themes which inform my theoretical position. It must be emphasised however that these themes can be discerned in all three cases, but rather than repeat similar theoretical observations *in extenso*, I have chosen to ground each discussion in the successive case studies. Thus, the argument that a causal theory of international migration can only be advanced by examining the structural and political forces operating in the regional political economy as a whole is pursued primarily with respect to the US and its neighbouring periphery (Chapter 2). The issue of the reproduction of labour-power (and by extension the modes of production debate and some feminist debates) is considered when dealing with southern Africa (Chapter 3). The third theme, on the postulated 'structural necessity' of migration to advanced capitalist countries (and the related debate on segmented labour markets) is discussed in relation to Europe

31

(Chapter 4). The case studies and additional empirical material are brought together again in subsequent chapters which examine the effectiveness of the state as a filter and regulator of the labour supply (Chapter 5), the way in which migrants are socialised to accept a capitalist labour process by the employers and the state and the attempts at resistance and self-organisation by migrant communities (Chapter 6). Finally, a discussion of the 'new' international division of labour, the export of capital and the creation of new subordinate sections of the global labour force on the periphery, is given separate treatment in Chapter 7.

2 Theories of migration: the US and its labour reservoirs

The law which always holds the relative surplus population or industrial reserve army in equilibrium with the extent and energy of accumulation, rivets the worker to capital more firmly than the wedges of Hephaestus held Prometheus to the rock.

(Marx 1976: 799)

When reviewing the literature on migration, one is confronted by an almost embarrassing plethora of general theories, middle-range hypotheses, laws, casual statements and propositions. Part of the difficulty of providing a general model thus derives from what level of theorisation is being attempted. It is also often unclear what precise phenomena are being included. Does one go along with Jackson (1969: 1) in his argument that migration is observed, 'albeit of a limited kind', when 'a child moves from cradle to bed, leaves home for his first day at school or goes courting in the next village'? Such examples, in my view, are absurd, but there are nonetheless real empirical difficulties in blocking out the parameters of the phenomenon. So let me quickly sketch some working boundaries to my study. I'm not concerned with children's motor development or *rites du passage*, let alone with romantic swains, but with men and women, typically men, who are crossing a recognised political or administrative frontier for the purpose of selling their labour-power. Other constant preoccupations in the literature are the questions of the distances travelled and the length of stay involved. Again, this can be resolved without too much discussion. Distance is nowadays more a function of the cost and speed of transport than the number of kilometres covered. With that in mind, I'm only concerned with those migrants whose original point of residence and present point of work (or work search) is far enough or expensive enough apart, not to permit daily or weekly travel. In Chapter 5, commuters working and living on both sides of the Mexican and Swiss borders are briefly discussed. However, the bulk of those discussed are migrants whose destination point is also in the process of becoming a place of settlement. There are, of course, numerous legal and political restrictions which inhibit this process, particularly in the case of seasonal or contractual workers, both discussed at various places in the text. Where such restrictions do not apply, or are evaded, spouses and dependants join the original migrant, a family is started, and a migrant community (see Chapter 6) is formed. But the transformation of migrant workers into a community (i.e, a settler group or ethnic group) may again be actively prevented by the state or resisted by discriminatory practices.

Established theory

Even if the phenomena under investigation can be narrowed in the above ways, they are still susceptible to a wide range of explanations. Some derive from attempts to evolve statistical laws or tendencies—a tradition usually dating from Ravenstein's celebrated papers read to the Royal Statistical Society in 1885 and 1889, and followed, with modifications, by modern demographers and geographers (for example: Lee 1969; Grigg 1977). One ends up with apparently *ex cathedra* statements which seem largely unconnected with any observable reality and which are characteristically hopelessly ahistorical. Thus: 'The great body of our migrants only proceed a short distance' (Ravenstein); 'Each main current of migration produces a compensating counter-current' (Ravenstein); 'The volume of migration within a given territory varies with the degree of diversity of areas included in that territory' (Lee); 'The volume of migration varies with the diversity of people' (Lee); 'The volume of migration varies with fluctuations in the economy' (Lee); 'The volume of migration is related to the difficulty of surmounting the intervening obstacles' (Lee). It is often difficult to rescue much of immediate explanatory value from such statements—but I do examine the last but one proposition, that the rate (I prefer the term to 'volume') of migration varies with fluctuations in the business cycle. The last proposition also hints at what I think needs very much more explanation, namely the role of the state. Lee (1969: 290) uses as examples of 'intervening obstacles' the Berlin Wall, and how obstacles were 'removed' in the post-1945 period by the lifting of immigration restrictions in the European Economic Community (EEC). Unfortunately, there is no sense here in which agencies of the state (or the employers) actively adopt policies to turn on or switch off the flow of migrants. Instead, the migrants are depicted as free-floating nebulae, attracted or repelled at their point of origin and evaluating the pluses and minuses of life at the proposed destination point. If the balance appears favourable, their decision to move is deterred only by some rather mysteriously appearing 'intervening obstacles'. Like the famous black boxes of cybernetic theory, Lee's black boxes have to be unpacked and spotlighted if the discussion is to proceed productively.

The first task is to decide what status to accord to the individual decision to migrate. This decision is often inferred unproblematically from censuses or immigration cards or derived from specially constructed sociological surveys asking individuals why they have chosen to migrate. As well as the many technical difficulties of assessing subjective evidence (especially, in this case, in view of the context of its collection), the major difficulty with a subjectivist starting point is that the researcher has to assume that the individuals concerned operate with a rational, decision-making model of the world, with which they weigh options and possibilities in an environment of free choice. It is apparent, however, that a freely-reached decision can only operate within the constraints of the opportunities on offer. This general proposition applies with particular force to the decision to migrate, where opportunities are tightly constrained and structured by such factors as rural emiseration, employment and housing prospects, transport costs, international law, immigration policies, the practices of recruit-

35

ment by agencies and employers, and the need for documents like passports, visas and work certificates. In short, the individual's resolve to migrate cannot be separated from the institutional context in which that decision was reached. Although, for this reason such ego-centred models are inherently flawed, it is worth drawing attention to one sophisticated attempt to use modern quantitative techniques of 'disaggregate choice behaviour' and 'collinearity diagnostics' to look at trade-offs between origin and destination, different destination points, economic gains, separation costs and risks (Mueller 1981).

No doubt the increasingly hard-headed methodology applied to subjective opinions will attenuate some of the objections I have raised to treating such evidence as having a causal status, but even at their best, individually-centred explanations can only tell us about the *incidence* of migration (the set of unique circumstances which induces a particular migrant to leave) rather than the *rate* of migration (the underlying factors which determine the volume, trends and patterns) (Mitchell 1959: 32). This distinction, which was used with powerful effect in African migration studies by Mitchell, has its roots in classical sociological theory. In particular, for Durkheim (1970: 51) the suicide *rate* referred to the 'statistical data express[ing] the suicidal tendency with which each society is collectively afflicted'. By deploying the distinction between rate and incidence, Mitchell was able to identify economic factors as causing the rate, and (a host of) personal factors as determining the migration incidence. The distinction is also a helpful one in that it clearly separates structure from motivation and allows the student of migration to decide which of the related—but separable— phenomena are in question. Without any apparent indebtedness to Mitchell, a more recent study, which seeks to develop a critique of existing theoretical positions on migration, nonetheless broadly supports his conclusions.

> Quite clearly, individuals migrate for a number of different causes—desire to escape oppression and famine, financial ambition, family reunification, or education of children. Nothing is easier than to compile lists of such 'push' and 'pull' factors and present them as a theory of migration. The customary survey

reporting percentages endorsing each such 'cause' might be useful as a sort of first approximation to the question 'who migrates'? In no way, however, does it explain the structural factors leading to a patterned movement, of known size and direction, over an extensive period of time. (Portes and Walton 1981: 25.)

The reference to push/pull theory is somewhat misleading in that a number of scholars of migration (for example Wilson 1972) use push/pull models to refer to general structural features of the economy, rather than the kind of particularistic desires and ambitions identified by Portes and Walton. In fact push/pull models of a structural variety are often linked to what Portes and Walton (1981: 26–7) call equilibrium theory. As they argue, such theory depicts a process of natural harmonisation as empty regions fill up, and full regions empty. By reducing the population in low-growth areas and increasing the supply of labour to growing zones, it is argued that migration acts to balance out excess human resources with the needs of the economy.

The functionalist logic is immediately compelling but, like all *laissez-faire* theories, is flawed by market 'imperfections'—imperfections so gross as to render the theory inoperable for all but the most insensitive adherents of neo-classical economic theory. As Portes and Walton (1981: 27) again point out, the equivalent sociological variant of equilibrium theory is no more plausible. The distinction between 'traditional' and 'modern' values is resolved by some individuals (presumably with an 'elective affinity') migrating to advanced areas leaving others behind who wish to cling to the past. As sociologists and anthropologists are wont to do, there is much beating of breast and wringing of hands at the human consequences of such a process. What of the people 'caught between two cultures', the 'marginalised men' (*sic*), the problems of adaptation and adjustment to new rhythms of work, new patterns of social interaction, new expectations and aspirations? These are not unimportant questions; they are simply posed in a way that is too voluntaristic, taking as an assumption that the individual inevitability incurs social costs in his/her restless quest for economic opportunity.

37

Alternative perspectives

In a paper challenging the whole tradition of migration theory applied to eastern and southern Africa, Murray (1979: 16) wishes to declare the rate/incidence distinction, used by Mitchell and other scholars, 'theoretically redundant', despite its 'illustrious intellectual ancestry and frequent citation in the literature'.

Some of his argument is special to the region where this tradition grew up, but his views have a more general import as well. On the arguments particular to his region, Murray (1979: 15) concurs with Wilson (1972) that there was an overconcentration on the structural factors impelling migration from the sending side, thereby ignoring the vital dynamic on the importing side:

> Indeed, investigation of economic cycles of boom and recession and of monopsonistic recruitment mechanisms would demonstrate that the supply of labour from the sending areas of much of central and southern Africa is to a large extent controlled by the South African mining industry. It was no accident that Mitchell ignored variables on the demand side, for they were precluded by the Durkheimian terms of reference in which he posed the question of explanation.

Let me put to one side whether this is such a damaging refutation of the rate/incidence distinction or of Durkheim's methodology. More important is that the example of the mining industry in southern Africa (about which a great deal more is said in Chapter 3), vividly demonstrates glaring weaknesses in much traditional theory. It is not so much that explanation is always supply-side oriented (this is not true, for example, of European studies), but that it is nearly always concentrated on one side of the migration chain or the other. This is understandable enough when pressing social policies are foremost in the minds of those funding research. Thus labour-power requirements or issues of race relations preoccupy metropolitan researchers, while most investigators in labour-sending areas are concerned with the lack of alternative employment prospects, or the costs and benefits of exporting what potentially is the most productive section of the labour force. The development of migration theory must, however, be predicated on a holism: sending and receiving areas being treated as a unit with causative structural factors operating on both sides. This is not to argue for an artificial symmetry on each side: in the majority of cases the determining force may well be the demands of capital in the labour-importing section of the regional political economy.

Another limitation to general theory thrown up by the southern African example is the lack of a specific set of institutional actors which galvanise the movement of migrants from one point to another. Modern migrants are not atomistic flies vaguely smelling the presence of aromatic sugar bowls. Nor do they simply flow to another receptacle when the cup of overpopulation runneth over. Recruitment agencies, companies, employer federations and states' administrative apparati, are actively involved in channelling migrants to a particular destination or preventing them from reaching it. In some instances, as in the case of certain illegal migrants, a rugged individualism still pertains, but the general rule is far different. In the modern world, migrants are organised, selected and controlled. Portes and Walton (1981: 25) make a related point in another way:

> The progressive disappearance of unincorporated areas and economic frontiers after the consolidation of world capitalism thus transformed immigration from a movement of 'advanced' populations settling backward lands, to one in which 'backward' populations were induced to fit the needs of more advanced economies.

While the thrust of this argument is correct, it needs to be qualified in two respects. First, the spread of world capitalism is not quite so global, or so flattening, or so unproblematic, as some world systems theorists appear to believe. The very processes of incorporation and transformation of pre-capitalist societies engender *different* outcomes. For some, conservatism and resistance (albeit ultimately doomed) to capitalist social relations and for others, dissolution and fragmentation to the point of genocide or total absorption as landless labourers. For many, a precarious set

39

of compromises with the power of advanced capitalism. Oscillating, temporary, contractual and seasonal migration are concrete examples of some forms of transaction between the capitalist mode and pre-capitalist forms of production. However, as the capitalist mode of production becomes more dominant, so (theoretically) does the tendency towards permanent migration increase—though this, of course, may be artificially held in check. Whatever the variety and timing of these outcomes, in explaining the causes of migration, we are forced, as Murray (1979: 21) argues, to recognise the historical particularities of incorporation and transformation.

The second qualification to a world systems perspective is that its adherents not only sometimes flatten historical specificities in favour of a naive globalism, they manage to elide or reduce the political level to a point below which even the crudest economic determinist would cry 'halt'. Zolberg (1981: 9–10) draws out the implications of this error for the study of migration:

> In Wallerstein's view, the world system is, by and large, devoid of any overarching political structure, and states are mere instrumentations of the capitalist dynamic ... yet it is evident that such a conception is fallacious, in that from the beginning of European expansion to the present, international political processes generated by the organisation of the world into states have interacted with the forces generated by capitalism in such a way as to determine complex configurations in which economic and political determinants are inextricably linked ... These are by no means incidental matters to the analysis of international migrations, since variations in regime form are directly related to exit and entry policies, and hence contribute to the determination of global patterns of international migration.

Let me summarise my theoretical orientation so far. I am interested in *structure rather than motivation* in that individual preferences can explain only why some people chose to make themselves part of a general phenomenon: they cannot explain the phenomenon itself. In this sense, despite Murray's reservations, the rate/incidence distinction remains useful as a signal that this book is concerned with macro-movements of population rather than micro-decisions on the part of a few individuals who happen to get interviewed by a persistent anthropologist or sociologist. However, any complete explanation must treat structural factors at both ends of the migration process, amongst which factors, demand for labour-power at the labour-importing end may well turn out to be decisive. Further, an insistence on structural factors does not simply stem from a pre-conceived anti-interactionist perspective, for modern migratory movements are policed by a more and more pervasive set of institutional actors, amongst which the labour-importing state is the most important. The state both legislates immigration policy and seeks to regulate the terms and conditions under which migrants can live, work and reproduce. Finally, I drew attention to the need for examining the particular historical circumstances under which an underdeveloped region becomes enmeshed in capitalist social relations.

This last theme resonates directly with the revival of Marxist theory applied to the field of migration. For Marx (1976: 796), as soon as capitalist production methods intruded into the rural world, the capacity to employ people in agriculture sharply diminishes. The result was that:

> Part of the agricultural population is . . . constantly on the point of passing over into an urban or manufacturing proletariat, and on the look out for opportunities to complete this transformation. There is thus a constant flow from this source of the relative surplus population. But the constant movement towards the towns presupposes, in the countryside itself, a constant latent surplus population, the extent of which only becomes evident at those exceptional times when its distribution channels are wide open.

The terminology deployed by Marx needs some further explication. For him, the 'relative surplus population' is, in effect, an 'industrial reserve army' and is as necessary to capital as the 'active army of labour' itself. The relative surplus population comprises three elements. The 'latent' group, referred to in the above quote, and the 'floating' and 'stagnant' sections. The exact distinction between these elements is rather vaguely depicted in *Capital* (Marx 1976: 794-9) and has given rise to a number of interpretations

41

(Godfrey 1977; History Task Force 1979: 36–51). Howeve in broad terms, the subdivisions refer to those potenti; workers whose labour-power can be activated by capital a and when needed ('latent'), those workers who are seasc nally, marginally or temporarily employed ('floating') an those, discarded from production, whose conditions of lif are poorer than that of the normal working class ('stagnant' All three sections of the relative surplus population, how ever, are bound by the same 'laws' of capital accumulatior In Marx's memorable words (1976: 799), which preface thi chapter, 'The extent and energy of accumulation rivets th worker to capital more firmly than the wedges of Hephaestu held Prometheus to the rock'. Capital holds the rural worl which it has penetrated in its thrall, not in some loose sens of a set of trade relations (the obsessive concern of depen dency and world systems theory), but because trade relation are a surface manifestation of a more important capacity that capacity to unlock a giant migratory stream of potenti; labour-power to help build capital's productive forces. Fo Marx, it is this capacity that occasions the dual functionalit of the industrial reserve army. First, it is held literally i; reserve, ready to be deployed in expansionist phases of th business cycle. Second, the very existence of a reserve arm; reduces the bargaining power of those in regular employ ment, both in respect of wages and condition of work. Th 'pretensions' of the working class can thus be 'held in check. (Cited in Godfrey 1977: 64–5).

I now have assembled all the major elements of m; theoretical argument. In the remaining part of this chapter, . will use my first case study, the regional political economy o the US and its labour reservoirs, to exemplify the structural historical and political aspects of international labour mig ration. While not ignoring these elements, Chapter 3 will be concerned with the issue of incorporation and transforma tion in southern Africa as labour reservoirs came into being for the use (primarily) of the mining industry. The functio nality of migrant labour and its status as a reserve army wil be discussed in Chapter 4 when describing the Europear political economy.

The creation of the labour reservoirs of the US

In a suggestive summary of the major phases of migration to the US, Piore (1979: 141–66) distinguishes between five periods in the development of a labour market for long-distance migrant workers and the evolution of four distinct streams of migrants which filled the vacant slots in the US division of labour, particularly those in the low-wage sector. Journeymen and apprentices supplemented family labour in the first period of household production. During the period of incipient industrialisation, agriculture and manufacturing existed in symbiosis with migrants arriving as family units or potential heads of households. It was in the next stage of factory production, particularly in the shoe and textile industries established just before the Civil War, that a demand grew up for unskilled, more or less transient, migrants. Finally, during the periods of industrial consolidation, in the late 19th and 20th centuries, Piore (1979: 144–6) maintains that large- and small-scale sectors of industry emerged with migrants being concentrated in the latter. With the growth of industrial unionism, the job market divided into secure and less secure segments, migrants characteristically filling vacancies in the second segment.

These periods of industrial expansion and labour market segmentation were matched by the evolution of four distinct patterns of migration: (a) the 'old' immigration from north-western Europe which dominated early economic development; (b) the 'new immigration' from southern and eastern Europe at the turn of the century; (c) the internal migration of blacks, Spanish-speaking Americans and rural whites, and the start of migration from Puerto Rico and Mexico from the end of the First World War to the 1960s and (d) what Piore (1979: 148) calls the 'new' immigration of the late 1960s and 1970s which is dominated by people from Mexico and the Caribbean basin.

I am interested here only in the Mexican and Caribbean cases (in my terms, the current labour reservoirs of the US regional political economy), not only because (as Piore notes) these areas provide the bulk of contemporary migrants, but also because, as I pointed out in Chapter 1, post-war migrants have become subordinate to political and legal restrictions in a way that is distinct from earlier waves of migration. This is not to say that Caribbean peoples and Mexicans are unusual in their position in the US division of labour. Their use in low-wage, low-skill jobs follows or parallels the similar use of blacks in the period after the Civil War, and the successive waves of Irish, Poles, Ukranians, Yugoslavs, Jews and Italians all of whom once formed part of a subordinate and poorly-organised labour force.

The peoples of the Caribbean and Mexico are also not the first victims of racially-specific immigration laws and policies. The first racially-explicit immigration legislation was in fact the Chinese Exclusion Act of 1882, an Act that was built, as Miller (1974) and Saxton (1971) convincingly argue, on a host of negative stereotypes of orientals orchestrated by conservative US lobbies. This act was followed by the 'gentlemen's agreement' to exclude the Japanese in 1907, the quota legislation of the 1920s, notably the Immigration Restriction Act of 1924, and the establishment of border patrols on the Mexican border in the same year.

For Mexican and Caribbean migrants who avoided the gradual encroachment of the US state on international worker mobility, or fitted within the quota system, the US was still a place of potential security and opportunity. Puerto Ricans also were unusually favoured in that since 1917, two decades after the US occupation of the island, they held US citizenship. But for most post-war migrants from the Caribbean and Mexico, the American dream remained flawed by their normally demeaning occupations and their holding of insecure and illegal statuses with limited access to the rights of citizenship and representation. In short, these migrants are part of the army of new helots and are some of the descendants of earlier generations of unfree workers. How they reached this condition is rooted in the history of incorporation and transformation of Mexico and the Caribbean by US capital. It is now necessary to periodise and characterise these transformations, bearing in mind my particular interest, in this chapter, in the supply of labour-power.

1848–1924 The Guadalupe–Hidalgo treaty of 1848 brought to an end the war between Mexico and the US, with Mexico ceding to the US more than half her territory inherited from Spain at her independence in 1821. The ceded territories included modern California, Arizona, New Mexico, Nevada, Colorado, Utah and a portion of Wyoming. In addition, the Mexicans were forced to approve the prior (1845) annexation of Texas. Along with the new territories acquired, the US also acquired the population of these areas, and with them a new population, variously described as Spanish-Americans, Mexican-Americans or Chicanos. A more recent attempt to construct a political identity between Spanish-speaking peoples which transcends their countries of origin has popularised the term 'Hispanics' or 'La Raza' (The Race) (see Acuña 1972; Servin 1974; Maciel 1977 and *Time Magazine* (New York), 16 October 1978). Strictly speaking, the notion of 'immigration to the US' in this early period is misconceived, as the Mexican presence in the US is as old as the United States itself. Various Indian peoples lived on both sides of the border and until 1924, when border patrols were established, came and went freely. The area covering the present-day south-west of the United States and the northern states of Mexico is, as Fernandez (1977: 37–74) has convincingly argued, more properly conceived of as a single economic zone. Nonetheless, within this zone, profound economic and social changes were effected by the hegemony of US capitalism and the consequent displacement of many native peoples from their land and their previous mode of production. Gonsalez (1977: 5–6) succinctly summarises these changes as follows:

> The process that emerges after the triumph of the American political and economic domination of the area is the conflict over the means of production—cattle vs sheep, fencing vs open range, landless vs land-owning cattlement, etc. Underlying all this was the land question as the key factor—as it had been in the earlier battles with the Indians and the Mexicans. At stake was the question of survival, because this struggle involved not

45

just who would 'own' the land, but which mode of production would predominate ... The results were of course to wipe out other groups economically by destroying the basis for their subsistence: the landless Americans, Mexicans and Negroes.

The mainsprings of what was later described as Mexican 'immigration' consequently lie in the dispossession of Mexican-owned lands by large US farmers and the penetration of north-west Mexico by other forms of US capital. Although legal land grants of the area existed, records were often inadequate or lost and the land was often poorly surveyed. Consequently, US farmers were able to find loopholes whereby they could expropriate large tracts of land from indigenous owners. Legal manoeuvres also discriminated against local farmers. As Samora and Simon (1977: 135) point out:

> Of the more than thirty five million acres claimed under land titles, the Court of Private Land Claims had approved a little over two million acres when it adjourned in 1904. The result of this situation was that many people lost their land and were thus pushed out into the labor supply and a wage economy.

The creation of a stock of labour-power for the capitalist mode of production within the US was paralleled by events with similar consequences within Mexico itself. The Mexican Revolution which began in 1910 and extended into the First World War, created considerable uncertainty amongst landowners and peasants due to land conflicts within Mexico. Land was confiscated, stolen and taken back, while the breaking up of *haciendas* into small agrarian plots, although threatened, was not actually carried out. The general discontent among the peasantry was matched by bitter resentment amongst workers in US-owned industries. In 1906, for example, workers at US-owned copper mines in Cananca, Sonora, came out on strike demanding, among other things, equal pay with US citizens and access to American-held jobs. The Governor of Sonora turned northwards for help and called in 275 armed American 'volunteers' from Arizona to suppress forcibly the strike, killing 23 Mexican workers (Russell 1977). The treatment of these strikers is a small illustration of a more general phenomenon: the continuing

46

difficulties of maintaining a radical trajectory in Mexico cheek by jowl with a more powerful, conservative neighbour. The egalitarian rhetoric of the Mexican Constitution, equally should not obscure the net effects of the revolutionary period. These included a demoralised and defeated peasantry, the continued existence of private property, and a dependent, crippled and ineffective labour movement. Together these factors contributed towards large numbers of dispossessed peasants and workers crossing the border into the United States.

During the First World War, the boom conditions in the south-west of the United States were marked by labour shortages in particular industries. The need for manpower in the armed services and defence industries created job vacancies in other (lower paid) forms of employment. Agriculture, in particular, lost many US workers to the defence industry. The expansion of commercial agriculture, the establishment of railroads and the development of a number of industries, including mining, in the south-west all provided employment opportunities for Mexican labourers now dispossessed of their means of subsistence. In an important early analysis, Handman (1930: 606) showed that it was only due to the existence of cheap labour that many farms in the south-west became viable:

> The rise in agricultural prices following the war resulted in a great expansion of agricultural production, but what is more important, it resulted in a great increase in the price of farm lands and inflation in farm values. Certain areas in Texas and California were opened up and sold at a price which could not possibly make them a paying proposition to the purchasers unless the purchasers could utilize cheap labor.

1924–42 The second period identified is marked by the attempt by the US authorities to intervene administratively to control the ebb and flow of migrant labour, first in response to racist demands and second in response to the needs of US capital itself. This policy engendered many contradictions. For example in the first .years after the Border Patrol was established (1924), the demand for cheap labour was still high, and the newly-defined 'illegal' migrants still crossed the border while ignoring the cumbersome paperwork and delays involved in becoming 'legal'. So long as the jobs were there to be done, US employers were happy to hire labour at the most advantageous rates—it made good economic sense to use migrant labourers when the US state and employers were not having to pay the price for the reproduction of their labour-power. On the other hand, the theoretical control of the border also provided the formal machinery which could be activated when labour was abundant and the need to import cheap labour decreased. This became dramatically evident during the Great Depression of the years 1929–39 when there were few jobs for the hundreds of thousands of hungry and destitute Mexicans and Chicanos, whose entitlement to public welfare would have greatly increased the social costs involved in the reproduction of labour-power. Appropriate administrative measures were brought into force.

This can be seen first in the number of illegal aliens apprehended. Whereas in the previous five-year period, 1924–8, an average of only 4329 illegal aliens were apprehended yearly, during the Depression years, 1929–39, the annual average of illegal aliens apprehended more than doubled to 10 311 (Samora 1971: 45). Second, deportations on a massive scale commenced. During the first four years of the 1930s alone, some 311 716 Mexicans were bundled across the border with such enthusiasm that the deportees included residents of 30–40 years standing; both illegal and legal immigrants, members of families who were forcibly separated from their spouses and children, and even US citizens of Mexican heritage (Guzman 1978: 500). The injustices of these repatriations led to great bitterness amongst Mexicans and those of Mexican origin on both sides of the border: a bitterness that was compounded by the clumsy arrogance of the US authorities. The US Commissioner for Immigration, MacCormack, for example, announced new security measures in these terms:

On the southern border extreme vigilance is now necessary to prevent the illegal re-entry of those Mexicans who during the depression voluntarily returned to Mexico, or were repatriated

48

at the expense of American communities. In seeking readmission, they would frequently present themselves as if they were returning after a temporary visit to Mexico, to a non-abandoned domicile in the United States. The most careful examination on the part of experienced inspectors is required to obtain the real facts. (Cited in Guzman 1978: 502.)

Whatever the private feelings of the Mexican authorities at the ignominious treatment of their citizens, they had little to offer in the way of alternative employment for the repatriates. When, therefore, the US war industry began hotting-up in anticipation of the war and the army was massively expanded, the Mexican authorities were only too relieved when, in 1940, growers in the south-western states petitioned the Secretaries of State, Labour, and Agriculture to allow them to recruit Mexican labour in the interests of national defence' (Craig 1971: 37–40). On the day after Pearl Harbor, the careful examinations by MacCormack's experienced inspectors were suddenly suspended and the border was once again open for business.

1942–64 Migration in this period was characterised by three principal features. First, illegal and legal migration for industrial employment accelerated, while migrants already in the US moved from agricultural employment in the south-west to swell urban Chicano communities elsewhere in the US, with notable concentrations in the *barrios* established in east Los Angeles, El Paso, San Antonio, Houston, Denver and Chicago. Second, an official agreement, the Bracero Program, was instituted by the US and Mexican authorities. Third, periodic deportations like that of the massive 'Operation Wetback' (1954) were instituted by the US authorities. The fate of the migrant communities properly forms part of the material covered in Chapters 5 and 6, but it is necessary to comment both on the Bracero Program and Operation Wetback to understand some major dynamics of the migratory process.

Although the Mexican government was somewhat apprehensive about the welfare of their nationals in the United States following the legacy of earlier repatriations, it nonetheless agreed in 1942 to enter into the Bracero agreement.

This agreement stipulated certain conditions to protect the wages and living standards of Mexican migrants, but these conditions were not strictly adhered to. The minimum wage stipulated in the agreement soon, in practice, became the maximum wage. Initially the agreement was intended as a temporary war measure—in fact, under pressure from the growers, it lasted until 1964. The numbers involved can be seen in Table 2.1 which also includes figures from 1965–68 when the Bracero Program was officially ended, but admitted aliens continued to be reported under the same category.

Table 2.1 Contract labour under the Bracero Program

1942	4 203	1956	444 581
1943	52 098	1957	450 422
1944	62 170	1958	418 885
1945	49 454	1959	447 535
1946	32 043	1960	427 240
1947	19 632	1961	294 149
1948	33 288	1962	282 556
1949	143 455	1963	195 450
1950	76 519	1964	181 738
1951	211 098	1965	103 563
1952	187 894	1966	18 544
1953	198 424	1967	7 703
1954	310 476	1968	6 127
1955	390 846	Total	5 050 093

Source: Samora and Simon 1977: 140

The close connection between the demands of the growers and the flow of migrants is shown by the fact that the peak of admissions under the Program coincides with the boom years of the 1950s, leading often to the displacement of local labourers who were not prepared to work for the pay and conditions provided for braceros. A labour lawyer active at the time, Ernesto Galarza (1977: 33–4), describes the conditions of the braceros in these terms:

They were based in camps and provided with barracks, cabins or tents. On rainy days or during lulls in the harvest the men lay on their cots under improvised indoor clotheslines strung with everything from socks to overalls. ... The braceros were marked off from the domestics in so far as they could be managed as a separate component of the labour force. The work assignments were arbitrary, lodgings were shuffled capriciously, meals were priced by a cost formula known only to managers, payroll records were coded.

Galarza and his fellow union organisers in the National Agricultural Workers' Union viewed the continued use of bracero labour with alarm. In 1957, of the labour force that picked tomatoes in the San Joaquin Valley, 92 per cent were braceros, as were 93 per cent of the lettuce pickers in Imperial County and 94 per cent of the celery harvesters. The union organisers responded by organising a long and intensive campaign to end the Bracero Program, an object which they finally achieved in 1964.

The substantial increases in the use of bracero labour in the mid-1950s has also sometimes been attributed to the expulsion of illegal (liberal opinion prefers the expression 'undocumented') workers during Operation Wetback, and the consequent need to employ more legally-contracted workers. In his well-documented study of the mass deportations of 1954, Garcia (1980) challenges many of the supposed benefits of Operation Wetback. Even if more officially-sponsored braceros were employed, the mass deportations 'did little to change attitudes, particularly in those areas where exploiting "wetbacks" had become socially and morally accepted' (Garcia 1980: 230). The result was that braceros were treated as if they were 'wetbacks', thus undermining what little contractual protection there existed in the formal agreements. As one grower callously remarked: 'We used to buy our slaves; now we rent them from the Government.' (Cited in Garcia 1980: 230).

Operation Wetback also dramatises the role of at least two major actors in the drama of Mexican migration: the Immigration and Naturalization Service (INS) and the Mexican-American community. Like many organisations the INS was beginning to act for organisational goals somewhat at a tangent to the purpose for which it was established. It was thus not surprising that the INS chose to inflate the number of departures resulting through deportation, repatriation or

51

'voluntary' exits in the period immediately before and during Operation Wetback. The INS claimed that some 1 300 000 Mexicans left during the (fiscal) year 1954 with over one million (see Table 2.2) being apprehended by the INS.

While modern scholarship (Garcia 1980: 227, 228) discounts the 1954 figures as exaggerations, such apparent assiduousness by the INS was rewarded with improved uniform, pay and status for the border patrols, and increased budgetary and political support from Congress for the INS's policy proposals. Seen from another perspective, Operation Wetback can also be viewed as a periodic, almost ritualistic, blood-letting designed to assuage engorged public opinion. In this sense it was the institutional response to a 'moral panic' (see Cohen 1972) generated by fears of an 'alien invasion'. Though one might expect such fears to be at their height during periods of economic recession (which indeed occurred in the 1970s), what is unusual about Operation Wetback is that it took place during a period of high demand for labour. (As I have mentioned, hirings of braceros went up dramatically.) An interpretation of these events, primarily at an ideological level, therefore seems inescapable. The

Table 2.2 Number of undocumented persons apprehended, 1951–64

1951	500 628
1952	543 538
1953	875 318
1954	1 075 168
1955	242 608
1956	72 442
1957	44 451
1958	37 242
1959	30 196
1960	29 651
1961	29 877
1962	30 272
1963	39 124
1964	43 844

Source: Garcia 1980: 236

vendetta against illegal Mexican entrants was phrased in what now have become the customary terms of debate—illegals were taking jobs, homes and social security benefits away from indigenous workers.

The effect of such a campaign redounded with great force on the Mexican-American community. Numbering probably about 12 million people and scattered over much of the south-west (Steiner 1979: 4, 14), they found themselves exposed to mistrust and hostility by mainstream Anglo society, simply by virtue of having a Spanish surname or Mexican 'appearance'. Even those Mexican-Americans who had travelled far along the road to assimilation (and who therefore were hostile or at best ambiguous about the continued flow of migrants from south of the border) found themselves effecting bonds of racial, class, linguistic and religious solidarity with those harassed by the INS. Trolled with the same broad net, the self-identification of many Mexican-Americans became 'Chicano', the writers and poets dreamed of an 'Aztlan nation', while the wild young men joined the 'brown berets' to fight for 'bronze power' (see Acuña 1972; Valdez and Steiner 1972).

1965–the present   The mid-sixties saw a massive and continuing pressure of migrants from the Mexican side of the border, a pressure that continues unabated today. The period was also marked by the attempt to 'stabilise' the border through the operation of the Border Industrialisation Program (BIP), which operated from 1965 to 1973. Finally, there have been a number of attempts by the US administration to 'deal with the problem' of Mexican migration, notable initiatives including those of Nixon's INS chief, General Chapman, in 1971–3, President Carter in 1977 and President Reagan in 1981.

The continuing propensity for Mexicans to migrate is frequently simply explained by the growth of population in Mexico. Superficially, this is a plausible view. Mexico had 25 million people in 1950, 65 million in 1980, with projections of 130 million by the year 2000. Population density is particularly visible in the band of northern Mexican cities near the Rio Grande. Tijuana's population, for example, has grown from 20 000 in 1940 to 165 000 in 1960 and was expected to reach 604 400 in 1980. Likewise, Cuidad Juarez has experienced a population growth of 700 per cent in the period 1945 to 1975 (NACLA 1975: 5). The cry of 'over-population' only, however, signifies more fundamental social and economic problems. As Marx and Engels (1971: 57) remarked of Ireland 'It is not population that presses on productive power; it is productive power that presses on population'.

This pithy dictum applied with great force to Mexico after the Second World War. Foreign investment in Mexico rocketed from US$583 million in 1945 to US$4275 million in 1974, the United States accounting for over three-quarters of the total. Unlike in the pre-war period when foreign investment was concentrated in mining and agriculture, nearly all post-war investment went into manufacture. This had consequent effects on the structure of employment; the percentage of the workforce in industry rose from 12 to 18 per cent, that in agriculture declined from 58 to 33 per cent (Baird and McCaughan 1979: 94). Agricultural production started falling in absolute terms. In the 1960s, the crisis on the land in Mexico's northern areas was so intense, it raised echoes of the pre-1910 revolutionary period. Landless peasants and impoverished farm workers attacked rural military posts and occupied private landholdings (*The Times* (London) 27 February 1976; *The Guardian* (London) 5 March 1977; NACLA 1975: 6). The government in Mexico City was alarmed at the rural unrest, but it was so beholden to foreign capital and domestic landowners that it could not embark on any fundamental programme of income redistribution or land reform. The landless drifted into the northern cities where unemployment averaged 30 to 40 per cent. Even when employment could be found, the wages paid were roughly one-third of the legal minimum wages in the US (Briggs 1978: 6). The temptation to slip across the border for many, was overwhelming.

The Mexican government, in alliance with the US authorities, sought to bring some stability to the ferment of the northern states by instituting the BIP. In brief, the plan was to establish a series of several hundred US *maquiladora*

54

(assembly points) located predominantly in a 20-km strip just inside the Mexican border. Though designed to mop up the surplus population on the northern frontier, in fact it seems likely that the BIP served only to accelerate the already high rates of migration to northern Mexican cities. The BIP could not provide enough alternative employment for those discarded by the ending of the Bracero Program, let alone the enormous number of new entrants to the northern cities. In particular, adult men were hardly affected at all, as the *maquiladoras* overwhelmingly employed young women on the lines, whose labour-power was cheaper and who were seen as a more pliable workforce. In addition, the BIP often played host to a number of 'runaway shops' which left when the best of the tax concessions expired, thus further compounding the unemployment problem. The generally negative assessments of the BIP (NACLA 1975; Fernandez 1977: 131–48) led to an extension of the programme to all underdeveloped areas of Mexico with the hope that the drift of migrants northwards could be halted. Despite Carter's promise in 1977 of US$1 billion to further expand US-led industrialisation in other parts of Mexico, containment of the drift north seems a futile hope.

Enough has been said to indicate the general dynamics of migration from Mexico. The fate of Mexicans once they have crossed the border and their functions in the labour market are subjects addressed at length in Chapter 6. The recent changes in US immigration policies are explicitly dealt with in Chapter 5. For the meantime, it is necessary to turn to migration from selected zones of the Caribbean which, together with Mexico, supplies nearly half the US's legal migrants and the overwhelming number of illegal migrants.

Caribbean migration: opening comments

As southern and eastern Europe dominated the migratory flow to the US at the turn of the century, so Mexico and the countries of the Caribbean basin have taken the largest share of the contemporary flow of migrants. If *legal* migrants alone are considered, Mexico and Cuba account for over half the

55

entries from the Americas recorded in the mid-seventie
while the Dominican Republic, Jamaica, Trinidad and
Tobago, and Haiti collectively add another 21 per cent. I
included in the term 'Caribbean basin' are all countries tha
border on the Caribbean sea (Mexico, Central America and
Panama, Colombia, Venezuela, Guyana, Surinam, French
Guinea, and all the islands in the Caribbean archipelago
some 88.2 per cent of American migrants to the US origi
nated from the basin area (see Table 2.3).

Impressive as these figures are, they considerably under
state the share of total migration that the Mexican and
Caribbean basin areas represent. First, on an extended
definition of the Caribbean such as that deployed by Krit
(1981: 209), Canada and Equador can be included as 'thei
regional orientation is towards other basin countries'. I don'
find this logic particularly compelling in itself. Rather
would point to the effects of step migration. A number of
reported 'Canadians' going to the US may well be Haitia
families who have used Montreal as an intermediate stop.

Table 2.3 Immigrants from the Americas admitted to the US by country of birth, 1957–61 and 1972–76 (000s)

Country/Region	1957–61	(%)	1972–76	(%)
Mexico	173.2	(34.7)	325.8	(38.5)
Cuba	54.9	(11.1)	118.3	(14.0)
Dominican Republic	6.8	(1.4)	67.0	(7.9)
Jamaica	6.8	(1.4)	55.9	(6.6)
Colombia	13.9	(2.8)	28.4	(3.4)
Trinidad and Tobago	—		31.0	(3.7)
Haiti	3.7	(0.7)	25.2	(3.0)
Other Caribbean	46.1	(9.2)	94.0	(11.1)
Canada	149.9	(29.9)	42.3	(5.0)
Ecuador	6.7	(1.3)	22.5	(2.7)
Other Americas	37.7	(7.6)	35.0	(4.1)
Total Americas	499.7	(100.1)	845.4	(100.0)
Americas as % of US total	36.2		43.0	

Source: Adapted from Kritz 1981: 215

Second, and much more important quantitatively, is the question of illegal migration. The major points of departure are Mexico, Haiti and the Dominican Republic although regional step migration (for example, Cuban and Dominicans to Puerto Rico or Haitians to the Bahamas) somewhat complicates the picture, in that points of origin and departure become conflated. The number of illegal migrants in the US was estimated at 8 million in the late 1970s, with a staggering estimate of a further one million illegal entrants annually (Wachter 1978: 80; *Time Magazine* (New York) 16 October 1978). The number of legally-admitted immigrants thus is likely to represent somewhat under a third of all entrants. The overwhelming majority of illegals are people from the circum-Caribbean.

But third, and finally, the dominance of the Caribbean in the US migratory flow is again underestimated by the peculiar status of the US Virgin Islands and Puerto Rico. The former does not supply a significant number of migrants, but Puerto Ricans in the US number in excess of two million people and in 1970 represented an outmigration of 40 per cent of the island's population (History Task Force 1979; Kritz 1981: 219). However, Puerto Ricans have never been counted in immigration figures, since, from 1917, they have had the theoretical right to freely enter the US. Some comments on the origin of this anomaly are in order, before dealing directly with migration from Puerto Rico.

Puerto Rico became a colony of the US in 1898 as a result of the settlement of the Spanish-American War effected by the Treaty of Paris. However, the island was never formally integrated into the US and its constitutional status is somewhat enigmatic. Dietz (1976: 3) simply characterises its relationship with the US as follows 'at a time when classical colonialism is on the decline as a means of control and exploitation, Puerto Rico remains a colonised nation and the Puerto Ricans a colonised people'. Despite various disguises and cosmetic legalisms, notably the Estado Libre Associado ('Free Associated State') Dietz's view captures the essence of the relationship clearly. The locus of all major decisions relating to investment, trade, foreign policy, immigration and emigration and military matters are controlled by Wash-

57

ington, as is the ultimate veto on all decisions in the political sphere. The granting of 'Commonwealth Status' under the 1952 Constitution, following pressure from Marín's Partido Popular Democrático, is now widely recognised as largely meaningless. Lewis (1974; 27), for example, writes: 'the so-called Constitution is little more than a municipal charter which permits Puerto Rico to exercise a degree of local autonomy no larger than that exercised by the local government before 1952'.

The authors of a major collective study insist that the substantive as opposed to the formal relationship between Puerto Rico and the US emerges particularly clearly in the case of migration. They write: 'It is finally beginning to be understood that the intense interaction and circulation of working people between the island and a growing number of communities in the US cannot be treated as just one more migration in the annals of US history'. Previous studies, they continue, contrive to juggle concepts 'in a sterile quest to rationalise a relationship of colonial exploitation' (History Task Force 1979: 26).

The insistence by a number of radical writers on the colonial character of the US-Puerto Rican relationship is clearly an attempt to circumvent the ideology of 'free association' and a way of formulating an alternative possible strategy—that of political independence (Puerto Rican Socialist Party 1975: 39–47). While the colonial dimension is important, Maldonaldo-Denis (1972: 302; 1976) further argues that:

> The problem of Puerto Rican migration should be seen as problem that transcends the relationship between Puerto Rico and the United States, to become a problem ... that hinges upon mass migratory movements within the context of the international division of labour in capitalist countries.

As I shall show below, some of the dynamics of rural dispossession and proletarianisation, i.e. the creation of labour reservoir at the edge of the regional political economy of the US, are as evident in the case of Puerto Rico as they were in Mexico. For these reasons, Puerto Rico's dissimilarity to the other labour reservoirs is more formal than

58

substantive at the economic level, though the dissimilarity asserts itself at the political level.

Puerto Rican migration

1898–1943   These years can be characterised as the period when a stock of labour-power was created and American capital successfully displaced the European mercantilist and underdeveloped capitalist division of labour on the island (Quintero Rivera 1973). Prior to the US occupation, a fairly stable system of local proprietorship still obtained, Puerto Ricans owning 93 per cent of the coffee, tobacco, and sugar farms. According to the Diffies (1931: 150) 'a great number of persons belonging to the rural population were homeowners and permanent residents of the island'. By 1930, 60 per cent of all sugar production was monopolised by four great absentee corporations while even more extensive monopolies were effected in tobacco (80 per cent US-owned), public services and banks (60 per cent) and shipping (100 per cent). From 1900 to 1930, US firms extracted $200 000 000 in profit from the sugar plantations, mills, factories, warehouses, docks and maritime services which they controlled (Maldonaldo-Denis 1972: 305, 6; Bergman *et al.* 1977: 40).

Agricultural workers and *jíbaros* (roughly 'people of the country') were uprooted from their small *haciendas* or coffee farms and constrained to work on the increasing acreages of sugar plantations. The authors, cited above, estimate that over the period of 1896 to 1928, the amount of land planted with sugar increased by 263 per cent while land used for food crops decreased by 31 per cent. *Jíbaros* rapidly were transformed into a proletariat—a large proportion of whom acted as a reserve army both within the local social formation and within the wider US-based social formation. By 1930, there were some 150 000 workers with 600 000 dependants who owned no land at all (Lewis 1974a: 95). Unemployment also moved in harness with capitalist underdevelopment, remaining steady at 18 per cent over the years 1899 to 1910, rising to 20 per cent in 1920, 30 per cent in 1926 and in the midst of the Depression, reaching 40 per cent; social conditions at

59

this point being so adverse that life expectancy dropped to 46 years (Bergman *et al*. 1977: 41, 52; US Department of Labor 1930).

The years 1898 to 1932 have been characterised by Lewis as the period of 'The Imperialism of Neglect', an accurate depiction in that social conditions remained unameliorated by any attempts at welfare measures. The depiction should not, as Lewis (1974a: 85–101) shows, blind us to the single-minded devotion of US companies in building up sugar production at the expense of the *colonos* (small planters) and *criollo* estate owners who effectively disappeared under the impact of American capital. What little escape valve existed for the erstwhile peasantry and unemployed labourers was cut off during the Depression when, during the years 1930 to 1934, there was a net remigration of Puerto Ricans from the mainland (see Figure 2.1 and Table 2.4) escaping the harsh conditions there. The development of 'New Deal' type public works during the 1930s, under the aegis of the Puerto Rican Reconstruction Administration provided some relief for the unemployed, but this was only a temporary solution, which also had the effect of further destabilising the rural population. A reminiscence of the late thirties period is provided by one Don Pedro who is quoted by Steiner (1974: 96, 92) to this effect:

> Farms were abandoned. When those dams and lakes and power plants were built everyone wanted to work there. There were good jobs. And money. So everyone looked to the power plants for work. No one wanted to work on the farms ... After the dams and lakes and power plants were completed we had no farm economy and we had no work. The electricity was not for us anyway. It was for the cities. We lost our way of living to progress. Progress brought us hunger.

The conditions of urban squalor, poverty and the growth of shanty towns in the metropolitan San Juan area were already well advanced by the 1940s, that decade also witnessing the heaviest migration to San Juan from the highland coffee region (Safa 1974: 1–21). For the most part, migration in this period was contained within the island—over the years 1908 (when figures were first recorded) to 1943, net

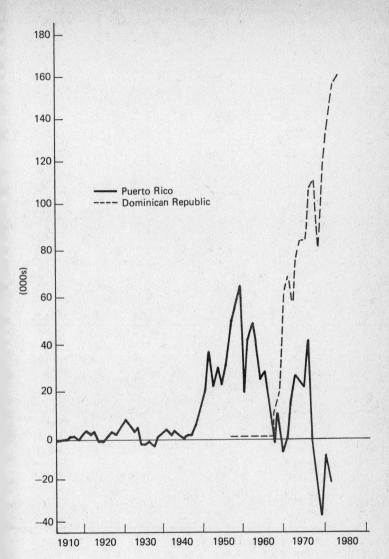

Figure 2.1 Caribbean migration to the US: Puerto Rico and the Dominican Republic, 1910–80

Table 2.4 Net arrivals from Puerto Rico and admissions from the Dominican Republic 1908–76

	Puerto Rico	Dominican Republic		Puerto Rico	Dominican Republic
1908	− 3 111	1943		7 548	
1909	− 3 500	1944		14 794	
1910	− 1 475	1945		21 631	
1911	− 195	1946		39 911	
1912	− 22	1947		24 551	
1913	588	1948		32 775	
1914	339	1949		25 698	
1915	− 33	1950		34 703	
1916	2 354	1951		52 899	1 000
1917	4 212	1952		59 103	1 000
1918	3 312	1953		69 124	1 000
1919	4 139	1954		21 531	1 000
1920	-612	1955		45 464	1 000
1921	-633	1956		52 315	1 000
1922	1 756	1957		37 704	1 000
1923	3 729	1958		27 690	1 000
1924	2 137	1959		29 989	1 000
1925	5 621	1960		16 298	1 000
1926	8 729	1961		− 1 754	12 147
1927	6 144	1962		10 800	22 830
1928	4 637	1963		− 5 379	66 919
1929	5 676	1964		1 370	72 013
1930	− 1 938	1965		16 678	62 142
1931	− 2 708	1966		28 753	85 373
1932	− 1 082	1967		26 553	90 305
1933	− 2 966	1968		23 853	90 323
1934	1 017	1969		43 060	112 124
1935	3 448	1970		− 1 154	115 998
1936	4 518	1971		− 12 901	86 876
1937	2 362	1972		− 33 656	122 605
1938	4 488	1973		− 7 515	138 449
1939	1 904	1974		− 18 378	159 192
1940	988	1975		—	163 452
1941	1 837	1976		—	155 930
1942	2 599				

Sources: Lopez and Petras 1974: 383; Maldonaldo-Denis 1976: 181; Mills *et al.* 1950: 44, 45, 185; Sassen-Koob 1979a: 316; Senior 1961: 26, 27, 38, 39; Vicioso 1976: 66.

migration to the mainland was only 65 798 (see Table 2.4), thus providing the basis for the growth of a Puerto Rican community in the US, centred in New York.

1943–the present As Lewis (1974a) suggests, 1940 can be seen as a major turning point in Puerto Rican political history. In that year, the Partido Popular Democrático was elected to power on a broad nationalist programme, a mood that was fostered by the collapse of the credibility of the New Deal social reformers. In Washington they were replaced by bureaucrats interested in matters of defence and international policy, concerns that even Tugwell, the new Governor who exhibited both unusual liberalism and ability, was unable to escape. What Tugwell's administration was able to accomplish, however, was the presiding over the relative decline of the old sugar giants and the beginnings of large-scale industrial development on the island. The central view the Governor shared with his army of experts and planners was that 'overpopulation' was Puerto Rico's principal problem and that the 'solutions' were threefold—opening up opportunities for emigration to the mainland, encouraging industrial capital to locate on the island and encouraging population control measures (Barlett and Howell 1944; Puerto Rico 1944; Tugwell 1947; Friedlander 1965).

The complex structure of economic, fiscal and tax incentives to US capital that was supervised first by the Development Company (founded in 1942) then by the Economic Development Administration (*Fomento*) resulted in what has come to be known as 'Operation Bootstrap'. It is impossible here to give a fully rounded picture of the effects of Operation Bootstrap. It certainly greatly increased industrial production and per capita income in the early years, the annual rate of growth averaging 6 per cent between 1947 and 1955. But these achievements have to be set against the increased dependency of the Puerto Rican economy on the mainland, the maldistribution of the income generated and the fact that the volume of employment generated has not kept up with the demand for jobs. By the 1980s, the enthusiasm for Operation Bootstrap had collapsed in acrimony, as the taunt 'Welfare Island, USA' gained currency. One US commentator (Heine 1981) put the matter bluntly: 'For too long the solution to Puerto Rico's economic problems has been to integrate the island more and more to the US economy. The results are there for all to see: 57 per cent of the population on food stamps and a 20 per cent unemployment rate.' In terms of employment creation, the industrial development projects on the island demonstrated a similar flaw to the BIP in Mexico. Migration to the capital, San Juan, was stimulated (even to the point of occasioning a rural labour shortage) while women workers, who were relative newcomers to the wage labour force, provided the bulk of employees. Thus the continuing problem of youth and male unemployent has not been solved at all.

What concerns us here is that migration to the mainland, one of the solutions to unemployment advocated by Tugwell's planners, was strongly encouraged by the provision of cheap air travel in 1943—thus permitting Puerto Ricans to enter the US on a large scale. Some 606 180 Puerto Rican migrants entered the US over the period 1944 to 1960. This was the first big wave of Puerto Rican migration, the second big immigration peak occurring between 1965 and 1969. The 'mild' recession of 1961 was accompanied by a trough in Puerto Rican migration in the first four years of the sixties, a trough which deepened in the seventies with the advent of the recession (see Figure 2.1 and Table 2.4).

To understand why the volume of Puerto Rican in- and out-migration corresponds so closely to the cyclical changes in the US economy, it is necessary to examine the place of Puerto Ricans in the US labour force and in particular to show how the jobs they fill are highly vulnerable to the booms and slumps characteristic of a capitalist economy. The most useful data available is in a US Department of Labor Survey examining the labour market experience, economic status and social characteristics of Puerto Ricans of working age living in central and east Harlem, the South Bronx and Bedford-Stuyvesant between July 1968 and June 1969. According to this survey (cited in Lopez and Petras 1974: 347, 8):

> Puerto Rican workers were the most deprived of all workers residing in the city's major poverty neighbourhoods. They were

64

far more likely than others to be unemployed or to hold lower paying jobs. Typically they held blue-collar or service jobs requiring relatively little skill . . . Lower educational attainment, unfavourable occupational attachments and concentration in industries with relatively large seasonal fluctuation in employment combined to make for high unemployment among Puerto Rican workers: nearly 10 per cent of them were jobless during the survey period, almost three times the rate for the city's white workers in 1969 and twice the rate for the city's Negro workers . . . Two thirds of all Puerto Rican families had less than $6000 in income—again twice the proportion for the city.

The vulnerability of Puerto Rican jobs can be specified further from data collected in the same report. Two-fifths of the Puerto Ricans (as opposed to one-fifth of other New York workers) held jobs in manufacturing industries, an employment sector that declined by 13 per cent between 1959 and 1969. Puerto Ricans are also disproportionately found in industries with high seasonal variation in employment. In the garment industry, for example, where many Puerto Ricans are employed, employment in 1969 fluctuated by 8 per cent between the peak and trough months, compared to 3 per cent in other industries. The jobs held by Puerto Rican women are also highly susceptible to slumps, their possible unemployment being made worse by the fact that fully one-third of them are heads of households. Whereas one-half of the city's women performed clerical or sales work, only one-quarter of Puerto Rican women were so engaged. Again, whereas only one-third of the city's women held service or blue-collar jobs, these jobs occupied two-thirds of Puerto Rican women—who often work in the 'sweated trades' (in particular the garment industry).

Sufficient data has been cited to illustrate the precarious situation of mainland Puerto Rican workers. It is also necessary to add that in respect of pay, the differential between the mainland and the island was seriously narrowing in the early 1970s, partly because of the increased class organisation of workers on the island. The authors of the study sponsored by the Centro de Estudios Puertorriqueños point out that in 1970 the average hourly earnings in manufacturing on the island were just over half the equivalent earnings in the US. But since Puerto Ricans in the US only earn on average three-fifths to three-quarters of the average wage in their occupation, the differential is substantially reduced. Taking the lower figure as the 1970 average, the difference would be 25 cents per hour—compared to 35 cents per hour in 1963 (History Task Force 1979: 168). I may add that though there is no systematic data on comparative expenditure patterns (that I am aware of), it is likely that the cost of housing, food, transport and a workers' tax liability is weighted against the Puerto Rican mainlander compared with his or her counterpart on the island. Where equivalent occupations are considered, the narrowing of wage differentials together with the increased cultural and political assertiveness of mainlander Puerto Ricans have led to a considerable level of return migration to the island since 1972. The exact balance of net migration must remain speculative as the 1980 census figures were subject to challenge on the grounds of under-enumeration of 'Latins'. Data collected in 1977 and 1978 suggested a net migration to the US, but early tallies of the 1980 census indicated that departures from Puerto Rico in the 1970s fell well below the 1960s level (Dominguez 1982: 9; Bonilla and Campos 1981: 150). On the other hand, the disproportionately harsh effects of Reaganomics on the welfare budget of the island, together with increased competition (from the Dominican Republic and Haiti especially) for Puerto Rico's brand of export-led industrialisation, have probably induced a slowdown in the rate of return migration. It may well be that some rough equilibrium has now been reached, with 40 per cent of Puerto Ricans being located on the mainland and the remaining 60 per cent on the island.

Migration from the Dominican Republic

The most important cases, numerically, of post-war migration to the United States have now been dealt with—that is, those of Mexico and Puerto Rico. Quantitatively, the next most important example is Cuba (see Table 2.3), but this case will find some coverage in Chapter 5, where the contrasting treatment of the Haitian refugees illustrates an important ideological dimension of state policy. It would clearly be unnecessary to elaborate on all the remaining cases listed in Table 2.3 in order to further validate my analysis of the dynamic of migratory flows in the US regional economy, but I do wish to provide some commentary on the Dominican Republic.

Not only is the country a major source of migrants (legal and illegal), Dominicans also provide an illustrative contrast to the case of the Puerto Ricans. Whereas the political and economic domination of the country by the US is of similar significance as in the case of 'colonial' Puerto Rico, the difference in their legal and constitutional status has forced many Dominicans into the illegal labour market where many have acted as replacement labour for Puerto Ricans, often in conditions of fear and insecurity.

Migration from the Dominican Republic trickled into the US at a fairly insignificant rate before the 1960s. The reasons for its sudden upsurge can ultimately be traced to the economic and political consequences of the US's involvement in the Dominican Republic's economy and political system in its quest for regional hegemony. A very close relationship between the Dominican Republic and the US has been enforced on the former ever since the early 1900s when the United States sent in customs' agents to secure the repayment of outstanding loans. When this initiative failed to achieve its desired objective, US Marines were landed. The US then undertook a unification drive and in the process managed to sever the Dominican Republic's traditional economic ties with Europe—replacing these with an economically dependent relationship with the US. As early as 1924, almost 70 per cent of imports into the Dominican Republic came from the US, while 30 per cent of their exports went to the United States (Vicioso 1976: 61). Over the years the US progressively gained more and more of a foothold in the Dominican Republic until in April 1965, when the US authorities saw a social democratic trend as threatening their control, they mounted a full-scale invasion, killing 5000 Dominicans. Subsequently, the US supervised the election of a friendly presidential candidate, Balaguer, the CIA having eliminated his discredited predecessor,

Trujillo, by means of an assassination authorised by John F. Kennedy (Vicioso 1976: 61; Gutiérrez 1972: 24).

Balaguer's regime served to solidify Dominican dependency on the US, with the economy being tightly integrated to US business interests. All sugar and mineral extraction was denationalised—nickel, gold and bauxite production fell into US hands, while Gulf and Western Industries acquired about one-third of sugar production. US manufacturing industry was induced to set up in the new 'tax-free zones' (see Chapter 7 for a full discussion of the capital-to-labour model) with wages undercutting the Puerto Rican rate for the job. As in northern Mexico and Puerto Rico, the local rural population have lost their capacity to survive in the countryside—unemployment is exacerbated by the US sugar giants who import even less fortunate Haitian migrants into the Dominican Republic. Current estimates are that nearly 90 000 Haitians live in the Dominican Republic, legally or illegally (Santana 1976: 129). Local peasants flock into the larger towns or cities in search of employment or are propelled to leapfrog this stage of their step migration by entering the US directly.

Political and economic domination by the US triggered two different kinds of migratory flow. The first significant wave was largely middle class in composition and came to the US in the 1960s, especially after Trujillo's assassination. Prior to this period, immigration to the US had been restricted by the Trujillo regime itself—over the decade 1951 to 1960 only 10 000 Dominicans were admitted. By contrast, during the period 1961 to 1976, 1 556 678 were admitted (see Table 2.4). In 1978, it was estimated that 400 000 Dominicans were living in New York alone (half of them illegals) and that one million Dominicans at home directly or indirectly depended on money remitted from the United States (*Time Magazine* (New York) 16 October 1978).

This sudden upsurge reflected the intensity of the rural crisis, especially from regions like Cibao where, according to Sassen-Koob (1979a: 318) 'almost everyone has a relative, *compadre* or friend in New York'. This tight network of kinship and association allows even relatively impoverished

68

migrants to find or borrow the $500 needed to acquire phoney documents to enter the US. Power (1979: 132) recounts the case of a Dominican family acquiring a one-way-only forged passport and tourist visa for $1200.

Because most migrants from the Dominican Republic are without legal documentation, even by comparison with the Puerto Ricans, they are highly exploited, having little protection through unions, social security, health insurance, and other benefits even though dues for these are deducted from their pay each week. A 1975 US Department of Labor study cited by Vicioso (1976: 68) showed that of 793 apprehended 'illegals', approximately 75 per cent paid social security taxes and federal income taxes (through employers' deductions) but only 4 per cent received unemployment compensation, 4 per cent had children in school, 1 per cent obtained food stamps and 5 per cent had received welfare. The same survey showed that 16 per cent of the workers were paid lower wages and 11 per cent received less than the minimum wage because of their illegal status. As another study by Hendricks confirms, the constant fear of apprehension also serves to isolate the Dominicans from mainstream society and forces them to forgo even the minimum protection of unemployment benefits and health care (Hendricks 1974).

Conclusions

The data cited on Puerto Rico, Mexico and the Dominican Republic partly support one proposition of established theory advanced at the beginning of this chapter and illustrate a number of the alternative perspectives I put forward.

Following Lee (1969), I asked whether the rate of migration followed variations in the economy. Though this is not stated, it can be assumed that the proposition was meant to apply to the labour-importing economy. When looking at Figure 2.1, it can be seen that the waves and troughs of Puerto Rican migration indeed closely follow the ups and downs of the US economy. This was noticed in an early study (Mills *et al.* 1950: 43, 44) where a correlation with the high coefficient of 0.73 between the pattern of migration from Puerto Rico and US 'business activity' was found over the period 1908 to 1948. During the early years of the Second World War some discrepancy occurs, but this is readily accounted for by the inadequacy of transport from Puerto Rico and the relative isolation of the island (sometimes surrounded by German submarines). With the institution of cheap air transport in 1943, the correlation reasserts itself with peaks occurring in the early 1950s and late 1960s and return migration to Puerto Rico occurring after the partial slump of 1961 (Alvarez 1967), and during the recession beginning in 1973. Though the data is still too vague for firm assertion, the negative effects of the Reagan period on the secondary labour market in the north-east and on welfare entitlements on the island seem roughly to cancel each other out in respect of net migration.

The ebb and flow of Mexican migration also seems broadly to follow fluctuations in the business cycle in the US, particularly with respect to the seasonal and periodic demands for agricultural labour in the south-west. However, a demand-side labour market explanation needs to be discussed within the context of the particular needs and demands of the growers, whose political interests were especially well served by Congress during wartime 'emergencies'. There is also the major problem of economic rationality being confronted by a powerful social prejudice directed against Mexican workers—which (as in Operation Wetback) can disturb any neat economic explanation. Finally, demand-side economics take no account of the enabling and releasing mechanisms, the mechanisms of incorporation and transformation, which structure the availability of Mexican workers of a particular background for work in particular occupations. The fact that these workers are normally undocumented, permits a level of exploitation at the point of production greater than can be accounted for by mere market forces.

Attention to the labour-exporting zone is also necessary in the case of my final example, the Dominican Republic. While an upward fluctuation in the demand for cheap labour can explain the strong growth of Dominican migration in the 1960s, the equally high entry figures in the 1970s (see Figure

2.1) during a period of recession have to be largely explained by the even more debilitating conditions existing in the Dominican Republic.

Thus, while the data cited can partially support the proposition that migration flows vary with fluctuations in the importing country's business cycle, any variations to this pattern impel us to consider auxilliary logics and explanations. Those that I have introduced, include the need to examine the historical patterns of transformation and incorporation by a rich country of its surrounding labour reservoirs. Thus, it does make a difference to the flow and fate of migrants that US *political* hegemony was expressed in colonial terms in Puerto Rico and neo-imperial terms in the Dominican Republic and elsewhere. Equally, the fact that great chunks of Mexico were annexed during the westward thrust of US capital had important effects on the nature of the 'border' and consequent notions of legality and illegality.

What does appear true of all three cases is that the penetration of US capital triggered a massive crisis in the rural areas, displacing peasant proprietors and impelling them towards the cities in search of work. Whatever the attempts to provide such work in the home country (the Border Industrialisation Program, Operation Bootstrap and tax-free zones in the Dominican Republic), they were never sufficient to provide alternative jobs for the rising populations and the displaced peasantries. These groups became part of the relative surplus population, 'riveted to capital', yet unable to always find a market for their labour-power. Their countries became field hospitals for the reserve army of labour that the employers and the US state sought to draw on as and when their labour-power was required.

I say 'sought to' in that a hegemony that resembles Orwell's '1984' must not be assumed. It is true that employers often have the whip hand in offering employment in the secondary labour market and turning to alternative sources of supply when one segment gains some level of class organisation. It is true too that the state has become increasingly sophisticated in managing and regulating the labour market and in policing the core zone of the regional political economy. But hundreds of thousands of workers, driven to desperate and sometimes heroic feats by conditions in their own countries, manage to evade these controls and live on the edge of legality and social acceptance. Such a fate, fearful as it is, is often preferable to coping with the debilitating conditions in the labour reservoirs. The reproduction of labour-power at the edge of the regional political economies and the effects of migration on social conditions in the labour reservoirs form the principal subjects of the next chapter.

3 The reproduction of labour-power: southern Africa

The labour-power withdrawn from the market by wear and tear, and by death, must be continually replaced by, at the very least, an equal amount of fresh labour-power.

(Marx 1976: 275)

For its existence and further development capitalism needs non-capitalist forms of production as its surroundings.

(Luxemburg 1951: 289)

In Chapter 1 Marx's injunction that labour-power has continually to be replaced was seen to be obeyed by the Nazi regime in a special sense. Rather than securing the conditions for the reproduction of labour-power from within the German economy, the Nazis fed fresh supplies of labour-power into the war machine from the conquered lands in order to service immediate expansionist goals. If literally unlimited supplies of labour can be hypothesised, such a strategy can be pursued over a longer period too. As will be shown, such a strategy was attempted by the mining companies of southern Africa in their search for cheap labour.

However, totally unlimited supplies of labour are something of an economists' fiction, despite Lewis's (1954) instructive insights into the relationship of labour supply to economic development. Barring some exceptional circumstances, nationally-based capitalists generally have to develop some capacity for the internal replacement of labour-power, if only because the cost of renewing the existing labour force has to be weighed against the cost of subduing, transporting and training raw recruits from far afield.

How is internal reproduction to be accomplished? Despite

73

Marx's acceptance of the relationship between the reproduction of labour-power and the long-term persistence of capital accumulation, feminists have rightly attacked him for failing to address the question of how precisely the proletarian family reproduced itself (Kuhn 1978: 46–51). Instead, Marx simply assumed that the reproduction of labour-power could safely be left to 'the workers' drives for self-preservation and propagation' (Marx 1976: 718). This Darwinian assumption was perhaps a natural one to make. For Marx, the fecundity of the working-class family was unproblematic and natural—indeed, his treatment of Malthusian theory is positively light-hearted. He thought that Malthus himself engaged in 'schoolboyish superficial plagiarism', though at least he was celibate unlike the other Protestant parsons, who contributed to the increase of population 'to a really unbecoming extent whilst at the same time preaching "the principle of population" to the workers' (Marx 1976: 766, 7). Despite the levity, the gap in Marx is yawning. Analysing the conditions of the reproduction of labour-power within the household unit is critical to understanding the dynamics of the capitalist mode of production itself. The importance of such an analysis is two-fold, one economic, the other ideological. In the former case, the modern debate, often referred to as 'the domestic labour debate', hinges around the issue of whether, and to what extent, unpaid female labour (in the private domestic sphere) acts to subsidise the cost of the commodity, labour-power, to employers operating in the public sphere of 'social production'. In the latter case, the family (or the household) is seen by many feminists as an important site for the reproduction of certain sexist relations of production/reproduction, which are often rather loosely referred to as 'patriarchy' (Kuhn and Wolpe 1978).

Both these debates are of relevance to the question of the reproduction of labour-power in southern Africa. However, it is necessary to widen the context of the debate and provide a short critique of each set of arguments. The domestic labour debate, for instance, became rather bogged down in an abstruse exchange about what Marx really meant about 'valorisation', 'productive', 'unproductive' and 'socially necessary' labour, etc. As asserted earlier, this is of secondary consequence to the fact that an analysis of the household unit is virtually absent in the classical texts. The protagonists to the debate were also coming to the argument with different political trajectories. Those who insisted that the point of production was the site of all meaningful political and class struggles, were forced into a position of arguing for the marginality of domestic labour except in so far as its *product*, labour-power, became an exchangeable commodity (Seccombe 1974; Smith 1978). Smith (1978: 204) goes further in making the rather cruel point that domestic labour is none the less performed even when labour-power is not exchanged, that is, when the wage earner is unemployed. Though this is superficially a clever riposte to naive feminism, the point is a weak one in so far as orthodox Marxism, which he defends, acknowledges the need to reproduce the *reserve* army of the proletariat, as well as those who are actively employed. For those who are broadly within an orthodox left camp, women's liberation lies in escaping domestic labour, becoming fully proletarianised and engaging in economic and political struggle together with the remaining (male) section of organised labour.

If this is indeed the logic of the orthodox view (and I believe I have characterised it correctly), millions of women in the domestic units of the advanced capitalist countries and in the peasant households of the backward countries must remain doomed to perpetual political and social oppression. For who now can believe that capitalism is in sufficiently vigorous a state to draw all humankind into direct productive labour? This scenario is worth considering, at least theoretically (see Chapter 7), but all realistic projections suggest that the ratio of those without formal employment to those in wage employment will massively widen into an 'unemployment time bomb'. Using approximate figures projected from ILO estimates, in the year 2000 there will be roughly 3250 million unpaid members of the world's population compared to rather less than 2600 million waged workers. The projections after 2000 increase the ratio exponentially (Kidron and Segal 1981: 52).

On the other hand, a number of feminists have argued that domestic labour is far less marginal than the orthodoxy would lead us to assume. According to this view, domestic labour is socially necessary labour, and is productive in the sense that it contributes to the exchange value of the commodity, labour-power, and therefore to the creation of surplus value. Though being productive labour in this indirect sense, women are central to the capitalist mode of production, and they can (and should) organise around their specific relationship to the means of reproduction. Their political trajectory should lie, not in entering the wage force, *pace* Engels, but in demanding 'wages for housework' (Smith 1978: 199; Dalla Costa and James 1975). Again the logic of this position leads to a rather unrealistic view of the contemporary world order. Can such feminists believe that capitalist employers or a capitalist state would willingly pay a wage for reproduction costs, when such costs can be avoided entirely by importing migrant labour or exporting capital to areas where a ready stock of labour-power exists in abundance? A good illustration of the unlikelihood of these costs being borne by the capitalist sector was provided by French scholars in 1973, who estimated that the market price for unpaid domestic labour could be costed at over three times the minimum French wage (Meillassoux 1981: 142).

In short, both positions in the domestic labour debate are flawed by their parochialism—in imagining that they are dealing with the possibility of growing proletarianisation on the one hand, or with a closed economy on the other. Yet, placed in a different context, these debates do bear on wider issues of development and underdevelopment, on the processes of labour segmentation and on the nature and logic of capitalist accumulation. For Meillassoux (1981: 95) the linking point is imperialism. As he writes:

It is by establishing organic relations between capitalist and domestic economies that imperialism set up the mechanism of reproducing cheap labour-power to its profit—a reproductive process which, at present, is the fundamental cause of underdevelopment at one end and of the wealth of the capitalist sector at the other. Socially and politically it is also the root cause of the division of the international working class.

Meillassoux argues (1981: 97–8) that the impact of the

imperialist relationship is revealed in a double-sided and contradictory manner. On the one hand, the domestic 'mode' of production is preserved as a means of social organisation from which imperialism profits. On the other hand, it is destroyed by virtue of the superior capacity of the capitalist mode of production to exploit and dominate pre-capitalist modes. With a charming Gallic ingenuity, the puzzle is solved: 'Under the circumstances, the domestic mode of production both exists and does not exist' (Meillassoux 1981: 97). I feel impelled to resist this kind of dialectical sophistry for it has become the basis of such a meta-theoretical mishmash that the authors of a lengthy work on *Pre-Capitalist Modes of Production* in the Althusserian tradition were constrained to develop an auto-critique of their own work two years later, which effectively denied it had any empirical or historical validity (Hindess and Hirst 1975; 1977).

The plain fact is that any scholar interested in reality, rather than theoretical discourse, has to exercise a historical judgement as to when the power of capital to dominate a pre-capitalist mode of production has reached a salient break point—in Marxist terms, the point when the pre-capitalist mode is not only 'formally' but 'really' subsumed under capitalist relations (cf. Taylor 1979: 215–23). I concur with Bennholdt-Thomsen (1981: 18) in finding this dividing line in three facets: (a) wage labour—where members of the rural household are forced to sell their labour-power for a whole or part of the year; (b) the market—where a 'peasantry' is created producing commodities for a national, regional or international market; and (c) credit—where sections of capital gain control of the rhythms of peasant production by the provision of loans, advance purchase agreements, extension programmes and the like. Obviously, the extent to which these factors are present varies a great deal from country to country and over time. In terms of my present interest in southern Africa, the most reliable historical accounts date the collapse of an autonomous African economy in South Africa between the years 1870 and 1913. The first named year marked the beginnings of the minerals revolution (the discovery of diamonds and gold), the second was marked by the passing of the Native Lands Act, when the African reserves were established. Though there was a period of successful adaptation by the African peasantry to the emerging commodity market, which has been much underrated by an earlier generation of historians, the period was 'crucial' in 'transforming the bulk of the rural African population from their pre-colonial existence as pastoralist-cultivators to their present existence as sub-subsistence inhabitants on eroded and overcrowded lands, dependent for survival upon wages earned in "white" industrial areas and on "white" farms' (Bundy 1979: v).

To return to my starting point. The domestic labour debate is of significance here only in so far as the unit of the reproduction of labour is conceived of as *both* the family in advanced capitalist countries and the peasant household in backward countries. It is of course perfectly possible, indeed it is quite common, that labour-power produced in the most backward areas of the regional political economy is destined to be deployed in the most advanced sector. This fact alone makes it necessary to link both sites of production and reproduction analytically. As Bennholdt-Thomsen (1981: 16) states: 'within the present capitalist world economy, housewives and peasants (men and women) are the main subsistence producers; in different concrete forms both reproduce labour-power for capital without compensation'. Though Meillassoux and other structuralist theorists have recognised the contributions to reproduction from both housewives and peasantries (thereby transcending many metropolitan debates), their work is flawed by anthropological and theoretical fictions like the 'pre-capitalist *modes* of production' which many historians (I have simply cited one on South Africa) would dismiss as anachronistic. The very fact that rural economies can only survive economically by reproducing labour-power for the advanced capitalist sector is testimony enough to the serious erosion of the domestic mode of production. To signify this enfeeblement I have used the term 'form' rather than 'mode' of production, to indicate that shell rather than substance is being dealt with in respect of the pre-capitalist economy.

However, because capital has generally (and certainly in

the context of South Africa) long abolished any autonomous economic capacity for the rural economy, this does not mean that I deny that many elements of the pre-capitalist world might survive at the level of social and cultural behaviour. Indeed, 'traditionalism' might be reconstructed, or even invented, to provide some ideological and social defence in the face of economic erosion or total collapse, or in the wake of military defeat. Such a context has provided the basis for millenarian and peasant movements in many countries. But popular reaction does not always take oppositional forms; adaptation to the new forces of economic dominance often produces an ideology functional or at least somewhat conducive to the changed material basis. This brings me directly to the second major aspect of reproduction mentioned earlier— namely, the reproduction of the *relations* of production.

Again feminists have opened out this arena of debate under the rubric of the debate about 'patriarchy', against a background of a merely nominal development of the arguments by Marx (see Henderson and Cohen 1982: 112–14). Again, however, the feminist debate is too narrow for present purposes, in so far as one of the major aspects of the reproduction of capitalist relations in peasant households, is the construction of an ideology supporting labour migration, an issue barely addressed in metropolitan debates. By contrast, Murray's comment (1981: 41) on Lesotho, one of South Africa's major labour reservoirs, typifies this phenomenon well:

> The paradigm of the successful migrant career for a man is to establish his own household and to build up a capital base, through the acquisition of land, livestock and equipment, to enable him to retire from migrant labor and to maintain an independent livelihood at home. Few men achieve independence in this way. Most must commit themselves in their declining years to dependence on the remittances of sons or of other junior kin who in turn engage in the oscillating pattern.

What is characteristic about this case is just as there are sufficient pop stars in England who become millionaires or sufficient black footballers in Brazil who become national heroes, so there are sufficient numbers of prosperous migrants to sustain the ideology of a successful migration. The myths of social mobility, equal opportunity and independent proprietorship all act to support and mentally alleviate the general extraction of surplus value from those who give credence to such myths. Listen, for example, to this idealistic young Lesotho woman's view of the relationship between migration and the reproduction of the domestic economy: 'On your first trip to the place of the whites you support those who brought you up. On your second trip, you take out money that counts as cattle for marrying a wife. On your third trip, you look after everything in your own homestead.' (Cited in Murray 1981: 60).

Regrettably such an optimistic scenario is rarely to be found. One-sixth of the total population of Lesotho is employed in South Africa at any one time, the earnings of migrants far exceed the gross domestic product (GDP), while about 70 per cent of the rural household income is provided for by regular remittances. Without *many* 'trips' to South Africa, the rural household (which provides only 6 per cent of GDP) would cease to exist and starvation would ensue (Murray 1981: 19). Unlike the young Lesotho women, those who have been ground down by the system of labour migration for a longer period both recognise their intolerable dependence and the strains it puts on both husband and wife. In a desolate song called 'I waste my energy' a Mozambican woman, Luisa Agosto Mbatini, laments her desertion, but sees that the need to migrate can produce an equally unhappy outcome for the man. An interviewer (First 1983: 164) records the reaction of her listeners to her song:

Your husband has not deserted you on purpose, it is the white men who are responsible for this! Stay where you are even if you have to suffer. Remain there and till your fields and take care of your small children! This is the advice which we fellow women give you and it is based on experience—we too have been suffering. It does not mean that your husband has deserted or left you; he is the victim of the white men's ways of life. He will return to find you here. [Luisa Mbatini replied] I remain alone here and waste my energy, tilling the fields and taking care of the family and when he comes back he tells me he doesn't love me any more. Today he comes back from 'there' [Johannesburg] and all my energy has been wasted! The same applies to men. They work and send money to build homes, but when they come home they find that the woman has gone off with another man.

These quotations from rural women in southern Africa provide helpful illustrations of my theoretical argument. At the level of ideology, capitalist social relations are not reproduced solely through patriarchy, nor are men invariably less oppressed than women. It does nothing to diminish the extraordinary difficulties women face in reproducing the labour force biologically, economically and ideologically to say that men too are victims. In so far as they continue to believe and act on the belief that they can reconstitute the material basis of the peasant household in the face of increasingly heavy odds, men and women have a common and not a contradictory relationship to the capitalist mode of production.

Though not producing much in the way of directly exploitable surplus labour, the peasant household nonetheless subsidises the capitalist mode of production in a number of concrete ways, all of which are involved in the concept of reproduction. What I have broadly characterised as the 'economic' and 'ideological' functionality of the non-capitalist sector can now be specified directly. The peasant household, with a special burden falling on the woman, is engaged in the biological reproduction of labour-power. The woman has to cope with the physical and psychological demands of sexuality. She has to sustain the image of a rural idyll in the face of isolation and 'desertion' by her man. (He too has the stress associated with male compounds and a very limited access to heterosexual relations.) In the pre-natal period she has to produce and cook food and look after her health, clothing and housing needs—with the help of her husband's remittances and occasional physical support (e.g. in house building). Customary obligations to the extended family, particularly the husband's parents, may impose an additional burden. Some of the activities associated with the pre-natal period (health, food and clothing requirements) are continued into the post-natal period which, however, adds

81

impositions like childbirth itself and the subsequent tasks of nursing, educating, training and socialising the child (cf. von Welhof 1980). Peasant households also renew, repair and service the reproduction of labour-power in other ways. They act as points of refuge, rest and recuperation for exhausted labourers. In the event of sickness, injury and disability (common in the southern African mines), they become field hospitals. When workers are fired, marginalised or reach old age, the peasant household provides a functional substitute for unemployment benefits, redundancy payments and a pension.

Simply enumerating the forms in which a peasant household meets costs, otherwise borne by employers and the state, provide a good indication of the dynamics of early capitalist accumulation in southern Africa, which political economy I have chosen to exemplify the question of the reproduction of migrant labourers.

The creation of the labour reservoirs of southern Africa

Modern southern African historians are agreed that the last three decades of the 19th and the first decades of the 20th centuries marked the incorporation of the last remaining African polities and the disintegration of autonomous peasant production. Bundy's (1979) views to this effect have already been quoted. Another reputable historian, Beinart (1982: 1–2), writes of the Zulu, Swazi, Sotho, Twana and Pedi kingdoms in these terms:

> Industrialisation and the accompanying development of transport, urban communities and large-scale agriculture set the terms on which the people of these chiefdoms were absorbed. During the first decades of the twentieth century the areas they inhabited were reduced by uneven but increasingly uniform pressures of change to reservoirs of labour for capitalist enterprises.

For exceptional reasons the area Beinart is especially concerned with, the Mpondo chiefdom, was insulated from

82

direct military incorporation. Thus entry into the labour market was more gradual and on more favourable terms than from the other chiefdoms mentioned. The processes of rural impoverishment also were somewhat delayed in Southern Rhodesia, where until 1912 the mines had to rely on forced (*chibaro*) labour. After this period, as van Onselen (1976: 117) writes:

> The decline of peasant workers, increases in populations and restrictions on the amount of land available were all forcing a growing number of African workers into the cash markets of the regional economic system. The decline of peasant independence on the periphery of the system was making cheap labour available at a rate that undercut even *chibaro* rates on the mines.

Whatever the variations in timing, it was clear that the demand for labour first on the diamond mines of Kimberly, and then for the gold mines of the Witwatersrand reef, impelled massive changes in the rural hinterlands. The scale of the changes wrought by the minerals revolution can be gauged from some statistical data. Within 15 years of the discovery of diamonds in 1867, gems to the value of £32 million had been exported. By 1881, the annual export value of diamonds exceeded the value of all other exports passed through the Natal and Cape ports, while some 17 000 Africans were employed as diggers (van der Horst 1971: 66, 85). The discovery of gold (1886) was to have an even more disruptive effect on the pastoral economies of the region. By the turn of the century, just short of 100 000 labourers were employed in the Witwatersrand mines (Wilson 1972: 2). The Boer War (1899–1902) caused considerable disruption to the supply of labourers for nearly all had returned to the rural areas when the mines were shut down. At the same time, a speculative gold boom fuelled the formation of 299 new gold-mining companies. The High Commissioner, Lord Milner, was desperate: 'I believe that when everything is done that can be, we shall still be short, and very short, of unskilled labour'. (Cited in van der Horst 1971: 168). His fears were grounded, for the Transvaal Labour Commission, reporting in 1904, concluded that the mines needed 197 644 labourers and had only successfully recruited 68 280 (van der

Horst 1971: 169). Though 'dead against Asiatic settlers and traders' Lord Milner thought 'the indentured Asiatic would prove controllable'. Accordingly, some 63 000 Chinese indentured labourers were recruited between June 1904 and January 1907 (Richardson 1984: 167).

The recruitment of Chinese workers was to prove a short-lived solution. Milner, as indicated, authorised it only under extreme pressure. It completely violated his grand plan to 'anglicanise' the country in the wake of the Boer War while the Liberal Government in Britain, under challenge from humanitarian lobbies, refused licences for the further importation of indentured Chinese after November 1906. Yet short-lived as this episode was, it demonstrated some of the laws of motion of the South African gold mining industry. Faced with a production crisis, a tap regulating the labour-power supply from a suitable labour reservoir, however distant, could be quickly turned on. If reduced production or politics intervened, the tap could be shut off just as quickly.

In a fascinating analysis of the origins of the Chinese workers, Richardson demonstrates that dynastic and social collapse, land scarcity, the aftermath of the Boxer rebellion, the exposure of the Chinese economy to international trade and finally the 'spill effects' of the Russo-Japanese war all made the northern provinces of China a particularly fertile recruiting ground for representatives of the South African mines (Richardson 1984: 167–85). But for the political reasons indicated, the Chinese could not provide anything but an intermediate stop-gap solution. In the longer run, it made more sense to try to regularise the process of labour recruitment from Portuguese East Africa (present-day Mozambique). Though labourers from the East Coast had already constituted a very high proportion (60 per cent) of the total mine labour force in the two years before the Boer War (First 1983: 16), there was a great deal of uncertainty by the Chamber of Mines as to whether this source could be relied upon. Wage rates fluctuated sharply, numerous contracting agencies tried to undercut each other to secure orders from the Chamber, the transport and security arrangements for recruits were inadequate and Portuguese officialdom was often corrupted by having to deal with the rival bids of predatory labour contractors. With some exasperation the mineowners complained that 'at Delagoa Bay everything is done by bribery and everybody from the highest to the lowest takes a bribe' (cited Levy 1982: 66). For the upstanding capitalists of the Chamber, themselves purer than the driven snow, a healthy dose of monopoly was called for.

The Chamber concluded that it was no less competent to procure labour than anyone else, while its influence would be more likely to yield positive results than the local touts, whose fees were exorbitant and whose hold over the Portuguese officials was uncertain (Levy 1982: 67). The first recruiting organisation established in 1896 by the Chamber was the Rand Native Labour Association (RNLA). The Chamber then tried to involve the Transvaal government in setting up a state recruiting enterprise and when that failed, set up the successor body to RNLA, namely the Witwatersrand Native Labour Association (usually abbreviated to WENELA for mnemonic reasons). It was this body that in a secret deal with the Portuguese authorities was given the monopoly over recruiting in Mozambique. There is some evidence that, in addition to freezing out the labour recruiters, WENELA was supported by the larger mining interests to throttle the supply of labour to the smaller companies. The mining group J. B. Robinson, for example, tried to circumvent WENELA's control, but the Portuguese, though pretending compliance at first, never produced a recruiting licence for the company (First 1983: xxiv, 18).

Though the management of the labour to the mines was henceforth to remain in the mining companies' hands, the colonial administration in South Africa (established after the Boer War), successive South African governments, and the Portuguese authorities were involved in a series of intergovernmental agreements around the issue of labour recruitment. A *modus vivendi* was agreed in 1901, which led to the Mozambique Conventions of 1909 and 1928. These were amended in 1964 and supplemented by additional agreements in 1965 and 1970 (First 1983: 17, 212–22). Governmental interests were involved in a number of areas. The South African state was determined to maintain the temporary form of migration, insisting indeed that three-year contracts be amended to one year. For their part, the Portuguese authorities used their control over the supply of labourers to extract a deal over the routing of goods from the Transvaal through the Mozambican ports and along her railways. The Portuguese went so far as to suspend recruitment before the colonial government in South Africa knuckled in to their demands. By 1928, not only did the Portuguese authorities obtain a guarantee of the flow of goods along their railheads, they also acquired the revenue from a native tax, levied at the mines, and paid to Lisbon in gold.

The Mozambique agreements are an especially stark illustration of some of the arguments advanced in earlier chapters. Any notion of freely-impelled, individually-motivated migration has to be set aside in the face of the juggernauts that organised this extraordinary trade in labour-power. The Portuguese government effectively sold the labour-power under its command as a means to acquire state revenue—revenue that was realised in Lisbon and not even in Mozambique itself. The nature of this transaction is almost breathtaking in its affront to human dignity and rights. Even Marx did not envisage such an outcome. For him, the most damaging effect that capital could wreak on a peasant economy was that the landless labourers had nothing to sell but their labour-power. In Mozambique, though a precarious attachment to the means of production in the labour-exporting areas still remains, officialdom contrived a its major *raison d'être* the sale of workers' labour-power *on their behalf*. Thus surplus value was not only realised at the point of production by the mineowners (the difference between the value of gold and the value represented b wages), it was also realised in the distribution points of th labour supply system (the proportion of wage costs paid t the Portuguese in fees and taxes).

It is difficult to fully get to the bottom of why the rura economies in Portuguese East Africa were in such a parlou state as to permit this level of exploitation. It is only recentl that studies oriented to the needs and activities of capit have been supplemented by studies committed to unravelling the picture from the labourers' point of view. Some answers to this question can be found in an examination of Inhambane province (First 1983: 115–27). This province provided from about one-quarter to one-fifth of the Mozambican mine workers until the late 1960s when the proportion dropped. The area had experienced a long period of foreign contact and colonial government, the authorities using (as elsewhere) a hut tax to defray the costs of administration and draw the peasants into acquiring a money income. What was unusual about Inhambane was that the peasantry was also forced to compete with Portuguese settlers who occupied the *machangos* (irrigated strips), increasingly forcing Africans on to the sandy soils, the cultivation of which was totally dependent on railfall. The larger Portuguese agriculturalists established *latifundia*, imposing a system of labour-tenancy on the peasant holdings they embraced. The peasant-tenants were required to pay rent either in kind or in cash from their share of production, to provide a period of labour-service, or both. As if these requirements were not onerous enough, a period of *chibalo* (*chibaro* in non-Portuguese areas), or forced labour for six months was held as a reserve power. Though little agricultural work was done by *chibalo* labour, its threat was an important inducement to go to the mines, particularly since signing on for minework provided an automatic legal dispensation from *chibalo*. In allowing this legal trade-off the Portuguese state revealed the contradictory interests operating upon it. For settler agriculture to succeed, a cheap agricultural labour force had to be assured, but a greater revenue could be obtained by selling workers to WENELA. The pressures to reconcile this contradiction induced the government to neglect the peasant sector, providing it with no technology, credit, seeds, fertilisers or pesticides. By this means it was hoped to meet the demands of both settlers and mineowners. Whenever this was not possible, WENELA was fed the first slice of the cake.

The story of Inhambane province is not necessarily a typical one, but the special pressures on peasant agriculture may account for why Inhambane provided such a large share of Mozambican mineworkers and why in turn (assuming

87

related phenomena operated elsewhere in the country) Mozambique became one of the largest reservoirs for mineworkers destined for the Witwatersrand. As can be seen from Table 3.1 the lowest numbers of workers from Mozambique ranged from 24 per cent (1961) to over 70 per cent (1906) of all African mineworkers during the period 1906 to 1971. The table does not contain data for the intervening years between 1971 and 1976 when the high proportion of workers coming from Mozambique continued—indeed in 1975 the number of Mozambican workers was higher than it had been for 20 years (First 1983: 33). This was due to a political crisis affecting the normal supply from Malawi (shown under the category 'Tropicals' in Table 3.1). After 1976, however, the new revolutionary government in Mozambique, led by FRELIMO, tried slowly and painfully to disengage the Mozambican economy from the enveloping clutches of South Africa. For its part, the South African government, as will be seen, devised a new means of obtainable 'foreign' workers by declaring parts of South Africa 'independent homelands'. Significantly, the share of African mineworkers coming from inside South Africa jumped from 22.4 per cent in 1971 to 57.3 per cent in 1979.

Reference to the category of 'foreign workers' illuminates one of the principal characteristics of the South African labour system, namely that the state has always contrived to declare a large proportion of workers 'foreign'—foreign signifying totally without rights of representation or access to what few social benefits are provided within South Africa. Legassick and de Clerq (1984: 142, 143) point out that even ignoring the ambiguities of the 19th-century distinctions which predated the unification of the South African state (1910), post-Union legislation was also eminently manipulable. The Admission of Persons to the Union Regulation Act (no. 22 of 1913) classified African workers from Mozambique and Malawi (Nyasaland) as 'prohibited immigrants' whose 'standards or habits of life' made them unsuitable for permanent settlement in South Africa. Such persons could enter the country only in terms of an inter-governmental treaty or an approved labour recruitment scheme such as that described operating in the case of Mozambique.

Table 3.1   Countries of origin of African mine workers (% employed)

	1906	1911	1916	1921	1926	1931	1936	1941	1946	1951	1956	1961	1966	1971	1976	1979
South Africa	22.80	40.32	44.32	38.69	38.23	49.80	52.18	48.17	41.26	35.29	34.71	36.46	34.04	22.40	43.88	57.30
Mozambique	70.79	51.59	43.73	47.08	47.54	32.71	27.83	27.00	31.54	34.45	30.78	24.22	28.43	26.52	13.44	7.87
Lesotho	2.60	3.82	7.63	10.56	10.93	13.62	14.46	13.10	12.49	11.67	11.93	13.02	16.77	17.78	26.67	22.81
Swaziland	0.70	2.07	2.05	2.28	2.12	2.24	2.21	1.93	1.81	1.84	1.61	1.57	1.13	1.25	2.38	2.09
Botswana	0.40	0.49	1.68	1.11	1.01	1.49	2.25	2.51	2.30	2.69	3.10	3.19	4.95	4.14	4.28	3.91
Tropicals	2.47	1.66	0.58	0.27	0.17	0.14	1.07	7.29	10.60	13.45	17.87	21.54	14.68	27.91	9.35	5.69
Total no. employed (000)	81	174	191	188	203	226	318	372	305	306	334	414	383	379	361	479

Note: 'Tropicals' are those recruited from north of latitude 22°S, chiefly Malawi. Figures are calculated as a percentage of those employed by affiliates of the Chamber of Mines on 31 December each year. Roughly 25 per cent extra can be added to the totals to measure all gold-mining employment (Bromberger 1978: 8).

Source: Böhning 1981: 14

The category of 'Tropicals' shown in Table 3.1 also requires some explanation. WENELA had been restricted from recruiting men north of 22° latitude at first because Portuguese settlers pressed the Mozambique administration to limit the South African recruiters. Later, when some modest supply of labour-power was authorised, the mortality rate, chiefly from pneumonia, rose to alarming proportions—some 67.6 for every 1000 recruited in 1911 (van der Horst 1971: 221). This led to a virtual ban on recruitment of 'Tropicals' until 1937 when it once again commenced on a large scale. A number of factors explain this change of heart. Medical research in South Africa is closely linked to production needs, and in the 1920s the South African Institute of Medical Research, set up and funded by WENELA, had developed the powerful Lister anti-pneumococcal vaccine (Wilson 1972: 68). The mining companies also continued to complain bitterly that they couldn't get enough workers from Mozambique, though there are some indications that production could have been maintained through technological innovation, enskilling and stabilising those Africans already on the mines (van der Horst 1971: 222). This, however, would have challenged both the privileged position of white miners and the traditional assumptions of mineowners—that surplus value could only be realised through large cohorts of unskilled workers breaking and hoisting the massive tonnages of low-grade ore necessary to mill a few ounces of gold. A major stimulus to successful recruiting also lay in the provision of improved transport facilities to the 'tropical' areas (much as the provision of cheap flights to Puerto Rico, discussed in Chapter 2, activated that labour reservoir for the US). Not prone to doing things by half-measures, WENELA established recruiting stations in Namibia (South West Africa), Botswana, Zimbabwe (Rhodesia), Zambia (Northern Rhodesia) and Malawi (Nyasaland), built a 1500-mile road linking its stations in Namibia and Botswana, established motor barge transport on the Zambezi river and laid on train and air services to Malawi and Botswana. By 1955, there were 32 flights organised by WENELA in or out of the Botswana capital each week (Wilson 1972: 69, 70).

90

Naturally, 'Tropicals' from all these areas were deemed foreign and 'prohibited immigrants'. On the other hand, workers from Lesotho (Basutoland), Swaziland and Botswana (Bechuanaland), that is the High Commission territories, were deemed to be part of 'British South Africa'. These areas were regarded as 'native reserves'. It was only in the 1950s and when the decolonising process raised the prospect of these territories becoming independent states, that (in 1963) labourers from the High Commission territories were also reduced to the status of 'foreign' (Legassick and de Clerq 1984: 142). The collapse of the Portuguese empire under the weight of national liberation struggles in Angola and Mozambique, together with the rapid dismantling of the British Empire, was an equally threatening prospect for the mines' recruiting policy. Though the labourers would continue to be 'foreign', negotiations would have to be conducted with nationalist leaders whose rhetoric occasionally included some anti-capitalist sentiments. Even so compliant a figure as President Banda, was impelled by public outrage to cut off the Malawian labour supply in 1974 when a plane carrying 72 Malawian mineworkers crashed, killing all the passengers. Though supplies were resumed in 1977, they never attained their former level.

As the pace of African nationalism quickened, so the South African government began the implementation of its Bantustan policy, that is the conversion of the 13 per cent of land within the formal boundaries of South Africa from the status of 'native reserves' to 'independent countries'. Needless to say this proclaimed sovereignty was recognised by no one but the South African government itself. By 1984, four Bantustans (Transkei, Bophuthatwana, Venda and Ciskei) had become 'nation states', one (Kwandebele) was set to attain 'independent' status within a year, while the remaining five 'homelands' were in various stages of progress toward their own 'independence'. While these peculiar entities can easily be regarded either as objects of farce or ridicule, or cosmetic concessions by the South African government to national and international demands for African representation, they confer undoubted advantages to the regime.

Here is how it works. Millions of South African blacks (many of whom are urban residents of two or three generations standing) are forced to assume an ethnic label. These ethnic identities are then given legal reality in the 'citizenship' of the various 'homelands' (Maré 1983: 75). The homelands are then given 'independence' or, when this is too implausible even for the South African authorities, they acquire the standing of 'national states'. Since 1970 under the Bantu Homelands Citizenship Act, every African is declared to be a citizen of a 'self governing territory' or a 'territorial area', so unless current political revolts force a rethink, 18 million South Africans are set to acquire the citizenship of other territories. Under the Bantu Laws Amendment Act (no. 12 of 1978) children born to parents from the independent Bantustans would not legally have entitlement to stay in urban areas. The extent to which this gigantic con trick can be pulled off successfully is further examined in Chapter 5. Here, it is simply necessary to discern the intentions behind the policy and to see what effects are already manifested in terms of the sources of supply of labour to the gold mines. The intentions of the South African government are well described by Southall (1982: 293):

> The envisaged scenario is that as each bantustan proceeds to independence, and with the eventual passing away of the pre-independence generations, the number of Africans with legal claims to permanent residence in the urban areas of South Africa will dwindle away ... In turn the continuing obligation of Africans to assume a homeland citizenship articulates with the renewed emphasis upon influx control and the resettlement relocation policy, whose objectives remain as 'the correction' of the increasingly unfavourable black/white population imbalance in the large urban centres, the removal from white areas of all Africans who are superfluous to the needs of the economy and the retention of the bantustans as labour reservoirs and compounds for the unemployed.

In respect of the mines' recruitment, although liberal commentary often assumes a disjuncture of interest between the 'progressive' mining capitalists and the 'reactionary' state, in fact the process of 'internalising' the labour supply showed a common purpose. In Stahl's view (1981: 37) the mines were 'virtually forced to recruit South African blacks' as Malawi cut off her supply and political uncertainties surrounded the supply of Mozambican workers. The switch to 'internal' supplies of labour can be clearly seen in Table 3.2.

In the short span of five years from 1973 to 1978, the proportion of workers recruited from inside South Africa had nearly trebled from 20 per cent to 54 per cent. For the mineowners, this dramatic shift in the historic recruitment pattern might have occasioned a collapse in profits as it coincided with a quadrupling of wages from 1972 to 1976— the result of the first effective action by black mine workers since 1946. Mammon smiled on the mineowners, however, for as the worldwide recession deepened, the price of gold in South Africa rocketed from R28.60 per fine ounce in 1971 to R168.90 per fine ounce in 1978 (a rand (R) roughly equalled US$1 over this period). Thus, despite the large rises in the wages of African workers, the profits per African employee rose from R1485 in 1972 to R4000 in the late seventies (Stahl 1981: 37). From the point of view of the government, the

Table 3.2   South African and non-South African sources of African mine workers, 1973, 1978 and 1982

	1973		1978		1982	
	No.	%	No.	%	No.	%
n-South African						
,esotho	87 229	20.66	104 143	22.85	99 034	22.09
Botswana	16 811	3.98	18 129	3.98	18 148	4.04
waziland	4 526	1.07	8 352	1.83	9 422	2.10
Iozambique	99 424	23.55	45 168	9.91	47 150	10.52
'ropicals	127 970	30.32	29 618	6.50	16 262	3.62
al non-South African	335 960	79.58	205 410	45.07	190 016	42.40
al South African*	86 221	20.42	250 311	54.93	257 954	57.60
al	422 181	100.00	455 721	100.00	448 970	100.00

ludes 'independent' homelands

rces: Murray 1981: 30; Lipton 1985: 385

switch towards the 'internalisation' of the labour supply by the mines was wholly congenial to the evolution of apartheid policy, about three-quarters of the 1978 South African recruits (Table 3.2) having emanated from the Transkei and the other Bantustans. These workers, shown as 'South African' in Table 3.2, had to all intents and purposes lost any effective claim on the South African legal system, polity and economy.

For nearly a century the supply of labour-power to the South African gold mines has been regulated and controlled by the employers often with the active support or passive acquiescence of the South African state. Fresh labour reservoirs—in Mozambique, in the High Commission territories, in zones north of the 22°S line, even in China, were activated, then deactivated as politics, disease or demand dictated. These fresh recruits, the new helots of the southern African regional political economy, remained on the margins of South African society—trapped in mining compounds, hauling out rock in dangerous and debilitating conditions and without access to legal representation, political rights or union organisation. Even as a more progressive capitalist strategy of the stabilisation and internalisation of the labour force began to evolve in the mid-1970s, in response to miners' struggles at the workplace and liberation struggles at the supply points, so the South African state contrived a strategy of 'externalisation' of its own citizens. The Bantustans have thus been added to the former High Commission territories (Botswana, Lesotho and Swaziland) as the principal sources of the supply of contract labour. The structural and sociological effects of this relationship on the labour-supply areas is the subject of the next section.

Effects of migration on selected labour reservoirs

The cases of Botswana, Lesotho, the Transkei and some less detailed references to Mozambique are used here to illustrate the effects of migration. By 1980, these four territories provided 4.8 per cent, 17.9 per cent, 28.6 per cent and 9.7 per cent, respectively, of all black workers employed on the

94

South African mines (Southall 1982: 215). As well as providing the bulk of mine workers, these areas are salient in that they include the largest remaining foreign supplier (Mozambique) and two countries whose status has changed from 'British South African' to foreign in the 1950s (Lesotho, Botswana) as well as the Bantustan which has been 'independent' for the longest period (the Transkei, 'independent' in 1976).

Murray (1981: 171–7) has drawn attention to the long tradition of anthropological analyses of the effects of migration on the areas in southern Africa from which the migrants are drawn. As he argues, G. Wilson (1941–2) anticipated the revival of Marxist analyses by talking in terms of 'disproportions' between town and country, and the impoverishment of the rural areas being caused by uneven capitalist development. But most of the anthropologists concerned wrote in a liberal vein. For example, Schapera (1947) and M. Wilson et al. (1952) were concerned about the destructive aspects of the pattern of oscillating migration on family life. The system whereby young men spent prolonged periods of work away from their homes generated, so these scholars maintained, marital instability, illegitimacy, economic insecurity, the breakdown of child-rearing arrangements and the undermining of the authority of the older generation.

All these effects of migration on the labour-exporting areas are still evident today. However, there are a number of dissenting anthropological and historical studies arguing that migration acted in one form or another to ensure 'tribal cohesion', to perpetuate the economic basis of the rural household and even to function as an escape valve for social contradictions inherent in 'tribal' society itself. Some of this argument is quite spurious and may be considered either evidence of wishful thinking or a form of ideological whitewashing for the apartheid regime. For example, Banghart (cited in Murray 1981: 173), writing in 1970, argued to this effect:

> I would like to reiterate that the effects migrant labour has on the homeland are not as great as most people would like to think. I believe that this can be attributed to the generally

conservative nature of the Bantu rural structure. In my research, both library and fieldwork, I found little or no evidence that labour migration is detrimental or disruptive, in any particular group's viewpoint. In most cases, I think, it can be shown that the opposite is the case, that labour migration has a stabilizing influence on the group and in particular on its social structure.

The 'most cases' argument is, certainly, fabricated, but reliable observers have documented a number of exceptions to the general rule that migration causes or exacerbates severe breakdown of rural social structures. Watson (1958) writing on the Mambwe of Zambia maintains that because there was no firm gender division of labour in agriculture, surplus male workers were able to leave the land without notably adverse effects and continued to value their access to land as a means of ensuring permanent security. Van Velsen (1959) writing of the Tonga of Malawi came to similar conclusions, emphasising particularly the continuing positive regard for 'traditional' values. Harris (1959–60) and Webster (1977, 1978) argued that the system of adelphic succession among the Tsonga of Mozambique left younger brothers and sons in a large household in a dispossessed state, thus permitting a harmonious 'fit' between Portuguese colonial policy, the labour requirements of South African capitalism and the local social structure. Again, Delius (1980) shows how migrancy amongst the Pedi of Eastern Transvaal arose as a means to acquire guns to resist the Boers militarily, a strategy that was successfully pursued until 1879. I have already cited Beinart's work (1982) on Pondoland to show that, because incorporation was delayed in that area, the 'terms of trade' between Pondoland and the hegemonic capitalist system were somewhat more advantageous to the Pondos than to other groups drawn into capitalist social relations. The result was that migration among the Pondo was used as a means to restock the cattle herds, thereby maintaining the integrity of the rural household for a little longer.

How is the salience of these examples assessed? The first point is obvious. These studies are not representative and do not conform to the generality of cases, usefully surveyed, for example, in a comprehensive volume describing the roots of rural poverty in eastern and southern Africa (Palmer and Parsons 1977). Even where the anthropological evidence is soundly based, it somewhat misses the point. It is quite possible for 'traditional' customs to survive or even be strengthened under the impact of (incomplete) capitalist penetration. In so far as Watson and van Velsen are refuting the conventional liberal view that Africans were always and inevitably injuriously 'detribalised' by contact with western 'civilisation', they are right. The capacities for cultural syncretism in such a complex ethnic milieu as southern Africa are almost unlimited. But the major refutation of such studies lies in their synchronic character. It is quite likely that small societies in Zambia and Malawi, lying on the very edge of the major recruiting zones, were able to effect a temporary and partial compromise within the capitalist mode of production and even create adaptive ideologies and social practices. (One that has attained an almost mythological status is the story that Africans go to the mines as a form of initiation into manhood. Tourist guides to the mines tell their clients that mine work has become a functional substitute for killing a lion—now too scarce—or engaging in tribal wars—now eliminated due to the wonders of western civilisation.)

The historians do not make the mistake of assuming a timeless functionality, nor do they treat the local social structure as an undifferentiated whole. Indeed, Beinart's major thesis is that although migration from Pondoland was principally designed to restock cattle to maintain the household, vastly different outcomes resulted, many of which simply show the delay in, and not the obviation of, rural poverty. Some migrants (going in this instance to the sugar fields of Natal rather than the gold mines) were, he says, quite unable to 'escape the downward spiral in indebtedness'. At the top of the social pyramid, the Christian and wealthier chiefly families 'were, to some extent, able to entrench their position through their political power, their cash income, their access to education and rural resources' (Beinart 1982: 148–50). The majority, 'probably over 80 per

97

cent' of migrant Pondo households, however, are described (Beinart 1982: 148) in these terms:

> Though they were able to maintain rural production, they were too short of labour and capital to innovate further or engage in petty entrepreneurial activities. Though they may have received help from neighbours in the shape of work parties at various phases of the agricultural cycle, they could not employ people to work in their fields nor attract clients. The women of such families who already had to spend more of their time on child care and the gathering of water and wood, probably gave more time to the wealthier homesteads in their location than they received back in the work parties they organised.

His account goes on to elaborate in careful historical detail what a number of scholars are now finding—mainly that early studies were on the whole insensitive to the processes of social differentiation and class formation arising from the effects of migration. Secondly, though the early liberal anthropologists did generally recognise the particular plight of women, they tended to cast their arguments in rather moralistic terms—which can now sound a little too like an idealised defence of the family, western nuclear, or extended. The plight of women has also severely worsened in recent years, with many having to assume increasing functions in rural production and many others being forced, like their menfolk, into the wage economy. Finally, it was often assumed by liberal writers that ending the morally indefensible system of migrant labour could only produce positive benefits. In fact, so dependent have some areas become that when labour supplies were switched (say from Mozambique to the Transkei) it was found very difficult to re-establish the local economies. Each of these effects—increasing social differentiation, greater pressure on women and what might be called the 'implosion effects' of a decline in migrant recruitment—merit further discussion.

Just as certain chiefs in West Africa and Arab slave raiders in East Africa profited from the slave trade, so the Portuguese colonial authorities and a number of African 'tribal' authorities have profited from the sale of cheap labour-power to the South African gold mines. In many pre-colonial African societies, one of the bases of inherited power and wealth was the capacity to exact 'tribute labour' from the chief's subjects. When capitalist penetration overlaid these customary rights, chiefs became additionally responsible, as Southall (1982: 106) writes of Transkei, for maintaining 'law and order, control of workseekers and unauthorised influx in urban areas, the impounding of stray stock and the dispersal of unlawful assemblies'. The powers provided control of the crucial aspects of the labour recruitment process. Together with their historic duties to allocate usufruct rights to land, they placed the chiefs in a powerful position. Many, as Murray writes of Lesotho (1981: 24), took the opportunity to enrich themselves 'at the expense of their subjects by abusing the principle of equity in the administration of arable land which is inscribed in customary law, and by exacting excessive tribute in labour from resident citizens, in fines and livestock from petty offenders and in cash from returning migrants'. The enhanced powers and greater pay accorded to the chiefs by the settler administrations were partly contingent on their acceptance of a reduced level of tribute labour in exchange for releasing labour for the farmers, then, later, the mining companies. An early manifestation of this relationship was that described by Delius and Trapido (1983: 66) whereby about 200 child labourers were provided to the Boer farmers in the 1860s by Swazi rulers, in exchange for hunting dogs, cattle, blankets, guns and horses. Such transactions are well bedded into the topography of South African unequal exchange. More colourful recent examples include the gift of a tractor to the Transkei State President, Chief Botha Sigcau, by the Sugar Industry Labour Organisation. (Eastern Pondoland, where Sigcau acts as Paramount chief, supplies the overwhelming bulk of cane cutters for the sugar estates.) Somewhat less expected was the announcement by the Transkei government that it held itself ready 'at a moment's notice' to arrange the documentation of 100 Transkei women for whom a white labour recruiter had found work as domestic servants in West Germany (Streek and Wicksteed 1981: 152–60). That these cases of chiefly connivance with the requests of employers and the state are not always accepted passively is evidenced by the 'Pondoland revolt' of 1960–1. The same Chief Sigcau, of tractor fame, was at the centre of a massive rebellion against the 'Bantu Authorities' system. Largely spontaneous riots occurred involving the death of Chief Sigcau's brother, another chief, five policemen and 15 headmen and bodyguards. The revolt was only crushed by incarcerating 5000 rioters and sentencing 30 to death for their part in the revolt (Southall 1982: 108–13). Despite such flare-ups and many less serious manifestations of resistance against the chiefs, the major impact of the system of labour migration is clear. The chiefs have sought to use their control over the allocation of land, their customary rights to demand tribute labour and their payments for recruiting or permitting the recruiting of labour, to place themselves in an advantageous position *vis-à-vis* their subjects. They are the first beneficiaries of the migrant labour system.

Also benefiting from the income derived from migrant workers' wages is a stratum increasingly being described as a 'middle peasantry'. Ruth First (1983: 128) in her research in Mozambique explicitly identifies two strata of 'middle' and 'poor' peasantries: 'What was clearly discernible was a differentiation between middle and poor peasantry, and in this process of differentiation the differing impact of mine wages was not a sole but often the most important determining factor'. These Mozambican middle peasants have better and larger land holdings, tend to own ploughs, oxen and grinding mills and produce for the market as well as for home consumption. More ambigious findings on the development of a middle peasantry have been reported from the other labour reservoirs under consideration.

Murray (1981: 88–99) points out that most men from Lesotho *have* to commit themselves to a working life in South African industry and that this trend is increasing. The trend is accompanied by the growth in landless labourers and by the increase in the number of very small farms. On the other hand, those who are able to maintain land rights, or those who are able to put their savings towards the purchase of land, are characteristically those with an income from mine wages. In so far as these holdings are not sufficiently stable to persist without continued investment in the form of remittances, a middle peasantry in the Mozambican sense has not evolved in Lesotho. It is perhaps fair to conclude that while migration has produced social differentiation in Lesotho, the differentiation is chiefly between poor and landless peasants rather than between middle and poor peasants.

A similar conclusion could probably be drawn in the case of the Transkei in that 50 per cent of families have no livestock whatever, and only 3 per cent have 15 or more cattle—estimated by the Food and Agricultural Organisation to be the minimum number for a viable homestead based on cattle (Streek and Wicksteed 1981: 166). The implication of these and similar land and income distribution figures (e.g. Southall 1982: 219–21) suggest that the number of independent or relatively autonomous farmers in the Transkei must be very small indeed—and probably largely confined to the chiefs, headmen and a few petty traders and businessmen who have bought land. This conclusion is in marked contrast to the reference by Innes and O'Meara (1976: 76) to a 'stable, rich peasantry' in the Transkei. Their analysis is a useful corrective to radical views which depict the Bantustan governments as totally without any social basis, but they seem to have exaggerated the extent to which such a class either exists or has provided the basis for political support of the Matanzima regime (Southall 1982: 175).

Whatever the extent of differentiation, the chiefs and middle peasants are a very small proportion of the population in the labour reservoirs whose lives have been severely disrupted by the migrant labour system. In the four labour reservoirs discussed here—Mozambique, Lesotho, Botswana and the Transkei—there is scarcely a household which has not been deeply affected by migrant recruitment to the mines. In Mozambique's three southern provinces, where nearly all the country's migrants are recruited, the total of mine wages paid out in 1967 was eight times greater than the value of marketed agricultural production. Wage employment outside agriculture was lower than the number of workers employed in South Africa and Zimbabwe (First 1983: 184–90). Figures from the remaining labour reservoirs

101

in the late seventies also indicate the level of dependence on wage labour: 60 per cent of all males in the Transkei were migrants in 1980; 17 per cent of Lesotho's total population were in wage employment in South Africa in 1976 and, in the same year, the comparable figure for Botswana was 23 per cent (Streek and Wicksteed 1981: 157; Murray 1981: 19 and Brown 1983:370). The very magnitude of this migration is an indication of the serious collapse of the capacity for commodity or even subsistence peasant production. The aggregate figures tell their own gruesome story. Once a granary, exporting 150 000 bags of maize in 1908, Lesotho had to import 320 000 bags 60 years later (Murray 1981: 18). Similar depressing statistics of declines in food production can be adduced from the other areas. The severe droughts of 1982–3, followed by the floods in southern Mozambique in 1984 have incalculably damaged the internal capacity to generate or regenerate domestic agriculture. The immediate events, following years of neglect, under-investment, soil erosion and a steadily worsening population/land ratio has meant that the overwhelming majority of migrant families and households may be on the brink of starvation or existing below the cost of their own reproduction. The political accord Mozambique reached with South Africa in mid-1984 was an inevitable result of this harsh economic backdrop.

This process of capitalist emiseration has borne particularly hard on women. The most complete and interesting data on this question has been collected in Botswana. Scholars are fortunate in having Schapera's detailed early studies (1935; 1947) of the effects of migration as an excellent historical base line on which to establish longitudinal comparisons. In a follow-up study conducted in the same ward as his earlier studies, Schapera and his colleague Roberts (1975), 40 years later, found that though the agnatic social structures had survived, many more men were away in the mines, there was a very high proportion of women who had never married (40 out of 73) and there was a high proportion of children (65 out of 162) who were born to these women. That these observations are broadly consistent with national trends is shown in an analysis of the Botswana National Census of 1971. This data revealed that of all women over 15 who had children, only 45 per cent were married, 36 per cent being single, 7 per cent were divorced or separated and 14 per cent widows. (Cited in Murray 1981: 110). The numbers of children born to unmarried women is especially noteworthy in that Schapera found that in the period before the European intrusion into Tswana life, the number of unmarried mothers was minimal, and these mothers were subject to strong public disapproval. By contrast, 'marriage offered social status, companionship, economic co-operation and for men, legal paternity of their children' (Brown 1983: 371, 2).

The rise in the number of unmarried women, and unmarried women with children, therefore violates Tswana custom which, in this case, conforms to conservative western cultural practices. On the other hand, what the arrival of western practices did occasion is the virtual disappearance of polygamy. In 1950, 43 per cent of marriages in Kgatleng district were polygamous: in 1978, none were found in the same district. Without polygamy, an unbalanced gender ratio of 63 men for every 100 women resident 'at home' automatically deepened the pool of unmarried women (Brown 1983: 372, 373). This discrepancy arose directly because of migration. A number of male migrants to South Africa never return home, despite the rigid laws that prevent their legal settlement. Again, men are marrying later probably because their rate of savings from mine wages, relative to the price of land, has dropped.

Brown's detailed study (1983) of 210 households in Kgatleng district documents the social consequences accompanying these demographic and social changes and these findings are now summarised, without further detailed citation, *in extenso*. The changes in marital patterns have had an obvious bearing on the woman's capacity to take on the burden of reproduction. The Botswana men, in any case (a finding that is somewhat surprising) appear to send the bulk of their earnings to their parents rather than the mother of their children. If they intend to marry the mother, the men tend to provide small payments as an indication that they accept paternity of the child and wish ultimately to marry the mother. Non-payment is an indication of a casual affair. In this case, the women can, and increasingly do, attempt to use

103

customary law like the *marebana* (seduction payment), payable to the mother's family for the first child. Modern law also recognises the mother's right to monthly payments under the Affiliation Proceedings Act. Many mothers do use these legal rights, especially the lump-sum *marebana* payment, but despite frequently winning their cases, it is very difficult, and often impossible, to enforce payment on the men. The number of female-headed households, a phenomenon barely noticed in the 1930s, has now reached 23 per cent in Kgatleng district. Again women have fought a long *de jure* battle to have legal claims to the land, but in practice they lack the resources, the labour, the tools and the cattle to make their land pay. Brown found that harvests in 1978 averaged 29 bags for households headed by men, 8 bags for single women and 6 bags for widowed women householders. The major success story in Botswana agriculture is the raising of cattle for beef production and here again female-headed households are particularly disadvantaged. They have few, if any, cattle, their plots are characteristically smaller and they need what few cattle they do have for ploughing. The result of these powerful demographic, social and economic changes has been to expose many women to enormous insecurity and individuation, forcing them to produce and reproduce with little help from the men and remarkably little (given customary expectations) from the surrounding community. Women, particularly younger and single women, have thus been forced into the wage market themselves, often in direct violation of cultural and legal sanctions. These women work in the Botswana economy and normally illegally in the South African economy, where they swell the numbers of women in domestic service, cleaning or in formal sector employment (Cock *et al*: 1983).

Migrant labour and the South African economy: the wider view

So far in this chapter, it has been shown how metropolitan and Third World debates on the reproduction question illustrate the advantages that mining capital in South Africa derives from utilising a system of migrant labour. It has also been shown how the labour supply from the surrounding ribbon of labour reservoirs was created, activated and deactivated, and with what effects to the inhabitants of these areas. The historic dependence of mining capital in southern Africa on large levies of migrant labour has attracted a large volume of comment on whether the system of migrant labour underlies the basic structures of the South African economy and conditions its distinctive social practices and political ideology, called, after 1948, apartheid.

One of the most ambitious theses along these lines is that advanced by Wolpe. His starting point is uncompromisingly materialist (1972: 429 [italic added]):

> The state has been utilised at all times to secure and develop the capitalist mode of production. Viewed from this standpoint, racist ideology and policy and the state now not only appear as the means for the reproduction of segregation and racial discrimination generally, but also as what they *really* are, the means for the reproduction of a particular mode of production.

He goes on to argue that whereas 'segregation' constituted the ideology appropriate to the pre-Second World War period when 'African redistributive economies constituted the predominant mode of rural existence for a substantive . . . number of people', apartheid was the ideology specific to 'the period of secondary industrialisation' allowing the maintenance of 'a high rate of capitalist exploitation through a system which guarantees a cheap and controlled labour-force, under circumstances in which the condition of reproduction of that labour-force is rapidly disintegrating' (1972: 432–3). His thesis raises valid objections to the older view that apartheid was simply the same thing as segregation in a different package. But it is flawed in a number of respects. First, it lacks a clear historical perspective and wrongly implies that the process of disintegration of the reserve economy was a post-1945 phenomenon or, in other places in his text, occurred 'in the 1920s and 1930s'. As has been shown, the process of disintegration can be dated from 1870 to 1913, much earlier than the development of secondary industrialisation.

Second, there is an unbroken line of continuity in the mines' recruitment policies from the 1890s to the 1970s, though the reservoirs that were tapped varied in their mix over the period. By concentrating his argument entirely on the supply of labour from the (South African) reserves, Wolpe misses the point that up to 1973 nearly 80 per cent of the African miners were from outside South Africa (see Table 3.2). Burawoy, in a lengthy but somewhat oblique critique, picks up this point and argues that the South African system is better explained in terms of 'a set of political and legal arrangements designed to separate the means of renewal from those of maintenance and at the same time ensure a continued connection between the two' (1976: 1059). Not only does Burawoy question Wolpe's excessive economism, he seeks to specify *in what respects* and *for whom* the system of migrant labour is cheap labour. These are pertinent questions even if the answer to the second is blindingly obvious. Migrant labour was cheap labour for the mineowners, otherwise they would not have spent the last century recruiting it. Burawoy is, however, right to suggest (if I have understood him correctly) that so far as the state is concerned the supply price of labour-power is not the only issue at stake. It is for political reasons (amongst which the protection of the white worker looms large) necessary to perpetuate the separation of the point of production (where the maintenance of the labour force occurs) from the point of reproduction (where its renewal occurs). A different state and a different economy takes much of the responsibility for renewal costs—but the South African state itself has to bear the cost of policing the boundaries between the systems of renewal and maintenance and the associated costs of restricting occupational and geographical mobility by black workers. I might add to Burawoy's observations, that when the supply of migrant labour from foreign states began to be threatened in the period after 1973, the South African state had to subsidise the cost of maintaining the 'foreign' states, like the Transkei, that it invented. In 1979–80, three years after the Transkei's independence ceremonies, the South African government provided R211.96 million budgetary suport, some 90 per cent of the Transkei's projected expenditure (Southall 1982: 206). In short, there are economic costs as well as benefits in reproducing South Africa's migrant labour system. Wolpe's materialist analysis has led him to conflate the economic benefits secured by the mining houses, with what are seen as the necessary economic penalties borne by the South African state for ideological and electoral reasons.

At the same time, what Wolpe's discussion does raise is the need to adjust our analysis of the reproduction question in South Africa in the light of changes in the material base and the distribution of labour-power between the mining, service and manufacturing sectors. I am not myself convinced that these changes were signalled or signified in anything but the loosest way by the change in labels, like 'apartheid' rather than 'segregation'. At various times 'separate development' has been proposed as an alternative, not subordinate (see Wolpe 1972: 433) term to 'apartheid'. White South African politicians used the legitimacy conferred by a social science label, 'ethnic pluralism', in the 1970s. Now we are told by the ruling party that it is 'culture' not 'colour' that defines differences between South Africans and that the country is 'multi-national'. Rather than directly reading off these shifting cosmetic façades from changes in the material base, it is more instructive to describe the changes themselves.

First, the significance of gold mining is declining. Though state revenue from mining increased during the 1970s, due to the increase in the price of gold, the proportion it contributed to state revenue steadily declined over the same period (Martin 1983: 8, 9). Employment in the gold mines is also declining considerably—from 479 000 African miners in 1979 to a projected 148 000 in the year 2000 (Bromberger 1978: 97). Between now and the end of the century, the projected growth in coal and other base metal mining will, however, more or less make up for this steep fall in gold mine employment. Part of the projected fall in gold employment was based on expectations that output would drop, expectations that are based on the likelihood of no new discoveries, but which may fluctuate with changes in the world prices of gold and uranium. Another explanation is that many of the

107

larger diamond and gold mines have finally begun to replace labour with technology, particularly in the crushing, sorting and milling operations. With the rise in the price of gold it also became economic to reprocess mechanically the massive mine dumps that ring the south of Johannesburg, recovering the traces of gold left from more inefficient days. In the diamond mines, the proportion of migrant workers dropped from 85 per cent of the total in 1970 to 36 per cent of the total nine years later (Wilson 1981). The gold mines look like evolving a more complex picture but one pointing in the same direction. The richer mines, particularly those owned by Anglo-American, are publicly committed to stabilising a large proportion of their workers, though the former chairman of Anglo-American regretted that he thought some underground workers would always have to be migrants (Lipton 1980: Foreword). The smaller mines, less able to mechanise and with low-grade deposits, clearly intend to pepetuate their overwhelming use of migrant labour. The increased wages that miners won for themselves in the 1970s (the real wage level trebled in the decade) both occasioned the move to mechanisation by the rich mines and also encouraged them, in addition to the factors mentioned earlier, to shrink the size of the labour force.

In contrast to gold mining, the employment of Africans in secondary industry accelerated rapidly after the war and especially in the 1950s and 1960s. In 1945, African employment in the manufacturing sector was only about 67 per cent of gold mining employment, by 1952 about the same numbers were employed, and by 1970 there were 864 300 African workers in secondary industry compared to 425 871 in gold mining (Wolpe 1972: 443); Bromberger 1978: 8). The boom in manufacturing industry signified by these figures led to widespread fears in the early 1970s by the administration and factory bosses that there would be damaging shortages of labour-power. According to a 1973 survey by the Department of Bantu Administration, to meet anticipated job demand the Transvaal would 'have to absorb an additional 1 997 000 workers within 5 to 10 years'. The Deputy Minister, Mr Punt Janson, lugubriously confessed his doubts as to whether the structure of apartheid could survive such a rate of urbanisation. He gave only token obeisance to doctrine in hoping that Africans would eventually accept the homelands as their 'fatherlands' but announced that he was 'enough of a realist to realise that it cannot happen in 20 years' (*Rand Daily Mail* (Johannesburg) 3 November 1973). In the same year, the Minister of Finance, Dr Nico Diederichs, included a commitment in his budget statement to establish 'an inter-departmental committee to investigate the feasibility of a system of training for African workers'. As the reporter for the business section of the Johannesburg *Sunday Times* (27 May 1973) sardonically commented: 'Training of Africans would be pointless if, once trained, they were shunted off to some outlying Bantustan. Why should Africans be trained for industrial jobs if they are to end up as subsistence farmers?' Liberal commentators were exultant. Alistair Sparks, the editor of the leading organ of the progressive section of capital (*Rand Daily Mail* (Johannesburg), 27 October 1973) argued that:

> The government's announcement that Africans are to be trained as skilled workers in the urban areas is the most portentous decision yet taken in its great retreat from apartheid . . . once a country begins developing, as South Africa is now doing very rapidly, into a modern high-technology economy, the whole picture changes. The need shifts to more and more highly-skilled and educated workers. And such labour simply cannot be utilised on a migratory basis.

Do the decreases in the numbers of gold miners and the increase in the numbers of stabilised manufacturing workers indeed portend the collapse of apartheid? Is South Africa to be seen simply as a 'late developer' eventually manifesting structures and institutions similar to western industrial democracies? It is not proposed to answer this question in full here, but merely to indicate that the hopes of progressive commentators that industrialisation would automatically alleviate conditions for the African population and put an end to the migrant labour system, are premature and in a number of senses, fundamentally misguided. That is not to say that the last decade has not seen the stabilisation of many Africans, rises in their living standards and better provision of educational training, health and housing needs. To a limited degree, this *has* occurred. But African unemployment remains high and indeed rose from 18.3 per cent of the labour force in 1960 to 22.4 per cent in 1977, never falling below 17.5 per cent even in boom years (Legassick and de Clerq 1984: 158). These floating and stagnant sections of the labour force inside the country are still supplemented to a very large degree by the continued activation and deactivation of latent rural migrant labourers even though the mix of origins of these labourers has changed. Finally, even within the urban areas, a sophisticated battery of labour regulations and bureaux have been established to continue to permit the state to intervene, control and perpetuate a helot/citizen division of labour. These devices, elaborately constructed by the government commissions chaired by Messrs Riekert and Wiehahn, are discussed in Chapter 5.

But the notion that migrant labour and an industrial division of labour are incompatible has also to be questioned at a more fundamental level. Comparative evidence from Europe after 1945 suggests that far from being incompatible with the growth of manufacturing industry, the use of migrant labour may have provided, at least for a generation, the determining condition for fuelling the post-war growth of the European economies. It is this case study, the third and final regional political economy, that is analysed in the next chapter.

4 The functions of migrant labour: Europe

A twenty-first century capital and a nineteenth century proletariat—such is the dream of monopoly capital in order to overcome its crisis.

(Castells 1979: 363)

As in all migration studies, statistical data on European migration are often inaccurate or lacking in detail, and especially difficult to use cross-culturally in view of differing definitions of the words 'migrant', 'immigrant' or 'foreigner' (some of the difficulties are discussed in Salt 1981). When dealing with cross-border migrants to the nine 'northern' (Italy is the reason for the inverted commas) countries of the EEC, plus Switzerland and Sweden, in excess of roughly 15 millon people are involved. This total is reached by adding to the $13\frac{1}{2}$ million shown in Table 4.1, an estimate of one million illegal workers, who would not be picked up in the statistics, plus an estimate for the net numbers of new migrants and their dependants who have joined earlier migrants in northern European countries since 1974, when most of the data cited in Table 4.1 was assembled.

In trying to characterise these 15 million-odd foreigners it is useful to start with Moore (1977) in setting out the various legal statuses of migrant workers. Such statuses are often conferred on the migrant workers' families and are closely related to their market situation, their place in the class structure and their civic rights status. Moore suggests a fourfold distinction. First, 'community workers'—whose rights and conditions are regulated more by European Com-

111

Table 4.1 'Foreigners' in the labour force and population of northern European countries

Countries	I Total foreign wage labour force	II Total wage earners	III Total foreign population	IV Total national population	Col. I as % of Col. II	Col. I as % of Col. III	Col. III as % of Col. IV
EEC							
Belgium	217 000	3 164 000	775 000	9 800 000	6.9	28.0	7.9
Denmark	36 000	1 995 000	55 000	5 000 000	1.8	65.5	1.1
France	1 900 000	17 108 000	4 043 000	52 500 000	11.1	47.0	7.7
Federal Republic of Germany	2 177 000	21 626 000	4 127 000	62 100 000	10.1	52.8	6.6
Ireland	42 403	1 119 531	137 296	2 978 248	3.8	30.9	4.6
Italy	44 000	13 437 000	176 000	55 400 000	0.3	25.0	0.3
Luxembourg	45 000	127 000	73 000	360 000	35.4	61.6	20.3
Netherlands	119 000	3 860 000	297 000	13 500 000	3.1	40.1	2.2
United Kingdom	1 665 000	22 790 000	2 274 000	56 100 000	7.3	73.2	4.1
EEC total	6 245 403	85 226 531	11 957 296	257 738 248	7.3	52.2	4.6
Non-EEC							
Sweden	–	–	424 200	8 267 000	–	–	5.1
Switzerland	–	–	1 065 000	6 376 000	–	–	16.7
Total	–	–	13 446 496	272 381 248	–	–	4.9

Note: Data for 1974, except for Sweden (1978). See also ILO (1984: 100) which, on 1980 figures, records higher total foreign workers for Belgium, Luxembourg and the Netherlands and lower figures for France, Federal Republic of Germany and the UK.

Sources: Power and Hardman 1978: 6; Slater 1982: 16; Hoffman-Nowotny 1982: 5

munity law than by national legislation. Equality of treatment with national workers—in respect of remuneration, dismissal, vocational training and rehabilitation, tax and social security benefits, trade union membership and rights, access to housing and rights to be joined by spouses and dependants—was embodied in Regulations 15 (1961) and 38 (1964). The major restrictions lay in civic rights, voting and access to employment involving 'the exercise of official authority' (Böhning 1972: 15, 16). In effect, a virtually free labour market developed between the original six members, then the expanded number of ten members of the Community. In practice, for two decades after the war, Italy was the only EEC country with a labour-power surplus. With this exception, net movements between countries tended to be small, and legal guarantees of access to the labour market may indeed have inhibited any propensity to permanent settlement. The essential equality of status and freedom of mobility of these workers, as well as their small net movements mean that such Community workers fall outside the scope of this discussion.

On the other hand, the three other categories of migrant worker which Moore identifies, namely 'foreign workers', 'ex-colonial workers' and 'illegal migrants', are very clearly in a more adverse situation than either the indigenous or Community worker. They characteristically enjoy less favourable civil, legal and political status. Their family life is limited or prohibited, their housing is inferior, their rights as employees are often markedly worse than indigenous workers, while in most European countries they are disenfranchised and unorganised in trade unions, making them 'subordinate and relatively defenceless in the economic and political spheres' (Moore 1977). As will be shown, even where ex-colonial workers, say in Holland or Britain or France, have obtained some *de jure* rights superior to foreign or illegal workers, their *de facto* status as minorities, subject to strong racial discrimination, has placed them in a comparable situation (see Braham *et al.* 1981; Miles 1982; Granotier 1973 and Marshall 1973 for some evidence in support of this proposition). While this point will be returned to later and the argument will be qualified, for immediate purposes it is

113

considered that foreign, illegal and ex-colonial workers share sufficient similarities to be analysed together.

Where, then, did these workers come from and how can their essential characteristics be defined? The majority of the migrants were drawn from the Mediterranean countries— Greece, Spain, Turkey, Portugal, Yugoslavia and the Mediterranean section of Italy (i.e. southern Italy). But in each case the mix going to individual countries was different. Greeks, Turks and Yugoslavs went to Germany; Algerians, Portuguese, Spaniards, Italians and West Africans went to France, while the initial influx to Britain and Holland tended to be more exclusively drawn from their former colonies— from India, Pakistan and the anglophone Caribbean in Britain's case, and in the case of the Netherlands from Indonesia, the rest of the former Dutch East Indies and Surinam. Belgium's 'foreigners' were largely drawn from Spain, Morocco, Greece and Turkey, while Luxembourg's non-EEC workers were mainly from Spain and Portugal. In the case of Sweden, the predominant migration came from Finland, but this flow has been joined recently by Yugoslavs, Greeks and Turks in descending order of magnitude (Power 1979: 1; Moore 1977; Hammer 1982: 9).

The geography of this population shift can also be examined from the point of view of the labour-exporting countries. Portugal, for example, exported 2 117 000 emigrants from 1945 to 1974, the majority of whom went to France (742 000) with, in descending order, other migrants going to Brazil, Venezuela, the US, Canada and West Germany. This constituted nearly a quarter of the total Portuguese population, not allowing for its African colonies (*New York Times*, 22 December 1974). Another dramatic example is the case of the small Caribbean island of Montserrat, where the majority of economically-active adults have left the island and all but depopulated it (Philpott 1973). As in the southern African case, there is a minority view in the literature about the supposed economic benefits that migration is meant to confer on the labour-exporting regions, but there are clearly some zones and countries where depopulation has been so extreme that even the reproductive capacity of local communities has been brought into question.

114

Mention of the reproductive capacity of labour-exporting zones also raises the question of whether earlier assumptions about the gender distribution of migrants were, in fact, valid. It was often unquestioningly thought that labour migration was overwhelmingly a male phenomenon, with females either staying 'back home' or arriving somewhat later, as dependents. With some justice, Sheila Allen, a British writer on race relations, referred to 'the sexist myopia which ran through almost all the published work on migrants'. (Cited in Morokvasic 1983). Subsequent work has done much to correct this image. Many migrant women are not simply the 'chattels' of men, as they are often considered in immigration law. A fair number left their home countries as single, widowed or divorced women, with the intention of working, not simply 'joining their husbands'. Since the late sixties, the number of women in the foreign population has expanded considerably, constituting some 40 per cent of all migrants and 25 per cent of the labour force. This last figure might well be an underestimate in view of the high level of unrecorded work (homework, illegal sweatshop work, or domestic service) characteristically found amongst migrant women. Rates of female participation in work may also vary considerably by ethnicity. Thus, according to one survey, 88.5 per cent of West Indian women in the UK are economically active, compared with 59.8 per cent of Indian women, 11.4 per cent of Pakistani/Bangladeshi women and 48.6 per cent of all UK women (Phizacklea 1983: 2, 102; ILO 1984: 53). In addition to gender and ethnic factors, the occupational and geographical spread of migrant workers provide further variations which are discussed later.

Why use migrant labour? The alternatives

How is the extensive use of migrant labour in advanced capitalist societies, such as those of northern Europe, accounted for? Both conventional wisdom and Marxist orthodoxy would suggest that a stabilised 'free' proletariat is a *sine qua non* of advanced industrial capitalism. Under this logic, the use of migrant labour might well be expected in the

115

early phases of industrialisation, or in settler societies such as South Africa. Yet that very epitome and shrine of modern western capitalism, Switzerland, with the highest per capita income in the western industrialised world, found itself in the late 1960s with 29.8 per cent of its labour force being foreign and anything from 21.5 to 63.2 per cent of its manufacturing industries staffed by foreign workers (Castles and Kosack 1973: 61, 69). So pronounced had the entry of foreigners to low-skilled, menial, manufacturing and service occupations become by the late sixties, that one respected Swiss academic (Girod, cited in Castles and Kosack 1973: 383) foresaw the development of a strange 'colonial' dystopia for his country:

> In the end, in fact, as some people fear, the Swiss could become a race of supervisors having at their service a labour force without political rights, dedicated to the least agreeable tasks, and victims of a more or less total segregation, which would be equivalent to a colonial state, with the difference that the autochthonous people would be the masters and the immigrants the servants.

While the Swiss case is atypical, both in the magnitude of its foreign population and in the virtual closure of the boundaries between the two labour markets for migrant and indigenous workers, all the European countries under review share similar features with the Swiss case.

To return to the question: Why did the import of migrant labour provide such an attractive solution to meet the needs of European capital? In an earlier paper with Harris (Cohen and Harris 1977), we tried first to identify what other solutions were available to European capital in the post-1945 period and what limitations inhered in each of these solutions. 'Solutions' also refers to a distinctive set of problems apart from those generally faced by capitalist economies in securing a stable base for capital accumulation. In classical Marxism, capitalism can never ensure balanced, full employment. The reduction of the reserve army of the unemployed which accompanied economic expansion would strengthen the bargaining position of the working class in their confrontation with the owners of capital. This in turn would lead to higher real wages, and a larger share for workers of total income. But this would pose a dilemma for capital, in that unpaid labour time would diminish and the rate of capital accumulation accordingly would be threatened. The essence of Keynesian economics was to discredit this notion and to argue that given appropriate macro-policies, full employment was at least a technical possibility. The attempt by monetarist theorists to attack the Keynesian argument from the right, actually confronts a very small part of his general theory and is likely to prove a passing ideological fad. The important long-term debate still remains between Marxists and Keynesians. It is not intended to address this debate directly, except to emphasise that the Keynesian model was the economic orthodoxy that informed economic policy in post-war Europe. But though the *economic* agenda was set, it was Kalecki's distinctive and important contribution to point out that Keynesian full-employment policies ran directly counter to the *political* and *social* requirements of capital. In his view, the maintenance of political and social control and the capacity of capital to respond to innovation and international competition, depended crucially on the employers' ability to deploy or discard labour according to movements in technology and capital (Kalecki 1971). This capacity was threatened by the increased class organisation of European workers, together with restrictions on available labour supplies (see pp. 118–20).

This then was the distinctive problem faced by European capital in 1945. Theoretically, four 'solutions' were possible: (a) employers could extend the participation (or activity) rate of the relative surplus population in the country, drawing in, that is to say, groups that had hitherto remained tangential to capitalist production; (b) employers could attempt to increase the rate of exploitation of the existing labour force by minimising production time, increasing output or lengthening the working day; (c) companies could invest more in labour-saving devices and methods (i.e. in Marxist terms, they could change the organic composition of capital); and (d) capital could migrate to underdeveloped countries or regions where the same constraints identified by Kalecki did not obtain or where Keynesian full-employment policies

117

were not even a distant prospect (cf. UK Government 1977: 183). These possible 'solutions' will now be examined in turn, pointing to the difficulties or limitations that were inherent in each.

First, *extending the participation rate.* In some countries it remained possible to continue to detach labour from the land. This applied particularly to latent sections of the relative surplus population in southern Italy which could be absorbed in the northern industrial triangle formed by Genoa, Milan and Turin. In the French case, there were the same 'pockets of labour surplus' in the overmanned service and retail trade. By European standards, a disproportionately large section of the French population also drew its livelihood from the land (13 per cent in 1971). Yet these sectors were a 'potent political force' which resisted government attempts to shake them out into the labour force (Böhning 1972: 102, 3). In West Germany, immediate postwar labour shortages were filled by refugees arriving from the German Democratic Republic—about three million had arrived in 1961. Britain continued to attract some rural migrants from its traditional labour reservoir in Ireland, but the supplies had been interrupted during the war and were now somewhat more uncertain. But for Ireland and East Germany, the crisis in the labour supplies to Britain and West Germany would have been more acute. As it was, it was clear that all major northern European countries had very nearly reached the end of the historical process of rural depopulation and urbanisation.

So what of that other obvious reservoir for the new mass occupations—women? With the war period excepted, female labourers had remained tangential to direct wage exploitation. When adding that ideological barriers had confined them to lower-paid, precarious and part-time occupations, they seemed ideal candidates for the job. However, here too there were difficulties. In Germany, France and Britain (in particular) there was an urgent need to reconstitute the indigenous labour force biologically and ideologically. This led to a number of contradictory attitudes by policymakers. Britain provides a good example. Faced with an acute labour shortage, estimated by a Cabinet manpower working part to be 1 346 000 in 1946, consideration was, at first, given to appeals to older male workers and women to remain in industry. The Cabinet even considered 'removing barriers to the employment of married women, providing crèches, flexible hours and part-time working' (Joshi and Carter 1984: 55, 56). Yet this prospect ran directly counter to the urgent problems of reproduction that had been highlighted in successive governmental reports. Already in the 1930s, studies conducted by Beveridge and Rowntree had concluded that capital accumulation was threatened by the fact that for decades a labour force had been reproduced unable to meet the demands of the more intensive production processes. Through sickness, malnutrition and following periods of long unemployment, the labour force had suffered serious debilitation. After the Second World War, with a reformist Labour party administration in office, there was likely to be a receptive governmental ear for social legislation concentrating on improving the conditions for the reproduction of labour-power. The Beveridge Report (1944) provided just such a manifesto. It laid the groundwork for the welfare state—constructed a 'social wage' with benefits and safeguards to ensure superior reproduction. Free orange juice, vitamin pills, health care, maternity benefits and milk coupons were instituted so that healthy physical reproduction was assured. Moreover, at an ideological level, there was much finger-wagging about the high levels of delinquency and illegitimacy that the war was thought to have caused. Women at work and women whose men were at the front were (it was thought) becoming dangerously alienated from the central social institution of capitalist society, the 'holy family'. It is in this light that Beveridge's insistence that unpaid domestic labour needed to be reinstituted and perpetuated must be interpreted. As his post-war report (cited in CSE 1977: 27) stated:

> In any measure of social policy in which regard is had to the facts, the great majority of women must be regarded as occupied on work which is vital though unpaid without which their husbands could not do their paid work and without which the whole nation could not continue.

119

All over war-torn Europe a similar logic obtained. As will be detailed later, the French were especially worried about the demographic skewing of their population towards older, dependent, people. It is perhaps instructive to contrast the situation of the USA and Japan. In the US, it was possible (in addition to absorbing large numbers of migrants from the surrounding labour reservoirs) to insert into post-war production 10 million married women, together with more than 4 million farmers, share-croppers and agricultural labourers. Japan, which is often treated with such mystification that it appears to escape the normal laws of capital accumulation, also had huge internal labour reservoirs to draw on to staff the post-war boom. Millions were drawn in from the countryside into the large industries, while the number of Japanese women 'gainfully employed' increased from 3 million in 1950 to 6.5 million in 1960 to 12 million in 1970 (Mandel 1978: 171).

By contrast, post-war Europe had exhausted, or was unable for ideological or demographic reasons, to further draw on its traditional internal labour reservoirs. Given this circumstance, could employers bear down more heavily on the existing workforce and *increase the rate of exploitation*? Some successes ('productivity deals') were achieved at the level of intensifying the labour process. This was easier in countries like France (where the industrial base was limited and could be built to new designs) or Germany (where much industrial plant had been wiped out during the war). It was more difficult in Britain, where any moves to displace labour, destroy craft demarcations or increase track speeds would have vitalised the class struggle—an outcome which a discredited Tory party under Churchill and successive social democratic governments were anxious to avoid. As a result of class struggles waged during the Second World War, the working class, through their principal class organisations the trade unions, had emerged with a new relationship to capital. This relationship inaugurated state consultation with trade union leaders on a wide range of political matters, not simply the incorporation of workers to social democratic politics. Fundamentally, what this meant was that there were serious political limitations which pre vented capital from 'decomposing' or 'recomposing' labour at will.

A third possible strategy to secure capital accumulation was to *change the organic composition of capital*, i.e. to install more labour-power saving machinery. But as Böhning (1972: 57) pointed out, it is difficult to thereby eliminate low-paid, undesirable jobs:

> Under current technological conditions the problem cannot be solved by automation because many of the socially undesirable jobs are not open to automation, particularly in the service sector, and because automation often creates new, low-paid jobs. The present usage of semi-automation in manufacturing industries has given rise to many boring and frustrating activities which do not attract sufficient indigenous manpower.

With the outset of the post-1973 recession and the installation of new technology some of this argument has lost its force, but it was undoubtedly true of the immediate post-war period. Again British capital was in a particularly acute crisis, given the historic tendency to 'underinvest' at home and 'overinvest' abroad. For specialised sectors, such as textiles or cars, it was cheaper to work existing plant more intensely (through night shifts, overtime and weekend shifts) than to rip out obsolete machinery and re-equip in a fundamental way. Moreover, advances in the reorganisation of the labour process permitted the complementary use of unskilled labourers side by side with skilled workers. If a skilled job could be de-skilled and parcelled out to two or more unskilled workers so much the better—wage costs would be reduced and that *bête noire* of European capital, the well-organised skilled craftsman, could be taken down a peg or two. Once more Böhning (1972: 59–60) understood this dynamic clearly:

> Employers in mass production processes who have hitherto not resorted to foreign labour realise that its easy availability in conjunction with an appropriate redesign of the production system would enable them to turn out far more goods than would otherwise be the case. They further divide many skilled jobs into simple components which can readily be taught to workers who have never before stood at a production line.

121

In short, whatever possibilities there were for changing the organic composition of capital, logic or immediate interest dictated a substitution or extension of unskilled work for skilled work, rather than a complete substitution of machinery for labour-power.

The final possible strategy mentioned for European capital to solve its problems of accumulation and the political control of the labour force was the *migration of capital to underdeveloped regions or countries*. As will be argued, particularly in Chapter 7, this was a strategy that became increasingly attractive to some sections of capital—the electronics industry, textile and toy manufactures were to prove particularly easy to relocate in low-wage areas where labour-power was cheap and the labour force more readily controllable. But this was a strategy that works particularly well with low-bulk, high-value goods where the cost of transport is not a significant factor. Some of the heaviest users of labour-power are inherently immobile—in the health services, the transport sector, the construction industry, the nationalised industries (post offices, gas, electricity). In other sectors like foundries, brick manufacturing and food processing, physical proximity to the market still remains an important condition for successful accumulation and valorisation.

Determined efforts were nonetheless made to relocate sections of capital within the European countries, often to correct regional imbalances—the north and east of West Germany, the Celtic fringe and the north-east of England and southern Italy being good examples. In each case, however, the impelling force was primarily political, not economic. Market and scale inefficiencies were bound to occur and though the companies eagerly seized regional relocation grants, tax incentives and other benefits, many such plants, started in the 1960s, eventually shut when faced with crises of overproduction and cyclical downturns in the industrial economy. One example would be the case of the American car firm, Chrysler, which never ceased to rue the day that the Labour party forced it to move to an underdeveloped region of Scotland, Linwood, as a condition for government assistance. The plant was shut in 1983.

If for some industries capital mobility was impossible or

only occurred within the domestic economy under political pressure, for other sections of capital, international relocation was made more uncertain by the unstable politics of the Third World. European colonial hegemony had been severely shattered by the destruction of the myth of European invincibility by the Japanese in the Far East, and by the growth of nationalist and anti-colonial movements all over Africa and Asia. Many of these movements adopted an anti-capitalist rhetoric and toyed with ideas of neutralism and non-alignment (see Worsley 1973 for a useful survey). For European capitalists, while rich pickings could be anticipated in the long term, the immediate post-war political prospects made large-scale relocation too risky.

Why use migrant labour? The positive benefits

So far the arguments have been negative—showing in turn that the alternatives open to post-1945 European employers in securing their profits and controlling their labour forces were without credibility as a short or medium-term solution. However, there were at least four positive benefits that were anticipated if migrant labourers *were* utilised.

First, a general association, rooted in classical economic theory between a large population and economic development, that is more hands meant more production. Second, savings in the cost of the reproduction of labour-power which, at least initially, could be avoided by the metropolitan state or metropolitan capital. Third, the advantages that accrued from deploying a labour force which was cheaper, less well organised, easier to hire and fire and had lower economic and social expectations. Fourth, the advantages that stemmed from introducing a racial and national division of labour and therefore fracturing the class composition (a term used to cover organisation, consciousness and bargaining strength) of metropolitan workers (Castells 1979: 361–72). Each of these expected advantages will be discussed below.

First, the general association between population and economic development. In a period when the present politi-

123

cal discussion hinges around 'repatriation', 'expulsion' and 'immigration control', it is perhaps necessary to be reminded that the conventional wisdoms of the immediate post-war period were very difficult. For example, one might cite a speech of a certain British Labour party politician in June 1946:

> We are not suffering in this country from a shortage of jobs at the moment [he said]. Have not the officials at the Home Office read the papers this morning and learned of the shortage of workers in this country? Have they not heard the Prime Minister's appeal to women to remain in industry? Have they not read the White Paper on Conscription, which refers to the overall shortage of men during the next few years? Do they not know that we are employing 350 000 prisoners of war who will presumably return to their own countries one day? We are living in an expansionist era. Surely, this is a Socialist Government committed to a policy of full employment? In a few years' time we in this country will be faced with a shortage of labour, and not with a shortage of jobs. Our birth rate is not increasing in sufficient proportion to enable us to replace ourselves . . . We are turning away from the shores of this country eligible and desirable young men who could be adding to our strength and resources, as similar immigrants have done in the past . . . It may be revolutionary to suggest that we ought now to become a country where immigrants are welcome, but that is really the logical development of our present position in the world . . . Who is going to pay for the old age pensions and social services we are rightly distributing now, unless we have an addition to our population, which only immigrants will provide in the days to come?

Thus James Callaghan (1946) in the House of Commons. Later that year a Foreign Labour Committee was set up by the Cabinet. Though the release of Public Record Office papers have now revealed that politicians and civil servants were clearly worried, as one put it, that 'there could be no authority for deporting coloured British subjects if they felt they wished to stay', the countervailing arguments prevailed. Commonwealth workers were cheaper then aliens precisely because they were British citizens. Since they would arrive 'individually and on their own initiative' there was no need

124

for the state to provide special welfare benefits or housing (Joshi and Carter 1984: 59, 58).

Across the Channel, the need to import vast numbers of migrants was an explicit policy and was, at first, freed from racist overtones. France had experienced a declining birth rate for many years. In the First World War she had lost $1\frac{1}{2}$ million soldiers and civilians and a further 600 000 in the Second World War. The age distribution was also radically skewed to older, therefore lower child bearing, ages. As Freeman noted (1979: 69): 'The consequence of this, many felt, could be catastrophic, militarily, politically and economically'. Government advisors like Sauvy and his colleagues at the influential Institut National d'Études Démographiques advocated a programme of permanent large-scale migration. Sauvy felt that France needed, at the minimum, 5 290 000 permanent immigrants. At the political level, de Gaulle and Michel Debré became ardent proponents of what was, in effect, the single most important plank of the recovery programme: repopulation. Even as late as 1962, de Gaulle talked in terms of a country of '100 million Frenchmen' and so desperate was the perceived need for repopulation that a proposal, subsequently rejected because of the political furore it created, was advanced to persuade German prisoners of war to stay in France. In West Germany, the same perceived imperatives operated a few years later—as noted above, at the end of the war some 13 million East Germans crossed to West Germany and therefore permitted Federal German industry an early start in the search for a plentiful labour supply.

The question of the reproduction of labour-power is discussed next. The theory relating to this question has already been fully discussed in Chapter 3. As in southern Africa, it would clearly be of enormous benefit to a European capitalist state and the wider capitalist economy, if the social wage (training, education, welfare benefits, etc.) either was not met at all, or was met principally outside the core capitalist economy. It is just such a possibility that migrant labour provided. Potential workers outside the national area could be biologically reproduced, nourished, housed, trained and provided with suitable ideological expectations of the capitalist labour process. If in addition it is noted that it was often planned that workers would principally be young males in the prime of their working life, pre-selected for physical fitness, unaccompanied by wives and dependants and then thrown back into the reproduction sector when their productive working life was over, it can be seen that, in theory at least, it was possible for the Europe capitalist economies to be solely responsible only for the formal wage at the point of production and to eliminate, or at least substantially reduce, the cost of the social wage. In practice, of course, this ideal situation (from the point of view of capital and the capitalist state) did not fully materialise, though approximations to the model can be seen in southern Africa, in the early *gastarbeiter* system in Germany and Switzerland and in recruitment of agricultural labour in the south-west of the United States.

The pure model depends on an agricultural economy viable enough not to compel workers to migrate, illegally or legally, the denial of rights of settlement, the denial of workers' demands to bring their families with them and the capacity of the state to register, control and habituate workers who are essential, and expel workers who are no longer needed. These issues are pursued in detail in the next chapters. In fact, modern states exhibit a great variety of capacities in these respects. Of the European states, Holland and the UK started off with particular 'disadvantages' in that they found it difficult to discount the obligatory legal responsibilities to their 'subjects' they contracted during the colonial period. Though these and other countries are now trying hard to extend the category of 'alien' through the manipulation of nationality, citizenship and immigration laws, in effect they have failed to prevent the emergence of a reproductive sector within their own boundaries.

It is perhaps necessary to be somewhat more concrete at this stage. It is still true that the social wage advanced to migrant communities is proportionately *lower* than that paid to the indigenous community. In Britain, for instance, as a number of studies have shown, migrant access to public housing is restricted and through a combination of pride, insecurity and apprehension at dealing with a hostile white

126

bureaucracy, migrants characteristically underclaim in respect of health, welfare and unemployment benefits. However, they do tend to need greater public expenditure in respect of education and child care, given the special needs and the age distribution of migrant communities (Rex and Tomlinson 1979: 62). These facts are in stark contrast to public attitudes—75 per cent of British respondents in an extensive 1966 survey believed that 'immigrants took more in benefits from social services than they contributed to them'. (Cited in Freeman 1979: 268). Public attitudes are equally harsh, and equally misguided, in France and Germany. In the French case, where a large proportion of the migrant population is illegal, there are compelling reasons to avoid claiming a share of a social wage—lest this leads to entanglement and deportation. A similar logic applies in Germany with the additional compelling factor that (in 1969) 44 per cent of Germany's foreign workers were recruited through official inter-governmental contracts which legally restricted settlement and allowed the possibility of deportation in the event that the workers became a charge on the state (Castles and Kosack 1973: 42).

If costs could be reduced or obviated by the state at the level of reproduction, employers scored a more direct advantage at the point of production itself. This point has been amply documented in the standard literature. Migrant workers are normally paid less, work in worse safety and health conditions, and are located in more dangerous and disagreeable jobs—usually ones which the indigenous labour force has deserted. There were, in addition, some special sectors of the economy where migrant labour-power proved to be the only kind available. It should not be thought, however, that this applies only to the service sector. Take, for example, the case of the British textile industry which was seriously threatened and continues to face stiff competition from Asian imports. Short of a huge investment in new machinery, which the textile industry was in no position to finance, competition with Asian imports depended on the ability to use existing machinery to the fullest capacity. But women, who dominated the industry, were legally barred from working night shifts. What was needed therefore was

127

an assured, steady, cheap supply of labour-power: and labourers, moreover, who were prepared to work a relay system and endure staggered rotas. Migrant labourers filled this gap. In the 1960s, one-third of black workers in Britain worked shifts—more than twice the percentage of white workers. Moreover, wage discrepancies by race can be seen by the fact that there was a differential of 8 per cent in favour of white workers, despite the supposedly higher earnings for shift work (Cohen and Jenner 1968). Migrant labourers also were strongly in demand in other areas of manufacturing: 47 per cent of migrants, compared to 33 per cent of indigenous workers, were employed in British manufacturing industry in 1971. Ford's largest plant in Britain (at Dagenham) was 60 per cent black, while an even greater proportion of Turkish workers is found in Ford's plants in Germany. Right from his early days in Detroit, Ford himself pioneered the use of immigrant labourers to enforce speed-ups and keep down wages, so the company's European plants follow established policy. But not only at Ford, but in other car factories, migrant labour-power predominates in both France and Germany (UK Government 1977: 31, 32; Cohen and Harris 1977). The adverse conditions that migrants face at the point of production can also be demonstrated by the lack, or low level of, legislative protection in respect of health and safety conditions for typical migrant, and often female migrant, occupations. Sweat-shops, homeworking and domestic service characteristically escape regulation. To summarise: the advantages to capital at the point of production comprise cheaper labour-power, a more flexible workforce prepared to work unsociable hours, a workforce that is easier to hire and fire in industries highly vulnerable to cheap imports or to cyclical or seasonal demands for their products and a workforce finally, that is not fully protected by legislation.

The fourth and final advantage of the use of migrant labour, indicated earlier, is the use of migrants to fracture the class unity of metropolitan workers. One starting point is provided by Castells (1979: 362) who argues that:

The racism and xenophobia diffused by the dominant ideology accentuate the cleavages derived by national cultural particular-

128

ities and determine the ideological isolation of immigrants. They are thus separated from their class and placed in a balance of power so unfavourable that often they fluctuate between an acceptance of the conditions of capital and pure individual or collective revolt. This cuts them off still more from the labor movement, in a sort of vicious cycle which tends to reproduce the fragmentation and dislocation of the working class in advanced capitalism.

While the question of the grip of racial ideology in the minds of workers is undoubtedly important in showing why migrant struggles often separate from worker struggles, it is essential also to show how the racial division of labour, generated by migration, reinforces the skill and craft distinctions of an earlier period. Thus, a white worker in a highly-industrialised economy, although not sharing a narrow racial consciousness, may nevertheless wish to defend his skill and relative control over the labour process by distancing himself from a migrant who is prepared to undertake a similar job at a lower wage ('rate busting'), under conditions dictated solely by the employer. This situation developed, for example, in the British foundaries which prior to the 1950s and 1960s, were traditional craft-based industries centred around the skilled work of moulders and coremakers. After that period, the employers were able to take advantage of the opportunity to undercut the bargaining power of the craftsmen, by de-skilling their jobs and introducing bulk casting mainly produced by migrant labourers (Cohen and Harris 1977).

Irrespective, however, of whether racism is diffused at an ideological level or rooted in a changing division of labour, there is little doubt that racism widely gripped many working class people in advanced capitalist countries who provided their share of the rank and file of Facist and nationalist parties—from the Ku-Klux-Klan in the US to the National Front in the UK, the National European Action Federation in France and the 74 extreme right groups estimated to be active in Germany in 1982 (Castles 1984: 42). The union movements in the European countries found themselves unable to oppose vigorously the racism of their indigenous membership. This is not to derogate the firm anti-racist stand taken by a number of unions (the Transport and General Workers' Union in Britain provides one relatively virtuous example), or the official declarations from senior Trade Union Congress officials. But as Freeman (1979:226) writes of British unions: 'Between the ideals of Congress resolutions and the reality of the shop floor there is a breathtaking gap. There is substantial evidence that discrimination against immigrants by local trade unions is widespread.' Freeman (1979: 244–58) gives a somewhat better report to French Socialist and Communist parties and unions on racial issues, but the relative tolerance of the French seems to have collapsed in the 1980s, when marked anti-immigrant postures were struck by Communist unions and politicians. Early in 1981, several Communist municipalities sent the bulldozers in to flatten migrant housing, apparently to secure popular support in the forthcoming election. As the *Le Monde* (Paris) reporter commented (14 February 1981):

> The Communist Party is dusting off and re-using the most shameful and dangerous methods (a bulldozer against a Malian hostel, public denunciation of a Moroccan family, quotas on immigrants in holiday camps and recreation centres) for protesting against the concentration of foreigners and flattering a segment of the population in the hope it might possibly pay off in votes at the presidential election.

Actions of this kind can be turned to useful political ends by the employers who are often able to represent themselves as liberals giving a disadvantaged minority a chance for a job. Shopfloor disunity also compounds the tendency to fragment labour protest into separate, and often weaker, racial segments. In short, the use of migrant labourers provided a substantial industrial advantage for post-war European employers.

Migrants to Europe: a structural necessity?

The positive benefits that accrued to European capitalists in their utilisation of migrant labour led a number of theorists

130

to argue that migrant labour-power had become so crucial to post-war European economic expansion that it was likely to become a permanent 'structural' feature of each European economy. This theme has been pursued by so many authors in diverse ways that there is some danger of misrepresentation in attempting to summarise so wide-ranging a debate.

Bearing this problem in mind, the first feature striking the outside observer is the *apparent* unanimity in the conclusions of most conventional economists, radical analysts and official governmental statements. The most comprehensive conventional study of the European labour supply question remains that of Kindleberger (1967). Though he starts from orthodox demand/supply analysis, his conclusions are close to those looking at the same problem through a different ideological lens. For Kindleberger, the European post-war recovery was crucially hinged on the availability of a large labour supply. Migration fed economic growth by relieving labour supply bottlenecks, by holding down wages (relative to costs and profits) and by serving as a counter-inflationary force. There are, however, some further subleties in the thesis. The French, for example, managed the respectable rate of growth of 4.6 per cent between 1954 and 1959, despite labour shortages, by rationalising production. Thereafter, the 5.8 per cent growth rate between 1959 and 1963 is to be explained in terms of the general model of labour abundance. Britain proves Kindleberger's case negatively, in that the relatively modest increases and characteristic 'stop-goes' of the British economy are to be explained by the low level of *net* migration to the UK, almost as many Britons leaving the country as were entering it. In this case, the argument is that growth would have been impossible without the new streams of migrants feeding the employment market from below (Kindleberger 1967: 60, 77).

As an example of a Marxist analysis with apparently similar conclusions, the views of Mandel (1978) can be cited—a book so ambitious in its scope, that it is rightly described by its publishers as a 'landmark in Marxist economic literature'. Mandel draws attention to the massive influxes of foreign workers in West Germany after the initial flux of East German refugees had been absorbed. In July

131

1958 these were only 127 000 foreign workers. But these numbers rapidly increased, passing the 1 000 000 mark in 1965 and the 2 000 000 mark in 1971:

> Without this exodus of labour from Southern Europe, which allowed it to reconstruct a reserve army at home, West German capitalism would have been unable to achieve its formidable expansion of outputs in the 1960s without a catastrophic decline in the rate of profit. The same is true, *mutatis mutandis*, of France, Switzerland and the Benelux countries, which in the 1958–71 period together absorbed another 2 000 000 foreign workers into their proletariat. (Mandel 1978: 170.)

Official and quasi-official comment in Germany and France was again quite open about the economic benefits conferred by using migrant labour-power. The Germans made the notion of *Konjunkturpuffer* an explicit policy. It was, under this view, perfectly legitimate to import foreign labourers during a boom and export them during a recession. As Herr Arendt, the Federal Labour Minister, explained in a homely analogy: 'If you are going to undress you take your jacket off before you take off your shirt' (cited in Power 1979: 82). If foreign workers could usefully be discarded like a jacket, their general function was explained in the report by the German Institute for Economic Research:

> Although opposition to the continual inflow of foreign workers is to be found here and there, it is necessary to realise that with a labour market cut off from other countries the pressure of wages in the Federal Republic would become considerably stronger, due to increased competition by employers for the domestic labour potential. This increased pressure of costs could hardly fail to affect the competitiveness of West German enterprises, both in the export markets and at home. (Cited in Berger and Mohr 1975: 137.)

In France the head of the Office National d'Immigration in his retrospective view of the period 1946 to 1966 defended his department's record by boasting that 'immigration has contributed a great deal toward starting up our economy, then towards its expansion'. This sentiment was echoed on a number of occasions by French government planners (Freeman 1979: 177, 8).

132

Only in Britain has official comment remained opaque, not to say hypocritical. For example, a UK Department of Employment report which is remarkable for its detailed statistical data showing how migrant workers are occupationally disadvantaged, yet *essential* to many segments of industrial activity, nonetheless retreats to an equally remarkable coyness when the anonymous authors essay 'Some Views on the Economic Effects of Immigration'. The diplomatic language deployed is pure Whitehall: 'Paragraphs 9–16 take as their starting point various ways in which it has been suggested immigration is likely to be detrimental to productivity growth and paragraphs 17–29 ways in which it is said to be beneficial' (UK Government 1977: 186). The most frequently cited 'detrimental study' which is also cited by the Department of Employment report just referred to, is a speculative article by Misham and Needleman (1968), followed by a more detailed argument by Misham (1970). The assumptions of the joint article were in fact quite ridiculous, that is 'large-scale net migration at a constant inflow of half a million a year'. On this assumption a rise in the labour-capital ratio would result, with consequent losses in productivity 'per man'. In fact the total net migration over the peak 13 years (1955–68) was 669 640 (Castles and Kosack 1973: 31); thereafter rigorous immigration controls dramatically slowed down net migration figures. While the model is therefore predicated on false data and assumptions, I would concur in a more modest rendering of their argument that in some segments of industry, capital investment in machinery has been delayed by the availability of cheap migrant labour (as already mentioned in the case of the textile industry). Misham and Needleman (1968) also argue that the 'social capital' (i.e. the reproduction cost of labour-power) needed for immigrants is high—similar to indigenous needs. Again, the data and assumptions are false in that the housing stock occupied by migrants was marginal and as already indicated, in general, the 'social wage' claims made by migrants are more modest than the equivalent claims made by native workers. However, there is some force in the long-run argument that the costs of reproduction between different ethnic groups will gradually move into harmony as migrant

133

communities are established. This point will be returned to later.

Despite official evasions and the slightly maverick views of the economists just cited, independent and left-wing commentators have no hesitation in placing Britain in line with its European neighbours. As Freeman notes (1979: 184–6), the mainstream journal, *The Economist*, was consistently open in proclaiming the benefits conferred on the British economy. Immigrants were far and away the best source of new labour; they were young, active, mobile and had fewer dependants. The journal was even open enough to disavow racism not because of 'woolly-headed idealism' but for the more material reason that racism 'constituted an artificial constraint on the free movement of the factors of production'. Writers close to the experience of migrant workers concur in seeing the use of migrant labour-power by UK capital as clearly beneficial to the latter, but unlike the leader-writers of *The Economist*, Sivanandan (1982: 34), the Director of the Institute of Race Relations, does not see racism as dysfunctional to the British capital.

> In the early period of post-war reconstruction, when Britain, like all European powers, was desperate for labour, racialism operated on a free market basis—adjusting itself to the ordinary laws of supply and demand ... racialism did not debar black people from work *per se*. It operated instead to deskill them, to keep their wages down and to segregate them in the dirty, ill-paid jobs that white workers did not want ... In the sphere of housing where too many people were seeking too few houses, racialism operated more directly to keep blacks out of the housing market and to herd them into bed-sitters in decaying city areas.

The work of Sivanandan and other writers (for example, Phizacklea and Miles 1980; Miles 1982) critical of earlier race relations research in the UK, have done much to link issues of political economy and the labour migration to the study of race relations in recent years. But still the best and most comprehensive survey placing the British case within the wide political economy of western Europe is the pioneering work of Castles and Kosack (1973). For these two authors, the contrasts often drawn between Britain and

134

continental Europe are exaggerated. The argument, for instance, that in Britain most migrants were permanent settlers unlike those in France, Germany and Switzerland is thought by Castles and Kosack to be somewhat overstated. Many migrants to Britain were *not* necessarily settlers while the pure guest-worker model in Germany showed early signs of breakdown. Nonetheless, even where this permanent/ temporary distinction is valid, they argue that the results are similar. As Castles and Kosack write (1973: 463):

> Immigrant workers will continue to be given the worst jobs, to be concentrated into the poorest housing and to suffer various social problems. Thus there is a permanent immigrant group with *rotating membership*. This rotation ensures that the group remains separate and subordinate. Rotation has the same effect on the position of immigrants in Germany, France and Switzerland, as does colour prejudice in Britain. In both cases immigrants continue to be the group with the worst jobs and social conditions long after the migratory movement first started.

The large numbers of migrants entering European economies in the 1950s and 1960s, together with the continuing evidence of segmentation between natives and migrants in the spheres of employment, housing and social relations, led a number of commentators to assume that European capital needed a permanent stratum of underprivileged workers, sometimes referred to as an 'underclass' or 'sub-proletariat'. In other words, migration was seen as a *structural necessity* for European capital. Castles and Kosack (1981), in an article first published in 1972, place the main emphasis of their argument on the use of migrants as an industrial reserve army and as a means of fragmenting the class conciousness of indigenous workers. On the first issue they write (1981: 45):

> Compared with early patterns, immigration of workers to contemporary West Europe has two new features. The first is its character as a *permanent part of the economic structure*. Previously immigrant labour was used more or less temporarily when the domestic industrial reserve army was inadequate for some special reason, like war or unusually fast expansion; since 1945, however, large numbers of immigrant workers have taken up key positions in the productive process, so that even in the case of recession their labour cannot be dispensed with. The

135

second is its importance as the basis of the modern industrial reserve army ... The main traditional form of the industrial reserve army—men thrown out of work by rationalization and cyclical crises is hardly available today. [Italic added.]

The issue of class fragmentation is also strongly emphasised by Castles and Kosack (1981: 55; 1973: 480, 481). According to their view the native workers have been granted the privileges of a 'labour aristocracy' in relation to the migrant workers. Xenophobia and racialism have been effectively diffused by ruling class control over the means of socialisation and communication. Thus large sections of indigenous workers 'objectively participate' in the exploitation of another group of workers. Those who think they are no longer the lowest group in society are less likely to take militant action, while the split in the working class allows one section of the workers to be played off against the other.

Similar arguments are advanced in Castells (1979: 358, 9) who, like Castles and Kosack, but in somewhat different language, insists on the *permanent* need for migrants by western European capital: 'Immigration is not a conjunctural phenomenon linked to the manpower needs of expanding economies but a structural tendency characteristic of the present phase of monopoly capitalism'. In addition to acting as a classical industrial reserve army and dividing working class, migrant workers are essential, Castells argues, to the management of modern economies. He draws attention to the sudden fluctuations in the European economies— migrant labour-power being precisely one of the anti-cyclical devices deployed by advanced capitalism to iron out these fluctuations and 'one of the basic elements preventing recessions turning into crises' (1979: 366). His argument depends on seeing the problems facing the European economies not in terms of the classical cyclical crises caused by overproduction (beloved by orthodox Marxists) but in terms of excess capital surpluses and wild financial movements linked partly to the *supra*-state activities of the multinational companies. This sort of crisis produces precisely the combination of recession and inflation (the so-called 'stagflation') observed in the 1970s. To overcome this effect, European economies need an ideal 'worker-consumer' who (a) must be very productive in the expansionary phase; (b) must be easily excludable in a recessionary phase and (c) must consume little.

This last point raises the important and neglected issue of the migrant-as-consumer. If, as Castells asserts, migrants 'underconsume' they reduce inflationary tendencies in expansionary phases and cushion the decline in demand when there is a down-swing. If expelled, their purchasing power will not be missed, thus productive capacity can be slowed with little change in effective demand (Castells 1979: 366, 7). To Castells' contentions it might be added that a number of studies written from the point of view of the labour-exporting countries have shown that many migrants and their families, either through remittances or severance pay, use their consumer power to buy goods from their countries of employment. Thus those planners in Turkey who supported the export of labour-power to Germany on the grounds that savings and new skills brought back by returned migrants would be productively invested in Turkey have been disappointed. Savings have been spent more on consumption than production, which in turn has increased the level of imports from Germany. As one Turkish study lugubriously concluded: 'Turkey has become progressively more dependent on migrants' remittances of foreign currencies to close balance of payments deficits and sustain her increased level of importation. Money that flows in thus soon returns to Europe' (Abadan-Unat *et al*. 1976: 382).

So far, the view cited from official sources, orthodox and radical social scientists, with some minor variations and exceptions, have tended to gravitate to similar conclusions. Migrants were not only good news for post-war European capital, their presence was essential to the fulfilment of capital's needs to accumulate, control the labour force politically and ideologically, and allow the state greater leverage in regulating the economy. This apparent unanimity, however, concealed an interesting tendential distinction between the orthodox and radical analysts. The former, often economists working in university departments or for government agencies, were encased in bland professional norms, or politically neutered by official responsibilities. They were thus protected, or had to ignore, political and social theory that disturbed or complicated their neat econometric models (thus rendering most of them quite limited for predictive purposes). On the other hand, a number of the Marxist writers, whose intellectual progenitor was often labelled as an 'economic determinist' in fact showed much more sensitivity to the political, social and ideological requirements of capital than did their mainstream counterparts.

Thus there is very little in conventional econometric analysis which serves to explain why, given the enormous advantages conferred on capital by the presence of migrants, there was a rapid rundown, then virtual stoppage, of the migrant streams in all northern European countries in the period after 1973. A demand/supply analysis in the wake of the outset of the recession is clearly inadequate, as it would have been in the interests of individual national capitals to cheapen their labour costs further as competition for scarce markets increased. The hint of an answer is given in one of the economists cited earlier (Misham 1970) where he argues in terms of the 'social capital' (i.e. reproduction) costs of migrant labourers. But, of course, the contours of this issue can only be established by a greater appreciation of sociological data—in particular the varying propensities and capacities to establish migrant communities in the face of the state's attempts to keep the advantages of the single migrant/ guest worker model (see Chapter 5).

Most Marxist and radical analyses are somewhat better in retaining some sense of a dynamic in the overall struggle between capital and labour, showing that it is necessary to remember what forms of resistance by labour are possible, as well as according credit to the extraordinary will and capacity of capital to decompose labour. Yet, I can only accord two cheers to many Marxist analyses, for there is no doubt that they too become subject to a kind of functionalist logic, showing more interest in what capital was doing to migrant and indigenous labour, than what contradictions were engendered by the process. Here and there, however, an alternative perspective does emerge. Gorz (1971), for example, clearly saw that for migrants to demand full parity nd equality with French workers was not a reformist but a evolutionary demand, in that the structure of the French conomy would be challenged and the essential basis of orking class unity would be forged. Migrant workers uld, he argued, be 'an *avant garde* "Fourth World"— hich is to say an eruption of the struggle of the "Third Vorld" within the imperialist citadel itself' (Gorz 1971: 87).

Sivanandan, writing on the UK, is equally explicit that the nti-immigration lobby grew precisely in harmony with the apacity of black workers to organise themselves—cause and onsequence being inseparable. A new Immigration Act and ndustrial Relations Act were both passed in 1971. ogether, the Acts threatened to lock the black working class nto the position of a permanent underclass. Hence, it is recisely in the area of black working class struggle that the esistance of the early 1970s becomes significant. But these vere not struggles apart. Because they involved *black* vorkers, they were tied up with other struggles in the ommunity, which in turn was involved in battles on the actory floor (Sivanandan 1982: 28). Though more cautious, Castells (1979) also concludes his 'structural' analysis by rawing attention to the possibilities of a dynamic political nd social contest between capital and migrant workers, ather than assuming the deck would always be so loaded gainst the migrants that they could be shoved about like awns on a chessboard. As he writes (1979: 375, 6):

The trial of strength between the immigrant movement and capital, which requires a certain status for immigrants, has started. It will be long and hard. All the more so since the immigrant movement is starting to escape its isolation and gradually to find its place again in the trade union movement through a reciprocal discovery of common class interests through common struggles.

The question of working class unity will be returned to ater, but for the meantime it is important to note that at least n outline, and in the case of Sivanandan (1982: 143–61) in nuch fuller terms, Marxist and radical writers were clearly ninting at a change in the basic logic and balance of advan-

139

tage facing European capital in the mid 1970s compared t
1945. This basic change in direction is analysed below.

The end to the migrant labour boom

There is no doubt that since the mid-seventies, the attracti
veness of the migrant solution to European capital has wor
off and we are witnessing an end to the migrant boom of th
1945 to 1975 period. In short, the supposedly *structura*
requirements of capital are no longer being met by th
continuous import of large numbers of migrants. The switch
in strategy is a result of two factors. First, at an economi
level, employers found that these structural requirement
could better be met outside the national economy. (Thi
question is discussed fully in Chapter 7: here it is onl
necessary to note that, for many companies, the export o
capital became more profitable than the import of labour.
Second, at the level of politics and social relations, th
structural requirements of capital were subject to contradic
tory tendencies. Some of these changes have been alluded t
earlier, but my explanation for the post 1970s shift ir
strategy will become clearer if the earlier train of reasoning i
followed, that is to show how in each case, where th
advantages of using migrants seemed evident, some countervailing pressures have since emerged.

First, the simple association between more hands anc
more production. Over the seventies, it became clear that i
was no longer necessary to bring workers to some sectors o
capital. It is true that in certain service and public-secto
industries cheap labour was still necessary, but importec
labour had already filled the major gaps in the labour market
the rest could apparently be filled by unemployed metropolitan workers, discarded from internationally uncompetitive
industries. With the increasing rates of unemployment,
some spare capacity could still be left over for an internal
reserve army. But with respect to some manufacturing (and
extractive) industry, if more hands needed to be set to work,
they could easily be recruited and employed within the
newly industrialising zones of the Third World itself. In

140

short, an internal racial division of labour could be replaced by an international division of labour, and the sites of production could be switched to take account of market, transportation and labour conditions.

Second, the cost of the reproduction of migrant labour-power is gradually rising in all metropolitan societies. The advantages in obviating reproductive costs are essentially only those accruing in an early phase of expansion, or (as in South Africa) where oscillation is possible. For the system to profit indefinitely, the process of marginalisation of exhausted labour-power and the new recruitment of fresh labour-power must go on continually. But in an age of the Universal Declaration of Human Rights, of the European Court of Justice, of the attempt by western powers to oppose their concern for human rights with that of the eastern bloc countries, there are clear legal and moral limitations beyond which the state cannot act. The agents of the state can, to be sure, expel some, repatriate others and attempt to cow the remainder of migrants, but in the end, most policymakers and politicians have been forced into the recognition that a permanent core of migrants will remain. Gradually, and as much through community action and political mobilisation as through the generosity of the bourgeois spirit, concessions are being won. The right to settlement, the right to vote, and right to reunite families, to acquire an education, housing and social benefits—all these are the terrain of migrant struggles within the advanced capitalist states. What is being witnessed at the moment is a grudging set of concessions, a weeding-out of those who are unprotected, and attempts to bureaucratically slow down the process of granting the rights demanded by migrants. It is known, for example, of the ploys by British officials in Bangladesh and Pakistan to slow down the flow of dependants to breadwinners in the UK by demanding forms of documentation, such as birth certificates, that aren't issued in the countries concerned. When, out of desperation, forged versions of the required papers are duly produced, these are immediately seen as sufficient cause to deny entry completely or to send the dependant to the back of the slowly-moving queue. It is known also of the secret police detention centre in Marseilles (now closed

141

down) which contained dozens of men, women and children awaiting deportation in crowded conditions and without access to legal help (Power 1979: 36). It is known that in Britain the rule of law runs skin-deep where 'illegal' migrants are concerned. During the first eight months of 1980 alone, 73 foreign nationals were detained in British prisons *after completing their sentence*, while 47 others were held, pending deportation, without ever having been sentenced (*The Sunday Times* (London), 17 August 1980). Franco Brustati's powerful film, *Bread and Chocolate*, has also been seen. This depicts the plight of an Italian migrant in Switzerland. When the swarthy hero of the film, Nino Manfredi, is released after a false accusation of murdering a lily-white Swiss child, he pisses in relief on the nearest wall—only to be deemed socially undesirable and a candidate for deportation. But all of this display of bureaucratic indifference, muddle and malevolence, is, in the end, rather Canute-like in the face of the fact that migrant communities are gradually showing the capacity to organise and defend themselves. In so far as this amelioration has taken place, in so far, in other words, as the migrant communities have improved their conditions of housing, established their families, utilised the educational and welfare system, so accordingly has the initial advantage to capital of the cheap reproduction of labour-power been undercut.

The third advantage to capital was the greater extraction of surplus-value at the point of production. Here too there have been a number of advances in respect of the development of worker organisations among migrant workers. Many migrant workers have shown considerable ability to organise strikes often in the face of indifference and hostility of their white co-workers. Some of these forms of resistance are discussed in Chapter 6. But two general points may be made here. First generation migrant workers began the task of self defence in protecting their jobs, and not permitting their employers as great a control of the labour process as occurred in the 1950s and 1960s. The second generation of migrants has often gone further in abandoning the attitudes of their parents in respect of the kinds of jobs and the kinds of conditions they are prepared to accept at the workplace

This is seen in a renewed cultural affirmation and in the rejection of what young West Indians in Britain dismiss as 'shit-work' (Henderson and Cohen 1982; Pryce 1979).

The fourth, and final, advantage to capital in the post-war period lay in utilising the migrant workforce to undercut the general conditions of labour and divide the working class. Here, the ideological advances by metropolitan workers have been limited, though not totally negligible. At a formal and national level, the trade unions have been loud in their damnation of racism. In Britain, resolutions have been passed and speeches have been made against discrimination at successive TUC Congresses in 1955, 1959, 1966, 1968 and 1974. At the same time, the TUC did not oppose the 1977 Immigration Act until two years *after* its promulgation. The most important limiting factor, however, has been the general insistence, both in Britain and in France, that migrant workers should subordinate their distinctive struggles to the existing organisational forms and skill distinctions which were developed without reference to the migrants' needs. The result has been a low level of rank and file membership, a low level of participation in routine organisational matters, and a serious under-representation of migrants at the leadership levels of existing trade union bodies. However, the growth of quasi-independent workers' organisations among migrants, together with the need for a common response to capital's recent general moves against labour, will probably propel a greater degree of class unity than that seen hitherto. At the very least, capital can no longer take it for granted that the labour force will remain split on racial, national and cultural lines.

Conclusion

It should now be apparent that the reasons for the great wave of migration in the post-war period have all but evaporated due to the countervailing ideological, social and political tendencies described. It is also clear that certain shifts in comparative advantage have propelled another twist in the changing international division of labour (see Chapter 7). The argument, in short, that migrant labour was a 'struc-

143

tural necessity' for the post-war European economies is belied by the virtual shutting-off of all non-EEC migration in the period after 1973. Some theorists have attempted to argue that the state is attempting through racist practices to reproduce a subordinate class within the domestic economy, rather than import further foreign workers (Hall *et al.* 1978; Miles 1982: 181; Duffield 1981). There is some truth in this argument, though it doesn't take into account the apparently serious attempts by the state to damp down race conflict in the interests of preserving law and order (Scarman 1982; Sivanandan 1982: 122–4). Nor does this argument sufficiently account for the high levels of work alienation experienced by migrant youth. Finally, the idea that internal reproduction has replaced external imports does not address Castells's central argument that the deployment of migrant labour helped in the management of 'stagflation'. Indeed, I would argue that 'monetarist' political practices have now assumed this function, while capital has sought richer pickings elsewhere.

In short, both orthodox economists and a number of Marxists became trapped into a timeless functionality and exaggerated the extent to which migrant labour was a permanent solution for European capital. Rather than seeing European migrant labourers as a 'structural necessity', a longer historical vision and a more international approach suggest that the period 1945 to 1973 was one where importing labour of a subordinate status was a preferred and helpful solution for European capital. As has been shown at earlier periods, capital characteristically deployed unfree labour-power at the edges of the regional political economy, a phenomenon repeated in the 1970s and 80s. The mix between free and unfree labour is spatially redistributed in a complex and continuously *changing* way in response to the mix of market opportunities, comparative labour-power costs, the course of struggles between capital and labour and the historically specific flows and supplies of migrant and other forms of unfree labour. Chapters 5 and 6 will assess the balance of power between capital and the state on the one hand, and migrant workers in the three regional political economies discussed, on the other.

5 Policing the frontiers: regulating the supplies of migrant labour

> *In capitalist society, the state is charged with the primary responsibility of defending the interests of the dominant classes: of managing the affairs, of mediating the needs, of capitalism and the capitalist class. These ends are accomplished through the removal or erection of obstacles which benefit or inhibit the functioning of a capitalist economy. The degree of relaxation, selectivity or stringency involved in the formation and enforcement of boundary regulations is illustrative.*
>
> (Petras 1980: 174)

The evolution of national boundaries is a relatively new historical phenomenon. Natural boundaries like rivers, mountains and oceans inhibited intercourse between peoples and regions, but, with odd exceptions like the Great Wall of China intended to protect the Ch'in dynasty from the Turkish and Mongol hordes, artifically constructed political borders did not exist prior to the 17th century. Political geographers have shown how the evolution of boundaries accompanied the development of the modern nation state. Where natural boundaries did not exist, treaties, laws and contracts created 'paper walls' dividing up land, sea and air into legally defined domains 'belonging to' legally recognised states (Prescott 1965; Petras 1980: 159).

For the older school of political geographers, much influence by liberal economic doctrine, the gradual hardening of political boundaries was very much to be regretted. Boggs (1940: 106) in a widely-cited work, noted that prior to 1914, passports were not generally required in going from one country to another, but after that date their use became the rule rather than the exception in Europe and America. In

145

a passionate denunciation of modern boundaries Boggs (1940: 110) claimed:

> If human beings could come and go as freely as they chose thousands would probably trek across their frontiers, almost anywhere, in the hope of escaping from almost unendurable psychological and economic pressures. Today the barriers to trade in Europe rise like walls between nations, slow the pulse of industry, rob artisans and labourers of a chance to earn a living, impoverish peoples whose ample capacities are thwarted, and instil fear and despair.

Nowadays, radical political geographers present themselves as more dispassionate and have sought to weld spatial divisions on to theories of the international division of labour and of uneven development. The connection between space, the state and the economy is thus considered to be the primary focus of research while, as one geographer in the new mould expresses it, nationalism can 'in one sense be seen as the cultural fall out from the economic explosion of capitalist uneven development' (Short 1982: 125).

While the contemporary line of analysis undoubtedly will yield a good deal of fruitful work on international restructuring, and industrial relocation (see Massey 1984), Boggs's moral outrage is not entirely inappropriate. He wrote as war clouds were looming in Europe and the tightening of frontiers prevented millions of innocent people from escaping the Nazi juggernaut. In our own time, and on our television screens, boat people from Vietnam or Haiti can be seen being brutally clubbed by the minions of the state, aspirant emigrants being denied passports by a number of the states in the Comecon bloc and long-standing residents of Nigeria being told to pack-up and return to their 'homes' in Ghana. Now, as in the late 1930s, workers seeking to earn a living are being denied the opportunity to do so by the restrictive practices of the state. The doctrines of 'de-regulation' and private initiative are applied highly selectively in our contemporary political order. Whereas rigorous attempts are made to control and restrict international worker mobility, the international mobility of capital is comparatively unfettered. Even where exchange control regulations obtain, these are frequently and easily evaded by transfer pricing, dummy registrations in tax havens and the general capacity of many transnational corporations to dictate terms to most of the modern world's nation states. By contrast, non-state sanctioned mobility by people is deemed illegal, and the undocumented worker is unable to benefit from the uneven spatial distribution of the world's productive forces in the manner perfected by the owners of capital. Currency speculation, foreign investment, repatriation of profits, and the development of global communications networks are just four of the ways in which transnational capital has superseded the historic bounds of the nation state.

While capital has an expanding global horizon, workers have been coralled into narrower pens, their physical and psychological frontiers being policed by the national state. This development has radically altered the context of celebrated academic debates about the role of the frontier in history. For Turner (1920), the frontier signified free land, a freedom from restraint and the possibility of recapturing the innocence of Arcadia, lost in the march of industrial civilisation. Such a vision, as Hennessy (1978: 6) has argued, was an attractive prospect for many: 'For European peasants burdened by feudal obligations, the West was the lure of free land, for workers penned in by industrial cities it provided the illusion of a carefree life, perhaps echoing a recently lost rural past'. But, he goes on, this dream can no longer be sustained: 'In Latin America there is no West no Frontier, there are only frontiers (ibid). Whereas in earlier days the borderlands were inhabited by folk heroes like Kitt Carson, Daniel Boone, Davy Crockett and General Custer, or romantic desperados, bandits, runaway slaves and *gauchos*, now the borderlands are peopled by pathetic work seekers' (Hennessy 1978: 158).

In the sections that follow, examples will be taken from each of the regional political economies covered (American, European and southern African) to show how the most powerful regional state has sought to engineer and refine the regulatory apparatuses directed against free worker mobility. In conclusion, the extent to which such controls have been evaded by illegal entrants will be discussed.

147

US immigration policy: the Haitians and Cubans

Despite its immigrant heritage, since the establishment of effective national boundaries surrounding the United States the country has never permitted untrammelled immigration. As Martin (1981: 4) notes, immigration law was predicated on an ever increasing list of 'undesirables' starting from the 1880s—prostitutes, convicts, Chinese, lunatics, idiots and contract labourers (1885) were followed by quantitative restrictions (1907) and national origins restrictions in 1921 and 1924. There are now more than 30 classes of undesirable aliens, including homosexuals and security risks, and a sophisticated seven-tier system of family and skill preferences overlaying country limits, hemispheric preferences and ceilings and quotas for various categories of would-be immigrants.

With such a battery of legislative controls it might be assumed that the pattern of migration to the US is highly controlled and predictable. In fact, over the last decade or so, the system of regulation is widely perceived to have been ineffective. In one poll, 91 per cent of US respondents supported an 'all out effort' to control illegal immigration while 80 per cent wanted further restrictions on the entry o legal migrants and refugees. This popular reaction was set in a context where the authorised number of 450 000 migrant for 1980 had been superseded by a further 358 000 legal immigrants, refugees and special entrants and perhaps a half million illegal migrants (Martin 1981: 1). In the 1980s, total annual immigration is thought to be exceeding the all-time high of 880 000 per annum achieved in the period 1901 to 1910.

Why then has the US state found it so difficult to implement the restrictive practices of its European and South African counterparts? Some of the difficulty is purely function of the practical problems of policing so large country—for example the shallow 1000-mile-long Rio Grande separates one of the poorest from one of the riche countries of the world. The sheer volume of passenger movements for purposes of trade, study and tourism also means that 'overstayers' are not quickly or easily detected

148

especially when internal state boundaries are crossed. But more important than these practical problems, is the certainty that any decisive political action by the executive will be opposed by determined pressure groups with an interest in exploiting cheap labour-power to the full. In addition to the state versus big business conflict, those occupying positions of political responsibility are cross-pressured by the need not to offend voters whose position may be challenged by an undiscriminating drive against their illegal co-ethnics (the Hispanics are a good case in point). Many politicians also wish to sustain the ideology that the US (unlike the eastern bloc) provides a haven for the tired, the poor and those who are seeking 'freedom' from 'totalitarianism'. The contradictions of these cross-currents are shown by the thus-far doomed attempts of successive presidents to produce master plans for the immigrant question, and well illustrated by the experience of trying to develop a consistent policy towards Haitians and Cuban migrants over the last few years.

The concern over immigration policy reached positively alarmist proportions during the Nixon presidency which was characterised by a virtual militarisation of the undocumented worker 'problem'. General Chapman, late of Vietnam, became head of the Immigration and Naturalization Service (INS) and he and Charles Colby (head of the CIA under Nixon) saw the US–Mexican border as 'the greatest threat posed to US national security' (NACLA 1977: 4). Massive deportations running at one million a year did not, however, significantly slow the level of illegal immigration. Moreover, the Hispanic communities, especially in California, were outraged at the selectivity of the INS's targets. The INS arrests were disproportionately directed against Mexican nationals. Whereas 45 per cent of undocumented migrants are of Mexican origin, Mexicans accounted for 95 per cent of the pick-ups. Again, whereas European undocumented aliens are given two to three months to leave 'voluntarily', Hispanic migrants are deported within five to six hours (Pandya and Schey 1981).

The attacks on undocumented workers served only to radicalise and politicise groups that had remained tangential

149

to mainstream US politics. It is greatly to President Carter's credit that he seriously faced up to the claims of natural justice which make it evident that the employer is as much of a party to illegality as the employee. However, this recognition was not given much in the way of practical sanctions in his 1977 proposals. The penalties proposed for employers of illegal workers were small ($1000), they would be charged with a civil rather than criminal offence and finally, the obvious 'let-out', the employer had to be 'knowingly' hiring illegal workers. Carter's 1977 immigration plan also included some of the package which has now become familiar in immigration debates in the US—that is a hard-line commitment to stopping illegal entry combined with a limited 'amnesty' for undocumented aliens. In this case, Carter proposed to provide a $100 million increase in the INS budget to provide for military equipment and a further 2000 border guards. Undocumented aliens who could prove seven years of uninterrupted residence could apply for legal recognition. Finally, Carter's plan also offered a package of aid and loans, aimed principally at Mexico, to reduce population growth, create employment and stabilise the border region (NACLA 1977).

There is little point in detailing the largely ignominious collapse of these proposals, as they were dragged through the mire of public and congressional debate. Agribusiness mobilised against the proposed employer fines, while sections of organised labour felt this measure would lead to the non-hiring of non-white workers, even where they were not illegal. Minority communities also mobilised against the second class citizenship applied in the amnesty proposals, civil rights groups directed more fire at the militarisation of the border area, while the ends of the balls of string tying the Mexican aid and loans package seemed largely to end up in the boardrooms of major US corporations.

The most Congress would accept was the establishment of yet another commission, the Select Commission on Immigration and Refugee Policy, set up in 1978 'to study and evaluate . . . existing laws, policies and procedures governing the admission of immigrants and refugees to the US'. Marti (1981) provides an excellent summary of the major recommendations, no less than 57 in total, in a 453-page report taking three years to complete. The report repeated some of the Carter package. Fines against employers, a one-time amnesty for illegal aliens in the US, and an increase in legal quotas combined with stronger enforcement procedures all made a reappearance. What was new, was the narrow vote in the Commission (8–7) in favour of a more reliable mechanism to identify legal workers in the form of a counterfeit-proof social security card. The analogy with the South African pass system (the new-style South African plastic-sealed passes are now ironically made by a US computer firm) was perhaps too uncomfortable for the dissenting commissioners. The Commission also proposed major changes to refugee policy some of which were anticipated in the Refugee Act of 1980.

The proposals of the Select Commission, the passing of the Refugee Act and the sudden development of a 'refugee crisis' in the summer of 1980, combined to expose some of the paradoxes and problems of US immigration and refugee policy. Though not the sole contributing factor to his downfall, the political difficulties of trying to ride the refugee tiger severely damaged Carter electorally. Whereas the official total for refugee admissions in 1980 was 50 000, during the spring and summer of 1980 alone some 125 000 Cubans arrived in the 'freedom flotilla', while another 20 000 Haitians sought asylum in the US. In both cases, the mix of ideology, economics and state policy proved explosive. At first, Carter endorsed the 20-year-old official policy welcoming refugees from Communist countries (indeed prior to 1980 the official definition of a refugee was one fleeing Communist countries, Communist-dominated countries and, oddly, 'any country in the Middle East'). In a well-publicised speech he offered Cubans an 'open heart and open arms', though he carefully qualified his statement by adding 'in accordance with American law' (Bach *et al.* 1981–82: 31). Somewhat to Carter's surprise, the political embarrassment facing the Cuban regime when a large number of its citizens demanded the right to leave, did not impel Castro to try to deter the would-be emigrants. On the contrary, he announced that the revolution was a voluntary one and that anyone who wished to leave would be free to do so. As Bach and his co-authors point out (ibid), unlike during the 'aerial bridge' of the 1960s, or during the prisoner release period a decade later, the Cuban government refused to discuss a *controlled* departure programme, unless the agenda included talks on the economic boycott, the continuing US occupation of Guantánamo and the end to spy flights over Cuba.

Castro had turned the tables by, in effect, proclaiming: 'You are the showcase of an opulent society whose keys you refuse to surrender. Agree to face the real problems, or we will unleash the starving pack' (*Guardian Weekly* (Manchester) 15 June 1980). Carter was a president who showed an unusual capacity, so the electorate decided, for shooting himself in the foot. But it was perhaps unexpected that beating the customary anti-Communist drum would have so little effect. Three major factors turned what could have been a propaganda victory for Carter into a moral coup for Castro.

First, he failed to take into account the general mood of xenophobia (see Chapter 6 for other examples) which always appears during a recessionary period. With high unemployment, inflation and bleak economic prospects, many Congressmen and large sections of public opinion interpreted Carter's statements as an open-door policy. He was seen as imposing another burden on the taxpayer and introducing another set of competitors for housing, jobs, educational and health facilities.

Second, this mood was greatly fanned by the depiction of many of the flotilla entrants as 'socially undesirable'. Widespread reports appeared that the Cuban authorities were emptying their jails and mental asylums and rounding-up street criminals to load into the boats at Mariel Harbour. One Democratic politician claimed, after a trip to Key West, that 'just about every adult male I've talked to admitted to having been in prison in Cuba' (quoted in Bach *et al.* 1981–82: 31). The criminal image was reinforced by the riot of 300 Cuban internees at a transit camp at Arkansas. However, as Bach and his colleagues show, the level of prior criminality of the entrants was vastly exaggerated—their profile of the 198 entrants did not differ significantly from earlier waves of

152

migrants. In their survey of Cubans in transit camps they found the entrants tended to be younger, with a higher proportion of black and mulattoes than earlier waves of Cuban migrants, though the additional percentages involved were not great. None the less, compared to the earliest cohort of exiles (in the 1960s), the entrants were drawn from more working class occupations or were more likely to be unemployed. About 16 per cent of the camp population they surveyed had been incarcerated in Cuba (Bach *et al.* 1981–2: 46, 7). A significant proportion of this ex-prison group would be described as 'anti-social' in the Cuban context, but it is doubtful that many of their activities (minor corruption, petty trading in the shadow economy) would have landed them in jail in the US. Equally, however, there were very few full-blown political dissenters. While a number of Cubans learned to recite lines appropriate to political refugees for opportunistic reasons, it is doubtful that more than a handful had any strong anti-socialist ideological convictions.

Third, a local factor intervened to turn Carter's propaganda victory sour. For the Cubans did not disperse throughout the country—they mostly landed in that hotbed of explosive urban politics, Miami. The city is the closest urban concentration to Cuba and had always been the major point of settlement for the Cuban community. In 1960, when the Cubans first started arriving in significant numbers, the city had a fairly typical southern ethnic mix— 80 per cent white, 14 per cent black and 6 per cent Hispanic. Twenty years later, the Hispanic element represented 47 per cent of the population, with a nearly equivalent proportion of whites. In a *Miami Herald* poll, only 17 per cent of 'non-Latin whites' thought the arrival of the Cubans was 'a good thing'. The black minority was so alarmed that sustained rioting began, ostensibly occasioned by the miscarriage of justice in the trial of a black man. According to a Harris poll, however, it was not the court case, but the arrival of the Cubans that provoked a black riot (*Guardian Weekly* (Manchester) 4 June 1980). A Florida businessman closely mirrored local public opinion when he declared in some alarm 'We're Castro's hostages!' (*Guardian Weekly* (Manchester) 5 June 1980).

Policing the frontier between the US and Haiti als[o] generated considerable political embarrassment for the U[S] administration. Over the period 1953 to 1976, 745 815 Hai[-]tians were legally admitted to the US (Buchanan 1979: 19[)] fleeing both the severe economic impoverishment of th[e] island and the political depredations of Papa Doc and hi[s] son, Baby Doc Duvalier. Graham Greene's novel, *Th[e Comedians*, brilliantly captures the atmosphere of rando[m] violence, beatings, sudden arrests, torture, property confis[-]cation and executions of dissenters' relatives perpetrated b[y] the informal arm of government, the Ton-Ton Macoute[s.] The Haitian government none the less gains staunch suppo[rt] from the US—half the government's revenue coming fro[m] foreign, overwhelmingly US, aid. While permitting som[e] legal migration from Haiti, the US authorities have clampe[d] down severely on illegal migration from the island. In law, a[s] well as in acceptable ideology, it was nigh-impossible t[o] admit that there could be such strange creatures as *refuge[es]* from a state dedicated to capitalism and propped up virtuall[y] entirely by US aid, investment and tourist receipts. Y[et] refugees many undoubtedly were—in 1980 some 20 0[0]0 Haitians risked their lives in overcrowded and leaky boa[ts] attempting the 700-mile windward passage from Haiti t[o] Miami. For the INS officials, the Haitians had a status 'n[o] different than that of the illegal Mexican alien who cross[es] the border on foot' (quoted in Bogre 1979: 9). For man[y] Haitians, however, they are folk heroes making a despera[te] bid to save their precarious plots from ruination and the[ir] wives and children from starvation. In one account, th[e] journalist, Art Harris, describes how a 39-year-old schoo[l] teacher borrowed $500 from his father-in-law and $14[0] from a loan shark to make an illegal trip to Florida where h[e] picked grapefruit for 'the shining Kelloggs-pack faces of th[e] US breakfast tables'. Harris meanwhile traced his wife to [a] tin shack with a muddy floor where she was hunched over [a] porridge of corn mush and peas. The children were sic[k,] there was not enough money to buy milk. While she awaite[d] a cheque from her husband, there was little to do but fig[ht] off the flies (*Guardian Weekly* (Manchester) 25 Januar[y] 1982).

154

The treatment of Haitian illegals followed the Mexican pattern favoured by the INS officials, until civic groups and attorneys representing Haitians began to publicise numerous cases which clearly fell within the terms of the 1980 Refugee Act. Under this Act, designed to bring the US in line with international norms, a refugee was someone unwilling or unable to return to their country of origin, 'because of a well-founded fear of persecution on account of race, religion, nationality, membership in a particular social group of political opinion'. As Nicholls (1986) argues in a careful summary of the argument distinguishing a political refugee from an economic migrant:

> An authoritarian regime may be quite as oppressive in certain fields as totalitarian government. Many Haitian boat people claim, for example, that they have been victims of injustice and oppression at the hands of local macoute leaders who are officials of an authoritarian regime. The Immigration and Naturalisation Service has generally failed to pay attention to claims of this kind made by Haitian refugees.

In an attempt to make the INS treatment of Haitian refugees consistent with its declarations, the State Department commissioned a study of Haiti which found, to no one's surprise, that 'most Haitian migrants come to the US drawn by the prospect of economic opportunity and [are] not fleeing political persecution . . . economic motives, however admirable do not translate, into a right under the Protocol to asylum' (cited in Bogre 1979: 10). When adding that this conclusion was reached by a study team comprising four white men, in Haiti for three weeks and basing their findings on interviewees publicly recruited through the government-controlled radio station, it is perhaps understandable that at least one writer (Bogre 1979) is sceptical of the validity of the report.

The immediate political crises surrounding the admission of Cuban and Haitian refugees over the last few years served to dramatise the general incapacity of the US state to translate its ideological utterances and elaborate regulatory apparatuses into effective administrative practice. President Reagan has sought to wrestle with the same inconsistencies

155

and has only made limited headway with his immigration proposals. As will now be shown, the European states and the South African state were better able to match their immigration policies and practises to the racism of their electorates and the labour-power needs of their industrial and service sectors. But even in these cases, as might be expected, no complete consonance is possible.

Guestworkers, settlers and citizens: European variations

Within Europe the state was generally able to act more effectively than in the US to insulate the metropolitan society from mass, uncontrolled migration from the edges of the regional political economy. But there were important limits to the scope of state action in Europe too. State intervention took two major forms—policing the outer frontiers of the hegemonic country by tigher immigration regulations and better border controls, and policing the internal state by more subtle yet more pervasive measures, particularly when prompted to do so in the wake of riot conditions. Germany, France, Britain and Switzerland (the four major European importers of migrant labour) have all implemented both sets of control measures, though in somewhat different ways. As the labour supply question is the primary concern here, the variations in respect of immigration policy are particularly discussed.

In the case of Germany, as argued in Chapter 4, the model of the post-war migrant worker was that of a temporary guest-worker—there to fill immediate gaps in the labour market and to be dispensed with when the guest's services were no longer required. Though the presence of large numbers of East German refugees at first filled the vacancies at the bottom of the labour market, the rapid expansion of the German economy in the 1950s, meant an equally rapid expansion of the recruitment of foreign labourers—from 95 000 in 1956 to 507 000 by 1961 and 1.3 million by 1966 (Castles *et al*. 1984: 72). The system to recruit foreign labourers was taken over virtually intact from war-time

156

recedents. The Federal Labour Office set up labour bur-
aux in the Mediterranean countries, encouraging German
mployers wanting labourers to pay this government agency
 recruitment fee. Selection, occupational testing, medical,
riminal and political checks were all carried out before
ntry. The work of the Federal Labour Office was, however,
oon supplemented by inter-governmental labour-supply
ontracts with Greece (1960), Turkey (1961 and 1964),
Morocco (1963), Portugal (1964), Tunisia (1965) and
Yugoslavia (1968) (ibid).

The final test of the guest-worker system was to come in
973 when there was a ban imposed on all worker recruitment from non-EEC countries. Ideally, the initial specifica-
ions of the model implied a permanently rotating labour
orce, so it should have been easy both to stop new entrants
nd to expel existing workers as the economy lurched into
risis. In fact, the figures show only a moderate decline in
oreign-worker employment after 1973, and an increase in
he number of unemployed foreigners, together with an
verall increase in the foreign population. The numbers of
oreign residents increased from nearly 3 million in 1970, to
.1 million in 1974 and 4.6 million in 1982 (Castles *et al*.
984: 76). In some ways this growth is surprising given that,
n common with Switzerland, Germany has some of the
arshest legislation pertaining to the settlement of foreign
workers and their families. The Foreigners Law of 1965
imply confirmed the importance of the 'Foreigners' Police',
ot likely to be the most sympathetic authority in granting or
withholding a residence permit. The instructions given to
fficials as to how to operate the 1965 laws (cited in Castles *et*
l. 1984: 77) are nothing if not explicit:

> Foreigners enjoy all basic rights, except the basic rights of
> freedom of assembly, freedom of association, freedom of move-
> ment and free choice of occupation, place of work and place of
> education and protection from extradition abroad.

Korte (1985: 16) considers the difference between the legal
tatus of 'foreigners' and 'Germans' to be of 'decisive importance' in generating inequality of treatment in that, 'the
ncertain legal position in which the individual foreigner

lives demonstrates to him daily his position as an outsider'. When adding that foreigners do not have the right to vote and that birth in Germany does not automatically imply a right to citizenship, it becomes apparent that the German state in the post-war period conceived its foreign workers, especially its Turkish workers against whom most discrimination is practised, in a manner similar to the Ancient Spartan state's relationship to its subject helot population. Why then did foreign population in Germany show such a marked rise?

First, it is relevant to recall that at the end of the war the constitution-makers of West Germany sought to distinguish *their* state from its communist counterpart. This resulted in an unusually generous constitutional provision for the admission of refugees. It was evident that this provision was intended mainly to benefit East Germans wishing to desert the joys of state socialism, an opportunity that many seized until they were physically prevented from so doing. In addition to providing a useful moral contrast with the political practices of East Germany, the refugee provision also helped to fuel the post-war West German economy with well-trained and compliant labourers. However, it was ideologically impossible to deny a similar right of admission to other refugees—who began to stream into West Germany in significant numbers. Some 300 000 Eritreans, Afghans, Indians, Pakistanis, Vietnamese, Chileans, Argentinians and Turks have arrived as refugees since 1979 and these Third World migrants constitute some 40 per cent of the foreign population. The word 'refugees' is used in quotes since there is little doubt that in many cases this description was self-interested and meant to circumvent West Germany's otherwise forbidding immigration regulations.

A second factor explaining the recent growth of the foreign population is that as Germany sought to represent itself as a morally enlightened member of the EEC, and as demands by the migrant communities began to escalate, so it became politically impossible to deny the right to many dependants to join their breadwinners in Germany. As this concession was granted quite recently in Germany's migration history (compared, say, with Britain where Common-

158

wealth citizenship permitted family reunification in the 1950s and 1960s for West Indian and most Asian migrants), the baby boom associated with the reconstitution of families is a phenomenon of the 1970s and 1980s in Germany.

Third, the rise of foreign residents was also attributable to the very adverse conditions obtaining in Turkey—a combination of economic collapse, brutal authoritarian government and arbitrary exercises of administrative power at the local level made many Turks in Germany reluctant to return, and propelled those who had relatives in Germany to join them before legislative restrictions made this impossible.

In sum, German migration policy represents a combination of strong controls at the level of manpower planning, relatively open access to refugees and some recent concessions on the question of family reunification. The result has been what some scholars describe as a dual policy. On the one hand, social integration of the migrant communities is pursued through the easier provisions for family unification and the naturalisation of second-generation migrants. On the other hand, the German government has fiercely restricted new entrants and had few scruples in introducing a scheme for repatriation assistance in 1982 (a policy that even the Thatcher government in Britain has shied away from). Not that the relaxations on naturalisation should be seen in too benevolent a light: such a measure is directed at defusing what is widely recognised as a 'social time bomb', the problem of alienated, sullen and rebellious migrant youth (Castles 1980; Phizacklea 1983: 99). In a sense, all that the latest round of reforms in Germany indicates is that, having started from an extreme guest-worker model where no rights of settlement or citizenship were recognised, the West German state has been forced to accept the social reality of migrant settlement, and has therefore begun to converge with its European counterparts.

During the d'Estaing presidency, the French authorities also sought to link the immigration question to issues of employment, social control and repatriation in a highly-systematic way. M. Stoleru, the French Immigration Minister, announced plans in July 1979 to reduce the immigrant population by 200 000 a year. First, the French government offered £1000 to any unemployed migrant ready to go home—an offer accepted by an estimated 30 000 people per annum in the first years. Second, the National Assembly gave approval to a law allowing the police to hold immigrants for up to 48 hours without charge and summarily to expel any immigrant whose papers were not in order (this potentially affected some 300 000 aliens). Third, it was decided that work permits would only be renewed for periods of one to three years, except for those who had lived in France for a full 20 years, who still wouldn't obtain permanent renewals, but ten-year ones (*Guardian Weekly* (Manchester) 15 June 1979). Finally, the Interior Minister, Christian Bonnet, set up a system of computerised records, which drew together residence and work permits on one unforgeable document. About one million foreigners were forced to carry such documents, each of which contained 40 items of information concerning details of nationality, residence, employment and dependants. The potential for police surveillance and ultimately mass expulsions was obviously much enhanced by this information. As a sober article in *Le Monde* (Paris, 17 February 1980) put it: 'Such a filing system is unprecedented in France, except perhaps for the register of Jews during the Occupation'. Fortunately, from the point of view of the migrant community, some of these provisions were modified or expunged in the wake of Mitterand's election. Now most of the children of migrants have rights of residence and are normally able to obtain a work permit. However, a work permit simply allows the holder to look for a job and does not supply one.

The difficulties of finding employment in a recession have pushed many second-generation immigrants into the shadow (informal) economy. The unregulated labour market in France is immense, with perhaps as many as 400 000 illegal workers. The French government, rather like the US government, offered a one-off amnesty to legalise some of the illegal workers. But the take-up was disappointing to the government and on one estimate would have involved less than a third of the illegal workers (Verbunt, 1985). To the 400 000 illegal workers are added perhaps another 250 000

160

political refugees and their families whose fate is determined by the Bureau for the Protection of Refugees and Stateless Persons. The French have a distinguished record in offering hospitality to the political refugees ever since Article 120 of the 1793 constitution proclaimed that France would 'give asylum to foreigners driven from their homeland in freedom's cause. They refuse it to tyrants.' Yet this record of tolerance is now undermined by the sheer numbers of refugees involved. Senior officials in the State Secretariat are quoted as saying: 'The refugee problem is insoluble ... France can't take charge of the world's 10 million refugees.' The result of this shift in the official mood is that the border police have been given a great degree of discretion in deciding who is a 'true' refugee (*Le Monde* (Paris) 18 January 1981).

In the case of Britain's Immigration Acts since 1962, these have been largely directed at slowly removing the rights of colonial and Commonwealth citizens to full British citizenship. The distinction between 'old' Commonwealth and 'new' Commonwealth was one clearly based on racial criteria and was intended to separate out the white dominions (Canada, Australia and New Zealand) from the Caribbean, black Africa and the Asian sub-continent. White Rhodesians and white South Africans of British descent had blotted their copybook by being associated with a Unilateral Declaration of Independence from British authority in the first case, and the creation of a Republic outside the Commonwealth in the second. So, although residual Commonwealth rights remained for these two minority white groups, their sins were such that their fate was linked to residents of the so-called 'new' Commonwealth or to wholly 'alien' beings. The categories 'new' and 'old' Commonwealth were cynically manipulated to discriminate against black entrants. Barbados, for example, had been British since 1627, whereas Canada had only been ceded to the British by the Treaty of Paris in 1763—yet the logic of immigration control deemed that the first be designated new Commonwealth, the latter old.

The first attack on Commonwealth entry came in 1962, when the Commonwealth Immigrants Act established a voucher system, linking entry to a prior employment offer. Just before the 1962 Act became law, immigration from the new Commonwealth rose steeply as dependants joined existing workers and others rushed to 'beat the ban'. The legislation thus served to precipitate family settlement, even when only temporary migration was contemplated. By 1964, only professional or highly-skilled workers were obtaining work permits. In 1968, another Commonwealth Immigrants Act was passed, mainly directed against some groups of overseas passport holders, like the East African Asians, who had complied with the Colonial Office's decolonisation plans in exchange for the award of UK passports. By the terms of the 1968 Act, possession of a UK passport did not entitle the holder to free entry. Three years later, yet another Immigration Act was passed, this time restricting the rights of dependants to join their families in the UK and further specifying the link between a work permit (issued now to Commonwealth citizens on much the same basis as to aliens) and permission to enter and reside. By 1982, the issue of work permits or 'special vouchers' to potential entrants had dried up to such an extent that 90 per cent of those accepted for settlement were dependants still trying to struggle through the labyrinths of bureaucratic red tape strung out to impede their entry. Another turn of the screw came in 1981, with the passing of the Nationality Act. The major remaining distinctions between Commonwealth citizens and aliens were to be phased out. Gaining citizenship by registration was to be replaced by the process of naturalisation—a process that takes five years, is discretionary, and subject to tests of language and good conduct (Castles *et al.* 1984: 46). Moreover, for the first time in English law, the principle of equating birthplace with nationality was changed. Now nationality and citizenship is also dependent on parental status, irrespective of whether a child is born in the UK.

While the Act links the fate of Commonwealth citizens to that of aliens at home, it also includes two new classes of citizenship for those with British connections in British or ex-British possessions abroad. These are British Overseas citizenship and citizenship of the British dependent territories. The first mainly covers holders of dual citizenship in

Malaysia. The new status will not permit rights of abode in any British territory, nor will it be transmittable to descendants. In short, it is an unmistakable invitation for the holder to take out local citizenship and abandon all hope of Britain retaining any of its colonial responsibilities (see Layton-Henry 1982: 30). The category 'citizen of the British dependent territories' is perhaps the most significant part of the Act in terms of possible future migratory patterns. My own view is that this part of the Act was directed very largely at the residents of Hong Kong, who fall under this new category of citizenship and do not have the right of settlement or entry to the UK. At first, some obfuscation of this target was successful. For example, in a parliamentary debate the British government vehemently denied that the Act was 'racist', and in order to demonstrate its impartiality included the (white) residents of the Falklands/Malvinas Islands in the same category of citizenship. When Mrs Thatcher went to war in defence of the liberties of these British subjects in their struggle against the iron heel of the Argentine junta it no longer became politically viable to deny the Falkland Islanders the right to enter Britain. So, at the end of the war, this prohibition was quietly dropped from the Falklanders' passports, but retained for the Gibraltarians, St Helenians and Hong Kong Chinese. It is perhaps worth mentioning that in the case of St Helena, where 5000 brown Britons live with no racial, cultural or national identity other than that derived from their British heritage, the Act violated an ancient royal charter promising equality of treatment with the King's subjects 'in this our realme of England' (Cohen 1983). The violation of principle in this case was important, but clearly the main intent and effect of the Act is to exclude the five to six million Hong Kong Chinese from entry to Britain in the event of mass panic as 1997 approaches. (1997 is the year when China is due to repossess her territory ceded to the British under what the Chinese call the 'unequal treaties'.) Though apparent unanimity has been achieved between the British and Chinese governments, it remains to be seen what Britain might do if significant numbers of Hong Kong residents claim refugee status.

163

The fourth, and final, European country discussed here is Switzerland. The country has a long anti-statist and open-door tradition in respect of tax matters and capital movements and had an almost equally long tradition of freezing out foreigners from access to the enviable material delights of a highly-successful bourgeois civilisation. Even in Switzerland, however, nearly half a million foreigners had by the 1980s managed to acquire residence permits. These are a group quite distinct from the *frontaliers*, about 10 000 of whom commute across the frontier each day and the 110 000 'seasonal' workers who are on permits of nine months or less (*Guardian Weekly* (Manchester), 12 April 1981). Whereas the *frontaliers* are often UN diplomats commuting to desirable residences in France and making savings on local income tax, the seasonal workers include many migrants who are simply on a rotating oscillating pattern, rather along the lines of their South African counterparts. Since 1931, when the Law of Foreigners was drawn up, the Swiss state has been vigorous in policing the frontiers. But so dependent were the post-war Swiss manufacturing and service industries on foreign labour that all the state could do was to try to regulate labour movements as tightly as possible. The Swiss citizenry, for its part, was apparently happy to benefit from the labour-power of the foreigners, but periodically activated plebiscites directed against what was known as 'over-foreignisation'. This has led to even tighter restrictions. Under Swiss law, a foreigner is allowed to be on Swiss territory only when in possession of a permit of abode, a permit of residence or a permit of tolerance. The permits of abode are the main instrument of control, and since 1970 the annual quota has been fixed at 10 000 a year. The permit is given for one year and is subject to a labour market vacancy and good conduct. Should the migrant manage to live with this net of regulations and decide to take up citizenship, the applicant would have to wait for at least 12 years. But individual communes and cantons impose additional periods which are non-transferable from one canton to another, while a number provide an additional financial hurdle by charging naturalisation fees of up to 70 000 Swiss francs (Hoffman-Nowotny 1982).

Influx controls and labour bureaux: the South African way

Some aspects of the system of labour control and regulation in South Africa were discussed in Chapter 3, but the focus there was on the evolution of the regional migrant labour system and its effects on the peripheral areas of the political economy. This section is concerned with the attempts, particularly the recent attempts, by the South African state to manage and control the supplies of labour-power to South African industry, agriculture and mining, as well as to control the growth of black urban townships.

At the heart of the present control system is the 'pass'—in effect, an internal passport which serves as an identity document, an indication of work and residence status, an indication of 'nationality' (including the fabricated 'homelands' nationality accorded to all blacks) and equally importantly, a police record. White South African officialdom is fond of using the term 'influx' (Latin, *influere*, flowing in) to describe the movement of African labourers. The term suggests a natural, spontaneous process which has nothing to do with the almost insatiable historical demand for black gang labour by the mines or the massive recruitment drives initiated by mines' recruitment agencies and other labour suppliers. In so far, however, as an 'influx' suggests an inanimate, depersonalised phenomenon, akin to a rising tide, it would seem only right and proper that the representatives of 'civilisation' should erect dykes and canals to control this threat. In fact, the control measures are implemented on an almost unbelievable scale. One study estimated that since the turn of the century, 17 million blacks have been arrested under the South African pass laws. Another showed that about 10 per cent of adult blacks in Cape Town are likely to be arrested *each year*. Women are particularly likely to be singled out as pass offenders as the authorities rightly see their presence as a harbinger for the establishment of black families in the area (*Lincoln Letter*; July 1984).

The implementation of the pass and other regulations in turn depends on the status of the arrestee under the provisions established primarily by the Bantu (Urban Areas)

165

Consolidation Act of 1946. Section 10 of that Act stipulates that no African may remain in an urban or peri-urban area for longer than 72 hours unless such a 'visitor' 'qualifies' to be there. Qualification lies in continuous residence since birth (Section 10/1/a), continuous working for one employer for 10 years (Section 10/1/b) or a restricted possibility for immediate family to join a male breadwinner (Section 10/1/c). Urban residents who qualified under these provisions can be considered the permanent, stable, urban residents who the post-1948 Nationalist Party government were forced to accept and could not be 'endorsed out' to the homelands or forced into the contract labour system. Consequently, such residents constitute the core of the black urban working class in service, domestic and manufacturing employment. The terms 'Section 10 workers' or 'Section Tenners' are often applied to such residents who have gained an entitlement to live in a black urban township like Soweto (the south-western townships) near Johannesburg.

In fact, Section 10 also provides a sub-clause qualifying workers to stay in the urban area with the permission of a local labour bureau, the functions of which are discussed later. But as the bureaux rarely give permission to anyone other than short-term contract workers, this provision is a way of controlling migrant worker registrations, rather than permitting another route into permanent urban residence. In 1968, the Regulations for Labour Bureaux made clear that a black could not qualify for urban residence by extending an initial short contract for successive years until the 10-year period (specified in 10/1/b) was fulfilled. A succession of contracts would not be regarded as continuous service (Wages Commission n.d.: 18, 19). This ruling was successfully challenged in a fascinating court case brought by a machine operative, Mehlolo Rikhoto, which went to the Court of Appeal in 1983. The Minister of Co-operation and Development, who estimated that 143 000 migrant workers might benefit from the Rikhoto decision, decided to accept the judgment, but block the loophole by other means. He insisted that such workers and their families be housed in 'approved housing'. As there was already an officially recognised housing shortage of 260 000 houses, this provided an immediately effective deterrent to any other workers wishing to emulate Mr Rikhoto (*African Labour News* August 1983).

In effect, the distinction between Section Tenners and contract workers hardened into a distinction between stable and migrant labourers, the latter being routed either through the mines' private system of recruitment (already discussed in Chapter 3) or through the state's system of labour bureaux. It is these labour bureaux that provide the institutional basis for the classification, funnelling and further regulation of labour-power and are, in substance, replacing the politically-discredited pass system. Labour bureaux have been in existence in embryonic form since the turn of the century, but their number and powers increased sharply as a result of the 1964 Bantu Labour Act, the 1965 Bantu Labour Regulations and the 1968 Regulations for Labour Bureaux. As a result of these measures a network of 1300 labour bureaux was provided to cover every city, town, village or rural area in the country. The bureaux, in turn, cover three types of area: 'prescribed', that is 'white' industrial and residential areas where Section Tenners are the predominant black labour force; 'non-prescribed', where the 'district' labour bureaux mainly supply agricultural labour to the farming communities; and 'homeland' areas. The homelands bureaux are hierarchised into 'territorial', 'district' and 'tribal' offices, and constitute the effective base of the system. It is important to emphasise two aspects of the homelands' bureaux. One is that they are directly accountable to the Central Labour Bureau in Pretoria, thus further exposing the apartheid myth that these areas are in some measure 'independent' (Wages Commission n.d.: 20). Second, the homelands' bureaux initiate the primary classification system. Thus the Tribal Labour Office is given the responsibility of classifying every 'workseeker' into one of 17 categories of employment—for example, 'agriculture', 'mining', 'domestic', 'construction' or even 'unemployable'. Registration as a 'workseeker' is *compulsory* for all adult males over the age of 15, but in a classic demonstration of Orwellian logic, workseekers are not allowed to seek work: they have to wait their turn at the tribal labour bureaux (Regulation 21 of 1968). This primary segmentation of the labour force is then reinforced by three further control measures. First, a contract, without which a workseeker cannot take up employment. Needless to say, the employee is given no opportunity to negotiate the terms of the contract, and is in no position to enforce its terms, even where the contract offers some modest protection for the worker. Characteristically, the terms of the contract are not known to the worker and compliance is assumed after a process of mass thumb-printing takes place. Second, the labour bureaux structures the *occupational* mix according to manpower demands by refusing to reclassify the workers' categories of employment, unless they select 'farming' or 'mining', the two most unpopular categories. Third, the labour bureaux control the *geographical* destination by only registering the worker for particular zones, where labour-power happens to be in short supply. Again, changes of zone would only be made to the most unpopular area.

The system of labour regulation, as described, worked reasonably well until the 1970s, when a period of unrest—including riots, boycotts, strikes and other forms of worker resistance—began to shake the structures of the apartheid system. The highlights of these protests included a rolling wave of strikes initiated by unorganised workers in 1973 (see Dekker *et al.* 1975; Institute for Industrial Education 1979) and an uprising in Soweto, commencing in 1976 (Hirson 1979). The state moved rapidly to try to repair the damage to political stability and a number of ongoing reforms were initiated at the constitutional level with accompanying changes to the structures of industrial relations and labour control. Because the commissions set up to review these structures were established in the wake of unrest and with a public rhetoric suggesting a reforming mood from the top (see *South African Newsletter* for examples) the extent of the change was frequently exaggerated. Often, the proposals simply sought to rationalise, consolidate and modernise existing state practices rather than provide a genuine alternative to them. In other cases, the commissions simply recognised that they could do little to reverse the level of class struggle and sought simply to channel it into acceptable directions.

The two commissions that pertain to the present concern are the Wiehahn Commission, whose recommendations resulted in the Labour Relations Act of 1981, and the Riekert Commission, whose report was submitted in 1978. The Labour Relations Act permitted Africans to organise and join *registered* trade unions. Moreover, these unions could be multi-racial in character. The qualifying adjective 'registered' was important in that it subjected the union to a wide range of checks by inspectors—of a financial kind, but also aimed at ensuring that the registered unions steered well clear of political organisations and involvement, had no significant foreign links, and would not grant strike pay to workers illegally on strike. In the course of parliamentary discussions these checks and restrictions were applied to 'unregistered' unions, as well, with the additional stick that they would find it impossible to operate a 'check-off' system without ministerial approval (Cooper 1981). The new labour relations order can be seen as a recognition that in the wake of the massive outbursts of industrial unrest, the state had no alternative but to accept the reality of unionisation and, given this fact, it was better to talk to legally-sanctioned representatives who might be amenable to state control, than to spontaneously generated leaderships, unknown to the Labour Inspectorate. Though the provisions of the new Act applied to all workers, migrant or Section Tenners, there is little doubt that the stabilised workers benefited more from the Act in that they were more likely to join and sustain trade unions.

The Riekert Commission (1978) reinforced the relatively privileged status of the stabilised urban population, but also extended and refined the system of labour control in a number of important directions. Not all the Commission's recommendations have resulted in current legislation, but the report is crucial in understanding the broad direction of change in the labour supply system, upon which the major planks of apartheid rest, It represents one of the most sophisticated attempts to design a segmented labour market by state intervention and therefore merits close attention by students of comparative labour regimes. On the question of the supply of manpower, the report (Riekert 1978: 24) states:

169

The most important question is whether the right quantity of labour at the right *quality* will be available at the right *time* and the right *place* to satisfy the demand ... [its] availability is determined by the following factors (a) the optimal allocation of the available pool of artisan and technically skilled workers in accordance with demand conditions; (b) the *timely* training of an adequate number of workers ... (c) the horizontal and vertical mobility of labour. The horizontal and vertical mobility of labour is determined mainly by the following factors (a) statutory, administrative and traditional constraints, (b) the preferences of workers and employers, (c) wage differences and (d) the availability of housing.

The systematic construction of this agenda prefigures systematic attention to each aspect in the report. The net result was to rationalise and harden existing boundaries between the different labour markets by reinforcing discretionary and statutory differences. White and coloured (mixed race) workers in artisanal or supervisory positions would of course retain their existing rights to organisation and labour mobility. (Within the constraints, in the coloured case, of having to live in a group area designated for them.) However, a new group was to enter these 'privileged' ranks (though of course at a lower level). Section Tenners would be given the right to join trade unions, more mobility in terms of influx control (for example the right to move between zones), increased access to housing and also higher wages (Claasens *et al.* 1980: 34). The housing concession is of particular interest in that, by strict apartheid doctrine, no black could ever *own* property in a 'white area', as freehold ownership would recognise a permanent right of residence. The compromise effected in the wake of the Soweto riots was to permit 99-year leases, with an option to renew. This satisfied apartheid doctrine on the one hand, and the recognised need for labour stabilisation and African demands on the other. The ideology will have to be readjusted again in the aftermath of the 1985 disturbances, when further concessions on property rights were presaged.

While Riekert undoubtedly strengthened the position of Section 10 blacks, he separated their fate strongly from other categories of workers—migrants, foreign workers, commuters and the unemployed. In each case, the Commission recommended improvements to the organisational and institutional structure that policed these areas. For example, far from recommending closure of the labour bureaux system, Riekert sought to argue that the South African system was fundamentally similar to the employment services provided in the UK, the USA and West Germany. It was true that 'the general image of local labour bureaux in the eyes of employers and workseekers is very poor for a number of reasons, including their link with: influx control, unpopular types of employers who cannot succeed in recruiting workers and workseekers who cannot find work for themselves, and staff who are not trained for this type of work' (Riekert 1978: 140–3, 144). On the other hand, these faults were not intrinsic. Staff had to be better trained, private employment offices should also be permitted to offer their services under the control of the Department of Labour, and separate service points should be established for professional, clerical and unskilled workers. In one area the Commission proposed a fundamental change, namely that workseekers should not be obliged to register at the bureaux (this placed men in the same status as women). However, Riekert (1978: 144) was in no doubt as to the continued relevance of the bureaux:

> A programme of action should be initiated to ensure the efficient functioning of the labour bureau system . . . because it fulfils an important role in connection with the orderly canalisation of labour and the supply of labour in accordance with the demand for it.

As with the more efficient functioning of the labour bureaux, so the report also tidied up other 'anomalies'. For example, three of South Africa's major industrial areas are located in Pretoria, Durban and East London, cities also close to the existing 'Bantustans'. Many workers from Kwazulu, Bophuthatswana and the Ciskei therefore tried to acquire Section 10 rights while commuting across these rather nominal boundaries. Riekert puts a stop to this by ruling that commuters should not be able to qualify for Section 10 rights. He equally rationalises the inter-state

171

treaties (similar to the post-war West German treaties) regulating the supply of labour from foreign African states. Finally, his report contains some forceful recommendations designed to cut down the extent of 'illegality', an issue discussed in common with the general question of the illegal worker in the next section of this chapter.

In essence, the South African system of labour regulation is one that polices the external frontiers through immigration checks and inter-state foreign labour contracts, and polices internal frontiers (between racially-defined residential and industrial areas) through influx control. The particular feature that attracts such opprobrium to the South African system is that the state apparatus set up to enforce influx control uses particularly brutal methods. In addition, in the past the state sought to use influx control measures as a means of turning the indigenous (and voteless) black population into a foreign population. The recognition by the Riekert Commission that Section Tenners are in effect irremovable, has stabilised and often significantly improved the conditions of life of the long-standing black urban population, perhaps 10 to 15 per cent of the black population as a whole. For the majority, however, the apartheid state continues to present a brutal and unremitting face.

Illegal workers: control and evasion

In examining the immigration and labour-control policies of the major states in our regional political economies—the US, the European states and South Africa—it was indicated how each had a somewhat different capacity to put into effect legislative measures designed to police their frontiers and enforce the will of the central authority. In each case surveyed, the state sought to regulate the flow of labourers through a battery of immigration checks and other administrative means. The US even at one point tried to imitate the builders of the Great Wall of China by using barbed wire, dogs, infra-red scanners and helicopters along the Rio Grande. However, it was a rather half-hearted attempt that was soon whittled down to some publicity-seeking, but ineffective border control measures. Why do these states—even so powerful and wealthy a state as the US, or so authoritarian a one as South Africa—find it so difficult to enforce their immigration and labour regulations? How widespread is the phenomenon of illegal migration and how is its nature and significance interpreted?

The case of the US is first discussed, where the scholarly and political debate about illegal workers is more sharply drawn, before making brief comparisons with the other powerful states in the remaining regional political economies. In the US, the extent of illegal migration was estimated at anything between 8 and 12 million people in 1978, with a further half to one million illegals arriving annually. Illegal workers hold about a third of the full-time, low-skilled jobs in the country (Wachter 1978: 80). In particular sectors, notably in agribusiness, the service sector, textile sweat-shops and some manufacturing industries, illegal workers are numerically so significant that these industries would be unabe to compete internationally without them. For example, in considering the competitiveness of the New York apparel industry in the face of cheap imports, deWind (1982: 12) writes:

> How have those garment manufacturers still in New York City survived? By producing short-run fast-moving goods and by cutting down labour costs—and that, very often, means hiring undocumented workers. Competing with international producers, New York employers have set wages too low to attract a full supply of American workers ... The undocumented workers who take jobs in the garment industry can hardly be accused of taking these jobs away from anyone else.

Such a depiction, which is common to a number of US academics, often with a liberal political orientation (for example, Piore 1975, 1979; Cornelius n.d.), assumes the existence of a dual labour market. This view, most articulately and forcibly argued by Piore (1975), in effect abolishes the problem of illegal migration, at least as far as immigration restrictions are concerned. If illegals are filling jobs in a labour market separate from that in which indigenous workers are competing, cutting down illegal worker entry

173

will not solve the domestic unemployment problem and may well damage sectors of US industry. Of course, even if the argument is conceded that the labour market for illegal workers is separable (or even largely separable) from the legal labour market, this does not mean that the widespread existence of illegal workers can be ignored by the authorities. As Rosberg (1978: 340) points out:

> Respect for the rule of law cannot be enhanced by the spectacle of widespread defiance of our immigration laws and the ineffectuality of law-enforcement efforts. And beyond the symbolic problem, the fact that many persons are now living outside the law as an underground labour force is itself troubling. To conceal their presence, illegal entrants may feel compelled to withhold payment of taxes, keep their children out of schools, tolerate substandard wages and working conditions, decline to seek badly needed medical attention, and take other steps that may injure themselves as well as those around them.

Such a view of illegal migration, as economically beneficial (or at least not economically harmful) even if there are major consequential social problems, is not, however, the view accepted by US officialdom. Even if they do not have impeccable logic on their side, such officials have a great deal of public support in their campaigns against illegal workers. When, for example, General Chapman, Nixon's head of the INS, argued in a notorious *Reader's Digest* article (Chapman 1976: 654) that 'the vast and silent invasion of illegal immigrants across our borders is reaching the proportions of an national disaster', there is little doubt he was articulating a common sentiment. Moreover, many US citizens would concur with Secretary of Labour Roy Marshall's statement (cited deWind 1982: 4) that:

> It is false to say American workers cannot be found for all the jobs filled by undocumented workers . . . no matter how undesirable the jobs may be . . . eliminating this displacement would bring unemployment down to 3.7 per cent.

While the balance of logic and evidence is behind those who argue for a dual labour market thesis, rather than those who adhere to a displacement argument, it is necessary to remind dual labour market theorists that the social condi-

174

tions that determine job choice are not static. It *is* the case that workers with job security, good wages, a recognised skill and union protection are hardly likely immediately to go down-market to a job characteristically occupied by an illegal migrant, even if faced with unemployment. However, if conditions become desperate enough, expectations can and do change and some job competition may arise. In addition to the problems of shifting expectations, both sets of theory largely ignore the institutional and sociological parameters that regulate and control the flow of workers and illegal migrants to particular job destinations. These intervening factors include the policies and practices of labour-related agencies in both sending and receiving countries, the degree of attachment by a worker to an existing community, the activities of the *coyotes* (labour recruiters), union closed-shop norms, prior training, and many other factors that make the labour market an imperfect one.

But overriding both shifting job expectations and the other non-economic determinants of the labour market is the role of employers in shaping the extent and contours of the market for illegal labour. As Petras indicates in the quote that opens this chapter, the state is charged with the responsibility of enforcing or relaxing border controls in the interests of the dominant classes *as a whole*. On the other hand, as has been show earlier in this book, it is apparent that the sectoral interests of many employers do not correspond with the hegemonic and collective interests of their class. This leads to constant wars of attrition between the state and sectional employer interests over the question of illegal migration. Now a blind eye is cast in the direction of agribusiness, now a threatening gesture to fine employers of illegal workers is made. But as long as this remains a subdued war of position, illegal workers will be able to evade state controls (often in very precarious circumstances) with the effective connivance of employers ready to exploit a subordinate cheap labour force. Given the powerful lobbying capacity of agribusiness (in particular) and the non-interventionist and pluralist philosophy of government that legitimates the US state, it is doubtful, despite periodic ideological and short-term drives against illegal migrants (see Chapters 2 and 6), that the US government will ever to able to grasp the nettle of complete control of the traffic in illegal labour-power.

Seen more analytically and comparatively, such total control implies five elements.

(1) *A tight border*, possible in the UK given it has no contiguous land frontier, but very difficult in the US given its land frontiers with Mexico and Canada, its proximity to the Caribbean archipelago, and the sheer volume of passenger movements for trade, tourism and educational purposes.

(2) *Public support* for a complete clamp-down. Such support was evident in the Swiss case where public plebiscites and action at the canton level against 'over foreignisation' forced the state into policing the system rigorously whatever the labour-power demands of Swiss employers. In the US, such support is periodically forthcoming but cannot be universal given the bonds of co-ethnicity that significant sections of the electorate share with illegal workers.

(3) *Employer penalties*. In the US, the employer has virtually always escaped significant attention from the law. Even when, in the last ten years, both the Carter and Regan administrations have made tentative moves to fine employers of illegal labour, such moves have been frustrated or turned into such insignificant penalties that they do not act as a strong deterrent. Again, in the case of South Africa, employer penalties have been weak historically and it is only as a result of the Riekert Commission recommendations that the government has moved more vigorously against employers of illegal labour. A bill before Parliament in 1982 raised the fine to such employers tenfold from R500 to R5000. The fine could be imposed as an alternative, or in addition, to a prison sentence for one year. (In addition, to moving against employers the bill also provided R500 fine for anyone sheltering 'unauthorised' blacks.) (*Guardian Weekly* (Manchester), 12 September 1982).

(4) *Police enforcement* of the laws against illegal workers is also vital to the success of a state's campaign to restrict

such workers. The Europeans offer interesting contrasts in this respect. Traditionally, Britain relied on tight border controls and fairly weak internal police surveillance; whereas the French operated the opposite system. In France, for example, the local gendarmerie usually had effective control over the issue of residence permits and tended to know all about the foreigners in their district. Over the years, a certain congruence has developed as France has strengthened her border controls and the British local police constabularies have been amalgamated and brought more firmly under Home Office Control. Considering only the number of pass offenders caught, the South African police can be seen as shouldering a sisyphean task with a dogged and ruthless determination. On the other hand, it is doubtful whether, given the confusion of authority between city, state and Federal police and the variety of identification documents accepted, that the INS in the US will ever be able to mount a campaign on the South African scale.

(5) *State labour recruitment* is important to circumvent the role of the employer in encouraging illegal work. In South Africa, the mining companies have been permitted to organise their own recruitment system since before the turn of the century and the Riekert Commission has further extended the private recruitment system. However, these agencies are under relatively firm state control and the state has a significant role in recruiting labour in its own right through the labour bureaux system. West Germany and, to some extent, France, has also recruited labour through inter-governmental contracts—with employers having to ask for labourers via government agencies. The Bracero Program in the US (see Chapter 2) is another example of governmental labour recruiting, but it only covered a limited number of workers compared to the flow of undocumented workers recruited directly by employers.

As can be seen from Figure 5.1, which summarises the above discussion, only South Africa can be seen as coming close to a complete control system.

177

Figure 5.1 Control measures against illegal workers

	Strong	Intermediate/ Intermittent	Weak
(1) Tight border	SA, UK	Sw, WG	US, Fr
(2) Public support	SA, Sw	Fr, WG, UK	US
(3) Employer penalties	SA	WG, Sw, UK	US, Fr
(4) Police enforcement	SA, Fr, Sw	WG, US, UK	
(5) State labour recruitment	SA, WG	Fr, US	Sw, UK

Key: US, United States of America; UK, United Kingdom; Sw, Switzerland; WG, West Germany; Fr, France; SA, South Africa.

Illegal workers who evade the traps set for them by the state can be understood in a variety of ways. They can be depicted in heroic terms—as people refusing to allow their potentials to be crushed by unjust governments, exploitative employers or adverse circumstances. Certainly, the gauntlet that has to be run by today's illegal migrants is far more formidable than that run by the immigrants of the turn of the century, whose stories have often been depicted in epic terms. Alternatively, the illegal worker can be seen more coldly, in terms of a calculating economic being—weighing up costs and benefits, risks and opportunities, in a rational decision to beat the system. Undoubtedly there are such individuals in the millions of illegal workers who evade state control. Unfortunately, however, from numerous biographical and observational accounts, it seems that the mass of illegal workers are usually neither romantic heroes of the wild frontier, nor amateur micro-econometricians. Rather, they are sad, fearful, pathetic individuals desperate to escape intolerable conditions at the periphery of the regional political economy, thrown about by forces they at first only dimly comprehend, and forced to accept conditions of housing, employment and health care that permits a maximum level of exploitation. Such individuals, like many other migrant workers, are ideologically habituated into tolerating, even if not accepting, such conditions and are only slowly able to build the structures of personal and collective resistance to their fate. These processes of habituation and resistance form the subject of Chapter 6.

6 Habituation and resistance: the experience of migrant workers

Considered over the longer term, a remarkable feature of the migrant labour pattern is its instability, in the sense that the unidimensionality on which it is founded cannot be maintained for very long. Sooner or later, any foreign worker comes to be conceived of not only as an economic actor, but also as a cultural, social or political actor ... and hence as a potential member of the society.

(Zolberg 1981: 13)

The reader may be forgiven for assuming that the depiction of migrants in this book has tended to portray them as chaff in the wind, blown about by forces too powerful for them to comprehend, let alone oppose. Chapter 1, for example, concentrated on how the capitalist mode of production has always been able to find functional equivalents of the unfree labourers characteristic of its genesis. Later chapters showed how powerful states and employers in the regional political economies were able to activate and deactivate supplies of labour-power from their peripheral areas and to keep these points of reproduction in an almost permanent state of stagnation. Next depicted has been the attempt by the hegemonic states of the three discussed regional political economies to use migrant labourers as pliant tools of industrial and economic management and to regulate their movements by internal and external policing. But also criticised throughout the text has been the too functionalist a view of migrant labour (whether this emanates from conventional or 'Marxist' functionalists), and it has been indicated that the conditions that oppress migrant labourers are not so deterministic that they can never be challenged or contested. It is time to be more explicit about this conflict. While the

179

political interests and economic forces that structure the life opportunities of migrant workers are indeed formidable, forms of resistance to these forces and interests can, and are, being organised.

What this chapter will seek to do is examine the ways in which control over migrant labourers is effected principally through the state and employers and how, on the other hand, migrant workers organise to resist the pressure upon them. When considering the question of control of migrants it is necessary not only to look at the complex of laws that govern the immigration of workers and their civic status, but also at the patterns of their recruitment for, and deployment within, the production process. Again, law and labour process are reinforced by the ideological hegemony of the powerful image-makers in society (normally the media and the politicians and the interests they serve). This ideological hegemony can, moreover, be accepted by the migrants themselves, at least to some extent. To try to encompass these various processes of control and self-control at a theoretical level, the notions of 'exterior conditioning' and 'interior determination' suggested by Lefebvre (1976) have been adopted and modified. In Lefebvre's account, exterior conditioning comprises the overt moves by capital against labour, normally at the point of production. In the case of migrants (particularly) it is also necessary to examine the role of the state in policing its frontiers (a task undertaken in the previous chapter) and to look at both state and employers' roles in labour recruitment. Lefebvre is followed more closely in seeing interior determination as those elements of the workers' culture and ideology that sustain and reproduce the forms of control generated at the exterior level. When it is necessary to indicate that these processes of control and internalisation are continuous, unsystematic and often unconscious the term 'habituation' rather than 'control' has been used, as the latter can suggest too conspiratorial a control strategy for labour. The case study taken for the examination of the habituation of migrant labourers is that of agricultural workers in the US, a group that so far has appeared in this book only as part of an aggregated category of migrants to the US (see Chapter 2).

With respect to the concept of 'resistance', a working distinction between 'overt' and 'hidden' forms of resistance has been used, which I first developed in the context of a more general article on African workers (Cohen 1980). Overt forms of worker resistance are those that are easily observed or accessible to measurement. Such forms may include the number, scope and duration of strikes, the number of man-days lost, the rate of labour turnover and the extent of worker participation in union organisations, radical social movements or street demonstrations. Hidden forms, by contrast, may include desertion, revolt by pre-capitalist communities, target working, task, efficiency and time bargaining, sabotage, the creation of a counter work-culture, accidents, sickness, drug use, adherence to other worldly solutions or theft. The principal case study of resistance will be the migrant miners of southern Africa.

Habituating US agricultural labour: the role of the government

The first point of intervention by the state is to regulate its outer frontiers through immigration policies and controls. Who is let in, in what numbers and for what purpose? Who is expelled? In so far as the state can regulate this process, it is able to activate or deactivate the outer labour reservoirs ('the proletariat at the gates') and therefore affect the bargaining position of agricultural labour within the US.

The situation facing agricultural labourers in the south-west, for example, was decisively altered in 1942 when the Bracero Program was initiated. The Program was essentially a government-to-government agreement stipulating conditions to protect the wages and living conditions of Mexican migrants. From 1942 until the period 1965 to 1968 when the Bracero Program was officially ended but 'admitted aliens' continued to be reported under the same category, a total of 5 060 093 braceros had been admitted into the US (Samora and Simon 1977: 140). The close connection between the demands of the growers and the flow of migrants is shown by the fact that the peak of admissions under the Program coincided with the boom years of the 1950s, sometimes leading to the displacement of local labourers not prepared to work for the pay and conditions provided for braceros. The usual pattern of labour market segmentation was somewhat violated during this period as job displacement and job competition between the indigenous and foreign workers occurred to some degree.

With respect to the immigration of agricultural labour into the north-east, the principal form of migrant labour is contract labour from the Caribbean. For example, a contract programme with Puerto Rico was initiated in the 1940s. However, given the fact that Puerto Ricans have the right to travel to the US, many arrived under their own steam. The estimated numbers of Puerto Ricans working in agriculture in the post-war period varied between 60 000 and 200 000. With respect to the numbers recruited officially, over 21 000 were recruited annually in the peak years of 1967 to 1969, but by 1977 annual recruitment had dropped to only 4191. The reasons for this drop are not difficult to find. Over the years the Commonwealth of Puerto Rico had attempted to tighten the contracts in the interests of her migrants. Thus the new contracts stipulated wage rates, hours of work, procedures for firing workers, housing standards, and housing and food costs. Most importantly, the contracts also included provisions against reprisals if a worker joined or assisted a labour organisation (NACLA 1977a: 22).

Even though the Puerto Rican authorities were unable to enforce many of these provisions, the growers were sufficiently alarmed by what they considered onerous contracts and a difficult workforce, to turn to Jamaicans—who are considered 'docile and diligent'. This characterisation of Jamaicans is of some irony in view of the frequently expressed view on the island that the heritage of slave revolt and the prevalence of single-headed households have produced a particularly violent culture (Lacey 1977). The Chairman of the Farm Labor Executive Committee, representing apple growers in the 10 states from Virginia to Maine was particularly explicit: 'Over my dead body will there be any Puerto Rican workers picking apples in Wayne County' (NACLA 1977a: 33). The US government responded by

182

providing temporary visas for alternative labourers from the Caribbean under Section H-2 of the Immigration and Nationality Act of 1952 (also called PL 414). About 20 000 a year came in under this provision, most of whom were Jamaicans harvesting sugar in Florida and fruit in the other eastern states. In general, the growers have replaced government-to-government contracts with grower-to-government contracts, over which they have more control. Growers send recruiting teams to the Caribbean to screen carefully potential workers, to eliminate poor physical specimens, test comprehension, investigate the worker's employment background and check local police records. A US sugar corporation in Florida recruits 800 workers a day in Jamaica through the use of this screening procedure (NACLA 1977a: 10–17). If a grower is dissatisfied with a migrant's work or behaviour, he has the power to recommend deportation. The ability to deport and the fact that it is easier to house single men, are the critical elements in growers' decisions to prefer West Indian to domestic or Puerto Rican labour.

Behind the officially-sanctioned Bracero, Puerto Rican and West Indian programmes are large numbers of illegal aliens, many of whom enter the casual agricultural labour force. Indicators of the number of illegals in relation to bracero and indigenous agricultural labour are hard to come by, but some early pointers can be given. Galarza, a union organiser for the National Agricultural Workers' Union, estimated that in 1948 there were 40 000 illegals compared to the 33 288 authorised braceros working in California. Again in 1951, a confidential check by an official of the Wage Stabilization Board indicated that 60 per cent of the total labour force involved in the tomato harvest were illegals (Kushner 1975: 99; Galarza 1977: 37). These figures suggest that the immigration policies and practices of the state act only as a first crude filter. This is not, however, to argue that immigration policies do not have powerful political and psychological effects—simply that many slip through the net, partly with the connivance of employers.

Those who evade immigration controls find themselves virtually totally unprotected by the state when they find employment. Illegal workers are especially at risk but agricultural labourers in general have found themselves victims of what might be called a principle of malign neglect. Occasionally public concern surfaces, as during the movement of destitute families from the 'dust bowl' to California—a migration graphically portrayed in John Steinbeck's *The Grapes of Wrath* (1975). But Steinbeck's vision remained significantly contained within a racially exclusive appeal to the plight of the archetypal poor white family, the Joads. Workers from other ethnic groups appear only fleetingly in Steinbeck's account, international migrants and illegals not at all; regardless of the fact that these groups constitute the bulk of the agricultural labour force. Despite periodic congressional committees set up from 1936 onwards, presidential commissions on migratory labour established in 1950 and periodically thereafter, and numerous other cosmetic displays of political concern at federal and state levels, legal protection against the conditions that afflict agricultural labourers remains woefully inadequate. Agricultural workers are normally excluded from unemployment insurance, workmen's compensation, minimum wages legislation and collective bargaining, and have poor health and educational facilities. (The question of housing is considered on pp. 190–1.

These exclusions and hardships can briefly be considered in turn. First, unemployment protection. The federal employment tax specifically does not protect migrant workers, while migrant farm workers are again excluded from state insurance programmes everywhere but Hawaii and Puerto Rico (where sugar workers are covered). In 1970 a proposed change of the Employment Security Amendments of 1970 would have extended unemployment coverage to some 40 per cent of farm workers (that is still excluding foreign contract workers, illegals and many others) but it was defeated in the House Ways and Means Committee (Marshall 1974: 168). Some recognition of the plight of agricultural workers was given by President Ford, who signed an 'emergency' Special Unemployment Act in 1974 which permitted weekly payments of a maximum of $85 in unemployment entitlement for a maximum of 26 weeks.

Second, workers' compensation. A field-worker's life spar

is 46 years compared to 69 to 75 for non field-workers, while field-workers suffer 22 per cent of all fatalities from work accidents, despite constituting only 7 per cent of the workforce (Kushner 1975: xii). The state nonetheless manages to avoid paying compensation that would be compulsory for workers in other industries. The farm worker is denied disability payments, subsidised medical services and rehabilitation payments to his family in the event of death or illness. To add insult to injury, burial benefits are also not payable. Coverage under the Social Security Act came in 1951, but again the regulations favour the more stabilised farm workers; there are few benefits, and only rarely a pension, accruing to seasonal or migrant labourers or those with an irregular legal status.

As to minimum wages legislation, coverage was non-existent until 1966, when Congress extended the minimum wage to most of the large farms under the Fair Labor Standards Act. These farms employed about half the hired farm workforce, including two-thirds of the migrants. Employers were required to raise the minimum hourly rate by 50 cents, phased in *over three years*. This less than onerous burden on the growers was, however, as Marshall (1974: 166–7) reports, 'widely violated, sometimes outright and sometimes by various subterfuges such as the use of piece rates. Moreover, many farmers pay wages in cash and keep no records, therefore making it difficult to prove their violation of the law'.

With respect to collective bargaining, farm workers in the US are specifically excluded from the National Labor Relations Act. While this does not legally prevent trade union organisation, the lack of statutory recognition means that farm workers have to develop struggles like boycotts, pickets and publicity for their cause—precisely the forms of struggle that migrant workers are normally poorly placed to undertake.

Finally, health and educational facilities. The incidence of infections and parasitic diseases as well as diseases of the respiratory and digestive systems are 200 to 500 per cent higher among migrant workers than among the population at large. There is further evidence of poor diet, a high rate of

185

infant and maternal mortality, low life expectancy, a high accident rate and enormous risks in farm workers' exposure to modern pesticides. The Federal Government has made some small efforts to address the special health needs of migrants. The Migrant Health Act of 1962, amended in 1965 and 1970, allows the Public Health Service to upgrade health services to migrants with the help of voluntary agencies. Migrant health centres were established following legislation in 1973 and 1975, but as Dunbar and Kravitz (1976: 74) note: 'centers are not required to offer pediatric and family services, including children's eye examinations, preventive dental care, prenatal services and family planning'. As for the education of migrant children, Marshall's (1974: 57) judgement of a special programme offered in Texas can be cited. In his view, 'the migrant education project has done very little, other than changing school schedules, to gear education to the value system and experience of migrant children'.

In addition to immigration controls and the lack of legislative protection, the exterior conditioning of agricultural labour by the state is also seen in the establishment of an ideological heremony over, even the construction of a demonology about, alien migrants. The recent statements by politicians and the media stand in marked contrast to some of the founding principles that provided the *raison d'être* of US nationalism. Emma Lazarus's inscription on the Statue of Liberty has only to be recalled, calling upon the nations of the world to send 'your tired, your poor, your huddled masses yearning to break free . . . the wretched refuse of your teeming shore'. In a less than poetic counter-proposition the US Attorney-General, William B. Saxbe, demanded an increase in the expulsion of illegal migrants to one million in 1975 because of the supposed 'severe national crisis' they constituted. Not of course that 'prejudice of any kind exists', he unctuously maintained: 'We oppose the entry of all illegal immigrants regardless of their race or country of origin' (*Los Angeles Times* 31 October 1974).

Such revised versions of the founding principles of American democracy depend for their general acceptance on the characterisation of migrants as constituting an uncontrol lable 'invasion'—a 'horde' of aliens. Numbers are exaggerated and negative individual characteristics are attributed to all migrants. Migrants are supposed to exhibit criminal traits, evade taxes, yet make exorbitant claims on welfare, medical services and housing, provide a cultural threat to mainstream North American values and deprive US workers of jobs that are rightfully theirs. The stigmatisation of migrants is of course widely shared and diffused through many sections of US society—the press, some sectors of organised labour and right-wing political organisations. But the state and its agencies serve both to condense the major ideological expressions of hostility and to lend them greater legitimacy. While the dominant racial ideology is directed against 'aliens' and 'illegals' in general, in so far as many migrants (and perhaps one-third of the illegals) are engaged in agricultural pursuits, the negative stereotypes, often derived from images of the rural world, have a particular impact on agricultural workers.

The very language of popular and official expression encourages the imagery of a puritan Rome being overwhelmed by a mass of barbarians. For example, Nixon's appointee as Immigration Commissioner, General Chapman (formerly a Marine Corps General in charge of urban relocation in Vietnam), in an oft-quoted phrase, warned of 'the growing silent invasion of illegal aliens ... forming power groups to influence American foreign and internal policy'. The numerous readers of the *Reader's Digest* were further cautioned by Chapman that 'action must be swift, for there is no time to lose' (Baird and McCaughan 1979: 156). Other press descriptions referred to 'great waves of Latin Americans', 'a surge of immigrants', 'a flood', 'a human tide', 'the war along the Mexican frontier', 'an army of the jobless overwhelming US defenses', 'an economic time bomb south of the Rio Grande' and 'a problem of epidemic proportions', to quote only a small selection of phrases used in the most respectable newspapers.

The primary forms of exterior conditioning of agricultural labourers by the state can now be summarised. Immigration policies act as a crude filter, a means of acquiring temporary seasonal labour-power, and as a means of isolating an illegal

187

and stigmatised, but indispensable, group. The legislative provisions for agricultural labourers do not even provide a protective fig leaf to cover the bare bones of poverty and exploitation. Instead, farm workers are exposed, virtually without state mediation, to a labour market wholly dominated by employers. Their weak economic situation is compounded by the ideological drive against migrants in general and illegal Hispanic migrants in particular. Even though the charges laid against this group—its supposed criminal propensities, its claims on the social wage, its fostering of a 'dollar drain', its threat to US jobs and to the hegemony of Anglo culture—are only marginally sustained by evidence, nonetheless the effect of negative stereotyping acts as a powerful habituating mechanism. Non-native agricultural workers are thereby isolated and find it difficult to escape the image of a parasitic pariah group.

Habituating US agricultural workers: the role of the growers

As has already been shown, the employers are the dominant force in the organisation of the labour markets for agricultural labourers. They were successful in pushing through the Bracero Program, in blocking any attempts to penalise employers of illegal workers, and have been adept in switching supplies within the Caribbean reservoir when their control over the conditions of work for Puerto Rican labourers was mildly challenged. The employers have also been able to use their economic muscle to ward off attempts by the state and the unions to limit their exploitation of foreign and illegal workers. The organisation of the recruitment of workers, the forms of housing provided and the direction of other elements of the labour process all illustrate the powerful position of the employers.

Since the 1920s, growers have evolved a system of recruitment using 'crew leaders' or 'labour contractors' as intermediaries between themselves and the labour force. Friedland and Nelkin (1971: 51) describe the role of crew leaders supplying labourers to the north-east as follows:

The crew leader establishes contracts with northern employers and assembles the crew. He must schedule the movement of his crew and arrange for their transportation to the north. Upon arrival in the north the crew leader becomes a camp manager, responsible for the direction and control of the crew in the camp. He is provider of food, tobacco, alcohol and a variety of auxiliary services, including transporation. He brings the crew to the work site, where he acts as supervisor, allocating tasks, directing work in the field, monitoring inspection procedures, and often managing all aspects of the operation until the produce is delivered to the packing house.

Very little regulation of the powers of crew leaders existed until 1963, when the Farm Labor Contractor Act provided that anyone who recruited 10 or more farm workers had to be certified by the Department of Labor. Crew leaders were enjoined to ensure their vehicles were insured, were instructed to give statements of earnings to their workers and to keep employment records. However, the fine for non-compliance was modest ($500 for 'wilful violation') and only about 2000 of the estimated 5000 labour contractors bothered to register. The law was strengthened in 1974, but non-registration remained the norm—first, because the compliance officers were thin on the ground (of the 950 relevant inspectors, none was specifically assigned to agriculture); second, because the law only covered inter-state recruitment; and third, because an offending labour contractor was able to continue in business by simply sub-contracting parts of the operation (Dunbar and Kravitz 1976: 88–9). One such operator is Jesus Ayala, a labour contractor who had been convicted of a number of violations of state regulations and one of whose buses with insecurely fixed seats overturned, killing 19 lettuce pickers. Although Ayala was under contract to the High and Mighty Farms to provide teamster workers, the foreman of the farm was disinterested in whether the workers were receiving union rates or were even union members: 'The workers on that bus? Hell, I don't even know who they are. I don't know if they were Teamsters or what because I don't know anything about them. I pay Ayala to take care of that'. (Cited in Dunbar and Kravitz 1976: 90).

The initial source of worker dependence rests on the labour contractor's control of transport, which severely restricts worker mobility. When and where to start work, how to reach the fields, when to knock off, how to gain access to entertainment or shops—all are dependent on the good-will of the contractor. Some of the smaller crew leaders may dispense their favours with a degree of paternalism and thus work through a limited form of consensus, but most use their monopoly of transport to enforce labour discipline. For the grower, using contractors for exterior conditioning has the benefit of deflecting grievances, thus limiting the terrain of protest for agricultural workers and allowing the employer to distance himself from particularly onerous practices when protests do occur.

One source of possible protest is the issue of housing for agricultural workers. It is difficult to provide a single typical description of housing conditions as the units vary from single-sex barracks, to cardboard shacks, tenant houses, trailers, cabins or (rarely) well-constructed family housing subsidised by family grants. Normally the grower, or a group of growers, provide housing for the period of the cropping—between one and five months. One of the students in a participant observation study of migrant agricultural workers (in Friedland and Nelkin 1971: 37) described his camp like this:

> My camp is a two-storey wood frame house on a dirt road a mile from the nearest phone and grocery store. The house is heated by a Franklin wood stove and has no window on the first floor. The rooms are created by paste-board partitions ... When I first arrived in the camp early in the season before it was crowded there were not many flies. But when people increased so did flies. Now when you sit down, your body literally became covered by them.

The lack of privacy combined with the isolation of the migrant camps leave workers with little alternative but to accept the existing rents, the common practice of selling food prepared by the labour contractor's wife and the sale of beer and wine at marked-up prices. By undermining the capacity of the workers to exercise any choice in their living arrange-

190

ments, growers are combining two aspects of habituation—at the point of production and at the point of reproduction. Mining compounds, plantations and company towns represent more complete versions of the fusion of work and residence in so far as the employers' control over residence is more continuous. Nonetheless, the growers' camps represent a severe restriction on worker mobility and on the consequent capacity to challenge poor conditions by withdrawal or the search for an alternative job.

As to the allocation of work, the crew leader system is again the dominant form of mediation between employer and migrant. On a small farm, the employer might directly hire and personally supervise six or eight workers. But in the great majority of cases, as Harper, Mills and Parris (1974: 284) show, 'the grower has relinquished his management of the work force to the contractor; he typically does not care how the work force is managed, as long as his crops are harvested'. These authors provide (1974: 285) a pen portrait of the *modus operandi* of 'Ernie', a labour contractor operating in the north-east. Ernie was big enough to employ two foremen to supervise the workers in the fields and orchards, and who kept records of worker productivity. Favoured workers were given jobs as yard men and truck drivers. Others assembled after breakfast for the assignment of their tasks, which were paid on a piece-work basis. Ernie himself, however, was paid on a lump-sum basis for a whole crop, thus obviating the need for the employer to keep a separate tally. (Another system used is for the grower to pay the contractor an 'override' for each hamper picked over an agreed amount.) In the fields each worker's productivity was recorded in terms of crates, hampers or boxes by the field foremen. Pay-day was Saturday, when Ernie, complying with federal regulations, gave each worker a list of his earnings, with deductions of rent, social security, meals (cooked by Ernie's wife) and items purchased on credit. Typical pay envelopes would record $60, $70 or $80 a week, but contain $10, $15 or $20 after the deductions.

The habituating mechanisms used by Ernie and other labour contractors rested primarily on the provision of apparently arbitrary pay envelopes and the close supervision

191

of the work task. But there were a number of subsidiary mechanisms too. Contractors purchased candy, soft drinks, liquor, beer, gloves and other items and sold them to workers, frequently at double their retail value. By extending credit for these items, contractors secured a convenient state of indebtedness and were able to discriminate between workers by withholding or granting further credit. Meals were also withdrawn for recalcitrant workers and a limited amount of breakfast provided to encourage early starters.

The exterior conditioning of the workers by the growers, in sum, can be seen in terms of the dominance growers have over the labour market, the control they derive from having their workforce housed at the point of production in debilitated and isolated conditions and their use of crew bosses to manage and discipline the labourers. The crew bosses derive their credibility with employers by exacting a strict regime and by delivering the right amount of labour-power at the right time to pick a ripening crop. In his day-to-day contact with the workers, the crew boss is thus the effective agent of exterior conditioning carried out indirectly at the behest of the growers.

Interior determination: US agricultural workers

Unlike in the case of exterior conditioning, which refers to the leverage exercised by the state and the employer on the worker, interior determination refers to those elements of a proletarian culture that internalise, transmit or even generate ideologies or forms of behaviour that are conducive to the workers' own continued exploitation. However, it is necessary to place some careful qualifications around the notion of interior determination. In one sense, evidence of interior determination would indicate successful socialisation (to use a related, and more conventional, term) carried out at the behest of capital. In another sense, interior determination can be seen as another version of a 'culture of poverty'—to use Oscar Lewis's much debated term (see Valentine 1968). In the popular use of Lewis's concept, what one is talking about is the forms of adaptation, or even more fundamentally acceptance, of the capitalist world view.

'Interior determination' is intended to suggest a more complex mediation between ideology and observed behaviour. First, while consciousness in work-related contexts often reflects and refracts elements of the dominant ideology, this does not constitute the worker's whole being—what happens after work, or after a return from seasonal labour, or what is clandestinely thought, felt or acted out. Where deviant behaviour is conscious, dissimulation is the basis of apparent compliance. Second, there is a complex relationship between forms of adaptation and forms of resistance. The very indices of an acceptance of adverse conditions may provide the means to assemble an ideology of resistance: a subculture becomes a contra-culture. Some examples of this process are provided later in the chapter when discussing patterns of resistance amongst migrant miners in southern Africa. For the moment, however, two aspects of interior determination observable in US agricultural workers are concentrated on. The first concerns the internalisation of the ascribed and heavily-promoted attribute of being an 'alien'. The second concerns varying manifestations of psychological disturbance and disorientation in the migrant labour camps and at work.

Being an alien is not, generally, a comfortable state, though the Hungarian humorist, George Mikes (1946) managed to ameliorate his own alien status by poking fun at England and the English. The acceptance of his observations, however, depended on a certain cosy consensus going something like this: 'Poke your fun, but poke it gently and we'll treat you not as a foreign threat, but a quaint curiosity'. Patronising as such an attitude is, it is preferable to the expression of xenophobic fears and hostility when confronted with an outsider. Many migrants to the US have had to face just such hostility. One common reaction is to wish to appear invisible so as to deflect the more brutal manifestations of racism. Bisharat's (1975: 23) characterisation of the typical Yemeni farmworker in California shows evidence of this reaction:

He is shy, definitely wary, hesitant to make any disclosure. He is Moslem. Though he does not observe the fast of Ramadan because of the arduous nature of his work, he does pray five times a day in the field and attend mosque whenever possible. He is married. His wife and children are in Yemen. He speaks no English and makes no attempt to learn it formally. He can read and write Arabic, we were told. He is seclusive and associates with few people outside the circle of his fellow workers. He avoids drinking, smoking and public entertainments. He is sure to avoid any situation that might cause trouble and to this end he polices his friends.

The effects of an alien status are clearly visible in this portrait, and it is status that applies to a high proportion of US agricultural workers. The inability to speak English is especially important as many Hispanic migrants are forced to accept the word of the labour recruiter, the employer or the crew boss. Workers are unable to communicate effectively with social workers or with the US Department of Labor inspectors, and have little access to information concerning their civic rights—even where these obtain. In one case, where the US Department of Labor set out contractual rights in Spanish, officialdom used the opportunity to stress what a great favour was being granted to migrants by the US state and employers. In translation, the *Guía para los Trabajadores Agrícolas Mexicanos* states:

> You are here because you are needed to help us grow and harvest crops on the farms of the United States ... When our farmers cannot find all the workers they need in this country, they are permitted to hire agricultural workers from Mexico ... Should domestic workers become available, however, they have a prior right to jobs held by foreign workers.

On no less than 10 occasions the guide reminds workers to consult their *employers* if they are dissatisfied; *thereafter* workers are advised to consult their Consul or a representative of the Department of Labor (US Dept of Labor 1959: 227–31).

Disillusionment with the employer and the authorities is often a shattering experience to migrants who have internalised at least some elements of the 'American Dream'. An

194

autobiographical account by an *indocumentado*, 'Pablo Cruz', provides an interesting insight into the experiential and psychological traumas of a Mexican worker. Despite growing up to think 'the United States was real bad because of what it had done to Mexico', Pablo Cruz was 'always dreaming to be inside the Statue of Liberty and [wanted to] walk through the arm to the hand holding the torch, the fire, just to get the feeling of America'. He recalled: 'I saw movies that disturbed my mind real strong. It was the *Egg and I*. And I thought if I could go to the United States, I could do something to become rich like the man in the movie story.' Pablo Cruz's aspirant identification was, however, rudely challenged. In his first illegal crossing, he was picked up and deported after two days. His initial jobs included one where the farmer paid-off Pablo and his co-workers unusually early in the week. The more experienced workers were immediately suspicious, but Pablo stayed on—only to find himself roughly bundled into a car at three in the morning and taken to the border. The penny had dropped. As Pablo Cruz ruefully recollected: 'This is the way they work in Indio [the US], you see. The Immigration and the farmers have a deal. The farmer can pick up and work the *alambres* [thin people] if he agrees to turn them in to the Immigration when he is finished with them' (Nelson 1975: 37, 38, 77).

As a consequence of their low and often illegal status the state and the growers are often able to widen a cultural and social rift between Mexicans and Chicanos. As Pablo Cruz put it: 'If a person is born in Mexico a Mexican-American laughs at you and calls you a dumb person, because you come from a dumb country. There is a lot of discord you see. We don't look like brothers. We are not united. We don't feel the brotherhood. Everybody is real hard and tries to take advantage of everybody else' (Nelson 1975: 168). This sense of social distance is amplified by the intra-class competition fostered by the hiring practices of the growers who typically can switch between different ethnic sections of the work-force.

The disabilities engendered by an illegal status and a minority language are compounded by the casual, intermittent and short-term nature of agricultural employment.

195

According to a Harvard psychiatrist, this leads to the development of a migrant subculture characterised by social isolation, extreme poverty, cultural deprivation and social fragmentation:

> The uprootedness which characterises their lives, falls not suddenly upon them (as it does upon the observer who tries to comprehend their manner of survival) but is a constant fact of life from birth to death, summarizing therefore, a whole life style, a full range of adaptive maneuvers. [Workers have] a tendency to feel not only weak and hard-pressed, but responsible for their fate. (Cited in Marshall 1974: 52, 3.)

The experiential data collected in migrant labour camps also reflects the consequences of impermanence, disorganisation and other dislocative elements in personal and interpersonal behaviour. For example, with respect to sexual behaviour:

> Women are disdained as nothing more than 'pussy' and virility is constantly reaffirmed. Discussions about sex are highly ritualized and repetitive and accompanied by much sexual license. At the same time, there is a high tolerance of sexual deviance; with most crews there were one or two homosexuals ... they are accepted with affectionate contempt. (Friedland and Nelkin 1971: 100.)

Popular psychology would interpret the reported constant obsession with the size of men's penises as evidence of anxiety, while the existence of homosexual practices is commonly reported in the literature on closed institutions. But there may well be deeper structural determinants that underpin these behaviour patterns and derive from a particular historic division of agricultural labour. There still remain strong vestiges of the feudal peon system which operated in Mexico and the south-west. In the classical system, the women (and children) were not only an instrument of labour-power of the patron, but a possession of their fathers and husbands. Elements of this subordinate relationship remain when a 'family wage' is paid to the male head of the family to include the labour-power of the women and children. Gonsalez, who makes this argument, further adduces (1977: 49, 50) that even where single male labour-power is dominant, 'the practices and ideology of capitalism have encouraged the retention of feudal patriarchal attitudes in Mexican-American communities. Sexism is thus common in migrant labour camps and serves to divide the agricultural working class into two subordinate sections.'

The filthy and debilitating conditions of the camps also encourage an attitude of self-neglect, fatalism and anti-social behaviour. One researcher reported the following friendly greeting: 'Joe, get you ass up. You've been drunk all the God damn day and all night, and you shitted right on the floor here.' As Friedland and Nelkin explain (1971: 105, 108): 'As a recognised object of taboo, faeces "out of place" is considered by some to represent a desire to create anxiety. Such behavior, reminiscent of Gulliver urinating on Queen Mab's castle, is a pungent symbol of contempt and defiance of order.' The labour process itself also encourages a degree of intra-class conflict. Harper, Mills and Parris (1974: 288) quote a field-worker to this effect:

> It's each man for 'isself. One day we're packing tomatoes. You pick a basket and leave it by the row. When you finish a row you call Stamp [the foreman]. Well, I was pickin' like shit and once't I looked behind me and there's ole Jack, who don't pick so good, taking one of my baskets and puttin' it in his row. You can't trust nobody.

Medical and religious practices equally show evidence of deviant conduct which inhibits the growth of collective consciousness. Where access to conventional medicine is, in any case, limited, great store is set on the efficacy of 'roots' and other home-brewed remedies. Religious observance rarely conforms to the practice of the organised churches. Instead, the dominance of a single 'preacher' tends to encourage a sharp distinction between the secular world (which is marked by an absence of control over one's fate), and the spiritual world (which has to be attained through absolute conviction and a belief that God works in mysterious ways). In one case, a preacher strongly criticised Martin Luther King for allowing people to believe that *social power* was relevant to their lives and the attempt to find 'the living God' (Friedland and Nelkin 1971: 120).

197

The dialectic between habituation and resistance

So far, it has been shown, both at the level of exterior conditioning and at the level of interior determination, how the cards are stacked against US agricultural labourers and held largely by the state and agricultural capital. But, by concentrating attention on the habituating mechanisms effected by the state and the growers, the points of conflict and tension have also been highlighted. State and capital are never able to effect a total hegemony over labour, nor do they always achieve a total congruence of purpose. Such is the dialectic of habituation and resistance that each point of pressure against the migrant agricultural workers is also a point of leverage and movement against the state and capital.

Without attempting a complete analysis of the forms of resistance practised by agricultural workers, let me illustrate the connection I have made between control and resistance. While the state uses tough immigration controls to regulate the flow of external and subordinate sections of the agricultural proletariat, its manifest inability to close the frontiers effectively exposes the authorities to ridicule and reveals the contradictory interests of the state and the growers. The attempt to deny foreign workers civic rights, has activated the government of Mexico and the Commonwealth of Puerto Rico to intervene on behalf of their citizens. Dividing off the racially different and unorganised section of the agricultural workforce from the stabilised indigenous workers has led some sections of organised labour to argue for the extension of bargaining and other rights to migrant workers (for examples, see Baird and McCaughan 1979: 167–70). Racial stigmatisation has served to generate affirmative national concepts like 'the Atzlan nation' and 'La Raza' to create communal bonds of solidarity. Again, weaknesses of bargaining power at the point of production have been somewhat offset by consumer-based protests and boycotts, carried out particularly by the United Farm Workers and its supporters.

Finally, at the level of interior determination, while many agricultural workers internalise negative stereotypes derived from their cultural marginality and illegal status, most are not so mesmerised by their circumstances so as to actually prefer farm work. In one survey, 77 per cent of a sample of Michigan migrants explicitly stated they would leave farm work if they could, while only five per cent wanted their children to work on farms. (Cited in Dunbar and Kravitz 1976: 89). Attitudes do not, of course, always translate into action. It is important not to exaggerate the possibilities of protest amongst agricultural workers in the face of the debilitating conditions described. On the other hand, there is a history of determined farm worker protest in the US which should not be overlooked (see, for examples, Kushner 1975; McWilliams 1971; Foner 1964; Galarza 1977; Kiser and Kiser 1979; Levy 1975 and Majka 1980). The struggles described in these sources demonstrate that the state or capital should not be accorded a degree of rationality and hegemony that they intrinsically do not possess and are unable totally to effect.

It is now opportune to turn to the principal case study of resistance, namely the migrant mine workers in another of the regional political economies, southern Africa. In a sense, there is a kind of perversity in wishing to analyse patterns of resistance in the southern African context. The literature on European and US migrant worker protest (some just cited), is very much fuller and until 1985, when new protest waves in South Africa began to attract the attention of the western media, the preoccupation of many observers and participants in law and order debates was with the threat posed to European and American cities by alienated second-generation migrant youth (US Dept of Justice 1980; Scarman 1982; Cross 1981). These points of conflict and tension are still of continuing importance as the 1985 riots in British cities indicate, but the southern African example provides, in a sense, a more challenging terrain for argument. In the first place, it is 'worst case' example—so if the genesis and development of patterns of migrant resistance in so unpropitious an environment can convincingly be portrayed, so *pari assu* can the capacity for resistance in less authoritarian states be assumed. In the second place, the southern African case provides useful illustrative material for three aspects, or phases, of struggle, each of which will be discussed in turn.

One, the hidden forms of resistance buried in the nooks and crannies of everyday life in the mining compounds and underground. Two, the struggle for representation and legal organisation, which is now reaching an advanced stage in South Africa. Finally, the struggle for stabilisation and acceptance within South African cities as resident (rather than migrant) workers with full social and political rights. If such a struggle is successful it will confirm the view expressed by Zolberg and cited at the beginning of this chapter that, in the long-run, all migrant labour systems are unstable and that ultimately the state has to concede recognition to migrants as social, cultural and political actors. As South Africa has practised probably the most successful migrant labour system in the world for about a century, its potential collapse, if demonstrated, will indeed provide irrefutable proof of Zolberg's proposition.

Hidden forms of protest: miners in southern Africa

Chapter 3 described how the South African mineowners attempted to set up a monopsonistic control of labour-power throughout the southern African region. Whenever scarcity threatened to diminish their supply of cheap labour-power, they cast their net further and further afield, as far as China until they were stopped, but at any event all over east, central and southern Africa. In fact, total monopsony was never quite achieved. The farmers put in a bid for cheap labour-power and, at times, their claims were recognised by the South African state. Also, the mineowners of Southern Rhodesia (the former name for Zimbabwe) were largely outside the labour-recruiting schemes and, given their poorer seams of gold-bearing ore, tended to be strong competitors for tiro miners, unable to hold out for higher starting wages. By 1925, real wages in the Rhodesian mines had fallen by a third over the previous 13 years. As van Onselen (1976: 32–3) argues:

> Fundamentally, it was the reduction in costs achieved at the expense of African workers' wages that made the most import

ant contribution to the continued viability of the industry. The large numbers of workers 'pushed and pulled' from the fringes of the regional economic system was systematically supplemented with Rhodesian Native Labour Bureau recruits to ensure that the industry was dominated by cheap immigrant [i.e. migrant] labour.

But detaching agriculturalists from the land was by no means an automatic process; the invisible hand of the market lived up to its description in a more literal sense than is usually implied by that phrase. Instead, as is suggested in the above quote, 'pushing and pulling' was a much more organised and more difficult process. This led to what might be considered the first major form of labour resistance—the withdrawal of the agricultural community into regions beyond the control of the recruiters and the frequent cases of desertion from employment. A colonial labour administrator (Orde-Browne 1967: 46), writing in the 1930s, commented on the reluctance of Africans to take up paid employment, as follows:

Especially it will be found difficult to create any enthusiasm for wage-earning among a tribe which has had experience of forced labour in any form; the dislike of compulsion outlasts the existence of it, and the man who has once been educated to regard work for an employer as a misfortune will take long to change his attitude. This presumably accounts for the many instances of tribes who are energetic in the production of crops, but who can only with great difficulty be persuaded to accept a wage ... in some cases indeed they seem to contract a sort of obsession, which makes them abruptly abandon even a congenial job near home if they feel that they have worked at it too long.

The supposed obsession was, of course, not so much a psychological ailment, but a clear preference for trying to sustain some kind of capacity for subsistence, for household production and, when the money economy became pervasive, some means of securing income without having continually to accept the miserable conditions and low wages of the mining compounds. This wholly rational strategy found another form in what is sometimes referred to as 'target working'. This notion in fact has a rather hoary history and was often used by colonial officers to justify the payment of low wages. Africans off the land, they argued, preferred 'leisure' to income, once they had reached a certain 'target' commensurate with their desire to purchase a fixed bundle of goods. A bicycle and a radio were frequently featured as the whites' idea of what Africans most desired. Target working was meant to result in a backward-bending supply curve of labour-power—the supply drying up as more and more Africans returned to their rural idylls, radios tuned in for their lives of leisure. With other commentators, I have criticised such a depiction, arguing that 'in fact the targets that workers set for themselves were much more elastic than the colonial administrators realised (or were prepared to admit), and there appears to be solid evidence to support the view that wage-earners responded favourably to monetary incentives once they were offered' (Cohen 1974: 189). In the case of the South African mines, these incentives were not offered for the first 80 or so years of the industry's life. Rather than pay more, the mining companies preferred to widen their net of recruitment. The result was that potential miners behaved not like target workers in the colonial sense, but as optimisers of the available alternatives. To safeguard their rural livelihoods, many workers dropped out or refused to offer their labour-power between August and Christmas, the first part of this period being when the rains fell, the latter when the first maize harvest was due. Equally statistically verifiable, was an increase in available mine labour when influx control measures were harshly applied—thus preventing workers reaching the towns—and a decrease when manufacturing wages outstripped those offered in the mines (Wilson 1972: 87, 81–3). Workers were thus essentially trying to widen their choice—between sub-sistence production, minework and industrial labouring.

Even within the mining sector there was a constant movement southwards towards the richer mines with better wages, safer working conditions and a more benevolent management. A local newspaper in Rhodesia, the *Herald* commented in 1901 that 'batches of boys' (i.e. African workmen) assembled outside the offices of the paper to listen to a literate co-worker read the news of the 'no-pass' and 'desertion' cases in order to appraise which employers were less likely to hand them to the police. (Cited in Phimister and van Onselen 1978: 23). 'Native policemen' had to be supplied to the mining companies by the BSA Company (the administering authority) to try to prevent desertions. A British visitor to Rhodesia in the 1890s was told that a worker who attempted to run away was taken to a native commissioner for 25 lashes: 'I found that the word "twenty-five" said in English to any of the boys was sufficient to make them grin in a sickly way—they quite understood what it meant'. (Cited in Phimister and van Onselen 1978: 31).

Once within the mining compound, other hidden forms of protest, more related to the place of work, began to manifest themselves. Quota restrictions, time and efficiency bargaining, go-slows and 'careless' work became characteristic of the early mining compounds. The nature of such protests recalls Genovese's (1967: 74) description of slave resistance in the southern United States: 'Side by side with ordinary loafing and mindless labour went deliberate wastefulness, slowdowns, feigned illnesses, self-inflicted injuries, and the well-known abuse of livestock and equipment'. As in the concept of target working, white managements either did not wish to, or were incapable of accepting, the rational and solidaristic basis for the miners' behaviour. This is well illustrated by Gordon's (1977: 107, 8) observations in a Namibian mine:

> White supervisors attribute quota restrictions by the workers to 'laziness' and point out that in terms of cash earning it is illogical behaviour since it cuts into the underground workers' bonus. Thus, it is felt that laziness must be inherent. But quota restriction, from the workers' perspective, has a logic of its own. It enables them to avoid fatigue by allowing them to work at a comfortable pace. They are thus able to establish a degree of control over their own work targets ... Quota restriction prevents competition at the work place which would disturb established interpersonal relationships and protects slower Brothers thus alleviating white pressure because it is believed that if one worker works harder, the white will also expect other workers to put more effort into their tasks ... walk-offs were quite frequent and entailed considerable Brotherhood solidarity.

Sabotage and theft also are common, and of necessit hidden, forms of protest. Workers characteristically ar trying to slow down the production process to reduce th level of their exploitation or to jinx the machinery to show it limitations as a substitute for labour-power. Mining prop erty was frequently smashed, compound huts set on fire an cattle, belonging to the company, maimed (van Onsele 1976: 242, 3). Richardson and van Helten (1983: 92) describ how miners reacted to a wage reduction as early as 189(merely four years after the opening of the gold fields:

> The mines manager's house at the Anglo-Tharis mine wa blown up by dynamite, and the secretary of the Meyer an Charlton mine, F. McMillan, was caught in his burning hous on the morning of the 24 October 1890 as the wage reductio had made the 'Kaffir' take an instant dislike to Mr McMilla who also discharged the duties of paymaster.

Within the Namibian mines described by Gordon (1977 183, 4), workers drew a distinction between 'theft', whicl was morally reprehensible as it involved stealing from fellow-workers, and 'taking', which was accepted, as i involved the company or whites in general. Whites were seer as having so much that a little pilfering would not be noticed Besides which, miners surmised that their wages were set s low because the management assumed that they would steal 'I am just paying myself' and 'This is in fact our money which was withheld by the Boss' were two of the comment made by Namibian miners.

The structure of workplace authority is also frequently undermined by the deliberate creation or amplification o social distance between miners and mine managers. In jokes, private linguistic codes, exaggerated deference, wal slogans and mocking songs provided the most commor means for workers to express their solidarity and suggest the grounds for their own moral superiority to the mine manage ment. Sometimes this creation of a counter work-culture took a quite practical form. In one Namibian mine, workers assumed four or five different names, including a 'white name used for potentially advantageous interactions with the management. The proliferation of names confused the management. If trouble loomed, workers could deny their identity or allow a particular 'name' to disappear (Gordon 1977: 127). Social and psychological distance from the management was also maintained through the adoption of religion or other worldly beliefs, particularly those stressing relief from suffering in the next world. Often such beliefs were not formally constituted but took the form, rather, of beliefs in chance, fate, a lucky break, or the evil machinations of other persons whose actions were wholly beyond control. In other cases, African miners followed 'nativist' or 'Ethiopian' sects. Such adherence to religious or superstitious ideas is commonly pictured in classical Marxist thought as a clear case of 'false consciousness' which would have to be stripped away to allow a 'true' political consciousness to emerge. This misses the point. In the construction of a pro-worker ideology on the mines, certain ingredients deriving from religious belief and practice were essential. These included ideas of asceticism, guilt, retribution and solidarity as well as, in the African context, a sense of pride in being black. Church organisation or prayer meetings also provided practical experience of organisation in a non-ethnic milieu. Not surprisingly, mineowners were apprehensive about the influence of the independent churches and frequently outlawed them from the compounds.

The final set of 'hidden' responses found in the South African mines to be discussed here are those concerned with accidents, sickness and drug use. These responses are often thought of as having little relation to the labour process itself and are often thought of as extraneous to the relations of production, even by the workers themselves. In fact, given the reckless use of labour-power in the South African mines (especially in the early years), the rates of accidents, illness and drug abuse become social facts (in Durkheim's (1970) sense) to which the miners have to adapt or respond. Wilson (1972: 21) reports that over the period 1936 to 1966, 19 000 men, 93 per cent of them black, died in gold mine accidents. While the white death rate was 0.97 per 1000 men, the black rate was 1.62 per 1000 men. The distribution of sickness is even more skewed. Beriberi (heart failure due to lack of thiamine), for example, is common among black miners, unknown among whites. Medical compensation, running at the rate of R10 million a year by 1967, went one-third to blacks, two-thirds to whites and 'coloureds' (Wilson 1972: 51). Reported sickness, what for managers constituted 'malingering' or 'laziness' is often a matter of self-defence as well as protest—denying labour-power to the mineowners, while trying simultaneously to cope with the debilitating conditions the employer has provided. Volition in respect of 'accidents' like clothing caught in machinery, eye grit, fainting, and muscular injuries is often difficult to establish, a reaction under stress, or when tired, might well involve an element of psychological resistance. In this sense, 'accidents' may not be so accidental—and may be used to evade work, slow it down, or escape a more serious accident or death. As to drug use, this almost always represents a form of psychological resistance, but social quiescence by workers. In the southern African mines the sale of alcohol was sometimes encouraged, and favoured miners were given preferential treatment by being allowed to brew millet beer. Violence stemming from beer-drinking tended to involve only the miners themselves, so was subject to restriction, but not complete prohibition. On the other hand, workers were frequently able to use the rituals associated with drinking to build forms of companionship and solidarity. In a context where tales of poisoned beer were common, workers of different ethnic groups sitting together drinking from common beer bins emphasised the egalitarian side of compound society and built up the basis for mutual trust.

Strikes and the struggle for representation: miners in southern Africa

It is self-evident that the hidden forms of protest just illustrated have certain limitations as a means of representing and expressing occupational and working class consciousness. Though these forms of consciousness are vital to an understanding of 'grassroots' resistance, and often overlooked in conventional accounts by industrial relations experts, it is an error to romanticise everyday events that by

206

their very nature can but be disconnected, spontaneous, individualistic and with short-term effect. It is to be expected that where legal and accepted forms of union organisation and representation are outlawed and restricted, the hidden forms may become more prevalent means of self-expression. This largely accounts for the widespread evidence of such hidden forms of protest in the mining compounds of southern Africa. But from an early stage black miners in southern Africa attempted to push beyond the limits of such protests to forms of collective action like strikes, and demands for the right to organise themselves into unions. The struggle for the legal recognition of African trade unions and, more importantly, for their right to bargain on behalf of their membership, has been an exceptionally prolonged and difficult battle that has only recently been won. All that can be done here is to highlight some of the major historical skirmishes that were joined between miners and the mineowners.

The earliest strikes involving black miners occurred in 1889 and 1894. The strikes of 1894 were met by a response from the management that was to become characteristic. Six miners were killed by the police and 300 dismissed from their jobs (Simons and Simons 1969: 3, 13). Moreover, the management were able to force the pace of the 'closed compound system' which effectively divided black 'unfree' workers from their 'free' white counterparts (Innes 1984: 37, 8). The offensive by the Randlords (as the mineowners came to be known) against the gold miners, who they recognised could be a threat to their power, was not met with passivity. Warwick (1981) documents a wave of overt industrial action by black miners during the period 1901 to 1902 at the Consolidated Main Reef, Geldenhuis, Langlaagte, and Durban Roodepoort gold mines and the Vereeniging coal mines. Although each event was distinctive, they were linked by a common attempt by the Randlords to cut wages and costs (like rations) and an attempt by the British Government to develop a harsher labour regime in the wake of the unsettled conditions obtaining during the Boer War. The most dramatic confrontation occurred at Langlaagte when, on 28 June 1902, 1100 workers armed with sticks, bottles and stones broke out of the compound protesting, as a police report later noted, at being 'thrashed on their testicles with a cat-o-nine tails' and 'shut up like dogs' by the compound manager (Warwick 1981: 26). The workers were eventually driven back by a detachment of the Johannesburg mounted police.

The compound system was seen as a cheap means of obtaining labourers necessarily recruited from afar, and as a way of controlling them. The system soon spread to all the mines of southern Africa and provided the site for almost unrestrained brutality by the managers and considerable deprivation on the part of the miners. As in Langlaagte, the sjambok (whip) was used to discipline workers, while the compound police were put in charge of allocating the meagre supplies of food and rations. In the early stages of pro-letarianisation, workers often had to rely on supplementary provisions from their families in the countryside. In the Wankie coal mine (Southern Rhodesia), regular outbreaks of fatal scurvy occurred before the First World War and it was this health risk, together with the outbreak of famine in the country, that precipitated a strike of 160 of the 1000 black miners in 1912. Even though one miner was provocatively 'flicked about the face with a stick', the miners marched to the office of the police to present their grievances with a 'quiet and respectful bearing' (van Onselen 1974: 285). For their pains, the workers were charged with insubordination, found guilty and all fined a month's wages. In the midst of a famine year, it is perhaps not surprising that they went back to work without being able to ameliorate any of the conditions that oppressed them.

The bosses did not meet such a compliant stance the next time round. As the inflation rate spiralled in the wake of the First World War, workers on the Rand demanding increased wages struck with increasing frequency and militancy. In July 1918 they had to be driven back down the shafts by armed mounted police. In December 1919 and in February the next year small wage increases (linked to a bonus scheme) were prised from the Chamber of Mines. But this proved insufficient to quell the militancy of the black workers, 71 000 of whom (out of a total black workforce of

173 000) came out on strike. Some 22 of the 35 mines operating on the mines were affected (Innes 1984: 77). The president of the Chamber of Mines recognised that a qualitative change had taken place in the nature of black protest. He called the events of February 1920 the first 'native strike in the true sense of the word' and saw the effective combination of workers as evidence that the African 'was advancing more rapidly than we had anticipated' (cited Simons and Simons 1969: 232).

What at first seems paradoxical was that these early manifestations of overt class action took place while there was still considerable evidence of a continuing ethnic consciousness amongst mine workers. It was perhaps natural that novice workers drawn from scattered areas should wish to stick together for self-protection against the unknown. Such workers often organised themselves into 'home groups' under the leadership of an induna (headman) who sought to represent their interests. It should not be assumed that such representations were always of the 'doffing-the-cap' variety. Morony (1981) reports many instances of work stoppages and refusals to start work, based on home group organisation. For example, in 1902, 192 Mapoch workers refused to commence work for 10 days until they were assured of better treatment. Again in 1907, Pondo miners refused to work underground on the South Randfontein mine because they claimed they had been recruited for surface work only.

While ethnic-based organisations do not therefore necessarily act in a way that is contradictory to class interests, protests that are solely organised along ethnic lines can act to divide worker from worker and can often be manipulated by the management to the same end. One example of this occurred in 1907 at the Premier Diamond Mines, when Basuto workers attempted to undercut the wage rate demanded for certain prized classes of work by Transvaal workers. The management was able to play one group off against the other and get their way by concealing the economic content of the protest under the label of an 'inter-tribal conflict' (see Morony 1981: 44). Such a management technique has served mining interests well over many years. Because levies of miners from different regions are incorpor-

209

ated into the labour process at different levels and at different times of the year, any special grievance or sectional interest can easily be dismissed as an 'inter-tribal conflict'. The induna system also allowed the mines to argue that trade unionism 'along European lines' was not relevant to the southern African context, as workers from the different 'tribes' would be better served by their own headmen than by representation by a stranger. Epstein's (1958) sensitive observations of the Luanshya mine compound in Zambia (Northern Rhodesia) in the 1950s shows how gradually the industrial context asserted its own logic on the surviving forms of ethnic organisation in the compounds, and how workers began to turn away from them in favour of trade unionism when the assertion of their industrial muscle demanded it.

Although black miners were gradually able to transcend their prior ethnic origins in favour of their more pressing class interests (a process which, though not yet complete, is none the less far advanced), they were quite unable to effect a bond of common unity with the (at first) considerable numbers of white miners employed in the industry. The decisive moment of separation was to come in 1922 with the so-called Rand revolt. A considerable number of white miners, in particular those who were not converted to the role of supervisors, were fired in favour of cheaper black miners. Whereas in 1920 the ratio of white to black miners was 1:8.1, in 1922 the ratio had altered significantly to 1:11.69 (Davies 1978: 87). With this threat to their livelihood, the white miners came out in a massive and violent strike, which was only halted and defeated by a considerable display of force by the South African state. The compromise that emerged was enshrined in the Industrial Conciliation Act of 1924, which regulated wage competition and institutionalised collective bargaining for white trade unions, but virtually excluded the black worker from any legislative protection. Black miners' contracts fell under the various 19th century Masters and Servants Ordinances which made any breach of contract a criminal offence. The result was a union movement which found it almost impossible to overcome the racial divide (see Lever 1981).

210

Despite this setback, since the early 1930s there were sporadic attempts, often at the behest of the South African Communist Party, to start a mine workers union for Africans. A nucleus was formed in 1931, and leaflets were issued in 1933 and 1935 urging the formation of complaints' committees in every compound, but an attempt to secure joint action with the white South African Mine Workers' Union in 1936 was met with a rebuff in the form of the *re-insertion* of a colour bar in the union's membership rules (Simons and Simons 1969: 512, 3). A viable union was not formed until August 1941 when, at the initiative of the Transvaal African National Congress, 81 delegates, mainly from Congress, trade union and Communist Party branches met to try to galvanise African miners into joining the embryonic union. A major grievance had arisen from the specific exclusion of African miners from the compulsory cost of living allowance paid to other workers as a result of war measure 28 of 1941. Their basic cash wage per shift was 2 shillings in 1942, as opposed to 2 shillings and 6 pence in 1890! So the material motivation for collective action was strong. Power station workers took the lead and when they struck, the government, fearing contagion to the miners, established a Witwatersrand Mine Natives' Wage Commission in 1943 to examine wages and conditions of African workers. The commission conceded little enough and the Chamber of Mines trimmed its wage recommendations even further. Official concern followed by the employers' neglect gave further impetus to the union's recruitment drive. By 1944, the African Mineworkers' Union claimed 25 000 members despite the harassment of its leaders and the prohibition of meetings on mines' property (Lodge 1983: 19). This prohibition, which covered meetings of any number over 20 people, was proclaimed initially as a war measure, but was annually renewed until 1956, when it was finally allowed to lapse.

Although the ban severely constrained effective organisation, the union none the less felt itself to be sufficiently strong to take on the Chamber of Mines. In April 1946 more than 2000 delegates from a representative scattering of shafts and compounds demanded a minimum 10 shillings a day, the repeal of the prohibition on meetings and the provision of adequate food. The last was an especial grievance in that, as a result of war shortages, canned meat had been substituted for fresh. Just a month earlier, miners protesting at their diet at the compound kitchen at Modderfontein East had been dispersed by police, with one death ensuing. By August 1946, the pressures within the union for a confrontation were at a high pitch, and the leadership risked its hand. According to the Chamber of Mines' own figures, 76 000 Africans stopped work. Twelve mines were brought to a complete standstill, nine others partially stopped. The police responded with overwhelming force, killing nine and wounding 1248 strikers. The leadership was rounded up and charged with various public order offences and such was the level of repression that Lodge argues that it 'effectively destroyed the African Mine Workers' Union' (Lodge 1983: 20; but see Simons and Simons 1969: 569–78).

Despite the force of the repression, it is difficult to explain why the collapse of organised black trade unionism on the mines was quite so complete for quite so long after the unsuccessful strike of 1946. Even as late as 1961, after clandestine meetings and pamphleteering, the non-racial central body, the South African Congress of Trade Unions, only claimed the miserly total of 100 paid-up members amongst African miners (Lodge 1983: 193). Part of the answer for this poor level of open organisation was that in the wake of the 1946 defeat a number of the representative African bodies shied away from trade unions in the direction of consumer boycotts, community organisation and the demand for civic rights. Inter-racial and cross-class political alliances were stitched together between whites, Indians, coloureds and Africans, this form of politics culminating in the adoption of the Freedom Charter in 1955. Legislation also severely restricted the role for any black workers organisation. The Bantu Labour (Settlement of Disputes) Act of 1953 basically placed white officials and employers at the bargaining counter to determine the level of black wages. Indirect representation of African views was permitted only via a works committee under the eye of the management. But these explanations for industrial impotence miss the struc-

212

ural dynamic underlying the growth of the South African economy in the post-war period. This process is well-described by Innes (1984: 144,5), who shows that the rate of profit on the mines had fallen during the war. Now that industrial expansion was hotting up, 'the state had to try to reconcile a new phase of expansion in manufacturing with the necessary expansion of the primary sectors (especially gold) on the basis of a sufficient supply of cheap labour-power'. This led to a much more intense control of the labour supply by the government which needed to switch indigenous black workers to secondary industry (without alienating its supporters amongst the white farmers) and to increase the number of foreign-born migrants destined for contract labour on the mines (Chapter 3 explained this mechanism in some detail). With respect to the present concern, all that needs emphasis is that the increased control by the state of the recruitment and segmentation of the labour supply as well as the increased presence of previously unorganised foreign migrants allowed a greater control over the workforce than would otherwise have obtained. In the wake of the 1946 strike the employers and the government (after 1948, occupied by the National Party) were not about to allow their advantage to slip easily.

The employers had become so relaxed in their workplace supremacy in the 1950s and 1960s that the wave of strikes by 13 500 contract workers in Namibia in January 1972 against the pass laws and the humiliating conditions in the compounds caught the employers and the authorities by surprise. Just one year later the secondary industries around the Durban–Pinetown–Hammarsdale complex erupted. Some 100 000 workers were involved in a set of protracted disputes, some of whom achieved the purpose of picketing (illegal in South Africa) by parading *en masse* while shouting the old warcries of the Zulu armies. Parallel events on the Rand involved the bus companies, the clothing industry, newspaper and milk delivery services and engineering concerns (Dekker *et al.* 1975: 207–38). Although the mines were not involved directly in the 1972/3 events, they benefited from the conflict in that the scale of disruption indicated that black workers were not prepared to tolerate deteriorating

213

living standards and the lack of representation at work. The
20-year-old Bantu Labour (Settlement of Disputes) Act was
revised to allow some Africans the right to strike. Even
though numerous restrictions still obtained, black workers
were to make more and more inroads into self-organisation
and representation at work. The strikes of 1972/3 were an
important psychological (as well as practical) victory in that
the sense of the employers' invincibility was shaken. A few
years later, in 1976, the schoolchildren of Soweto provided
another decisive challenge to white supremacy. Again, the
miners were not involved; the authorities even attempted to
use them against the urban rioters. But again the argument
for black representation were raised and answered on the
streets. One of the young men who gained his political
initiation in the Soweto uprising was Cyril Ramaphosa, later
the principal organiser of the National Union of Mine
workers.

The industrial awakening of the miners from their long
slumber was seen in the late 1970s and early 1980s. At first
the stories were small items in the South African press.
Angry hostel inmates, whose rents had been raised from R1
to R15, from the Simmer and Jack mine 'set fire and
virtually destroyed East Rand Administration Centre, then
went on to smash and loot a nearby shopping centre', said
report in the *Rand Daily Mail* (Johannesburg) (8 April
1981). The General Mining Corporation dismissed all 1600
black mine workers from the Buffelsfontein gold mines 'due
to irregular behaviour, lack of co-operation and the necessity
to maintain discipline' (*Cape Times* (Cape Town) 23 May
1981). In the next year the West Drieffontein mine management issued a statement that 'About 4000 men from no.
hostel refused to go underground. They surrounded, and set
on fire, the hostel offices and looted a concession store
(*Sunday Express* (Johannesburg) 4 July 1982). Gradually
some perceptive observers and journalists realised that the
'troubles on the mines' were much more extensive than the
Chamber of Mines or the companies had admitted. One
report claimed that during 1982 there were 'at least 70 000
men on strike. It was the largest action to hit the mining
industry since 1946' (*Golden City Press* (Johannesburg) 1

214

September 1982). Thirteen mines were stopped, in one by 120 black miners sealing themselves in a tunnel. Some of the racial bitterness and class consciousness behind these largely spontaneous outbursts of industrial might can be discerned in a remarkable letter written by a black 'team leader', who had worked in the Carltonville mines for 25 years, and published in the Johannesburg *Sunday Times* (11 May 1982):

> The white miner today is the fellow who prefers to sit on top of his lunch tin at a stope entrance yawning the shift away ... A black man sweats blood and sometimes dies so that a white man can get a fat cheque and bonuses for 'good productivity' at the end of the month. But mining today is a black man's world. Black mineworkers will soon group together to form an organisation that will show Mr Paulus [the leader of the all-white Mineworkers Union] who the real gold producers are.

This sentiment was to prove prophetic. The Chamber of Mines quietly conceded a number of wage claims, such that the average money earnings of Africans on the mines moved from 5.47 per cent of white earnings in 1972, to 17.79 per cent of white earnings a decade later (MacShane *et al.* 1984: 51). Although the Chamber was by now also prepared to recognise a black union (whatever the white miners did), it tried at first to find a compliant organisation in the Black Mineworkers' Union (recognised in 1982). Other unions that began recruiting in the mines included the Metal and Allied Workers' Union, The Black Allied Mines Construction Workers' Union and The Federated Mining Union (active in the diamond mines). None of these unions succeeded in capturing the heart and minds of the mine workers in any numbers until the Council of Unions of South Africa (a black consciousness-orientated federation) sent Cyril Ramaphosa to the mines as an organiser. He established the National Union of Mineworkers (NUM) in August 1982 and within ten months had gained recognition from the Chamber of Mines who 'found it easier to deal with recognised leaders than to confront an angry mob' (MacShane *et al.* 1984: 102). Ramaphosa capitalised on the high levels of militancy amongst African miners and, using the sympathies of the team leaders, was able within two years to boast the largest black union in the country (70 000 members in 1984). An estimate in May 1985 (Golding 1985a: 101) put the membership at 130 000, by August another 20 000 members had been added (*The Sunday Times* (London) 4 August 1985). The upsurge in membership took place despite the deepening recession in South Africa, normally a hard time for workers' organisations. Though the NUM is arguably one of the fastest growing unions in labour history, it has still to reach the approximately 400 000 remaining unorganised miners.

The achievement of the NUM is, however, not only to be measured in terms of its growth in numbers, but also in terms of the commitment of its membership and its advances in bargaining rights. These facets are best illustrated by the escalating level of tension in the Anglo-American mines in the western Transvaal over the period November 1984 to April 1985 and the build-up to a major strike in August and September 1985. Legal strikes in September 1984 led by the NUM were followed in November 1984 by boycotts of taxis, sports events, liquor outlets and concession stores. Workers were both symbolically defying the old order of closed compounds and company hegemony and also pressing for further wage increases. One miner drew an interesting comparison between the upsurge in militancy in the mines and the equivalent events in the urban township: 'The township people thought we were stupid [he said]. They thought we were scared and did not want to fight for our rights. All this has now changed. They respect us' (cited in Golding 1985a: 99). In a number of incidents, the mines' security force and the police were used to enforce order. One worker who was injured in a skirmish declared his loyalty to the NUM: 'The union will free us from mine slavery . . . we cannot retreat now from the union . . . it is our organisation and we must fight to defend it' (ibid: 113).

These struggles moved to a climax in April 1985 when 17 000 workers were dismissed in the western Transvaal, 13 337 from Vaal Reefs, the biggest mine in South Africa. Workers were taken by bus back to the homelands and to neighbouring states after a protracted tussle. The challenge to the company was made in the period leading up to crucial wage negotiations and there is little doubt that the strong response by Anglo-American, which owns Vaal Reef, was equally designed to show toughness before the negotiations. In the event, the companies climbed down considerably. In its annual statement, Anglo-American announced it took back 10 519 of its 13 337 dismissed workers. The company defended its dismissals by claiming that it 'represented an unavoidable response by management during a very difficult period of transition from what might be called a paternalistic system to one of conventional bargaining' (*The Sunday Times* (London) 14 July 1985).

The union's increased strength is shown by the company agreeing to take back the overwhelming majority of its dismissed workers, a course of events that would have been inconceivable a decade earlier. Anglo-American also took the lead in trying to settle the mid-1985 demand by the NUM for an across-the-board 22 per cent wage increase. At first the Chamber offered and unilaterally implemented an increase of between 14 and 18 per cent. Later, under the threat of a large-scale strike against five companies owning 29 mines, Anglo-American broke ranks with the other companies and offered between 17 and 22 per cent, together with increased holiday pay allowances. The Afrikaner-controlled company, General Mining Corporation, and some other mines where the union was weak, decided to slug it out and precipitated a two-day strike (supported on the first day by 28 000 miners) in early September 1985. The usual pattern of dismissals and eviction from the hostels followed, though this time the union has taken the companies to court to prevent such conduct. By splitting the Chamber of Mines, forcing a favourable settlement in the mines where it was strong and showing its teeth even where it was weak, the NUM has made a decisive intervention into industrial relations. The exclusive white privilege of the Blaster's Certificate which permitted the placing of dynamite only by skilled workers, will soon be phased out, and further organisational advances and successful legal challenges are expected.

Conclusion

In this chapter an attempt has been made to convey some of the experiential quality of being a migrant worker, whether in the fields of North America or the mines of South Africa. In the first instance, how capital seeks to subordinate and habituate agricultural labour was examined, in the second, how migrant workers gradually learn to fight back—initially hesitantly, secretly and often in individualistic ways, then later and on other occasions in a more open, organised and collective manner.

By taking the case of the migrant mine workers of southern Africa, it was hoped to use a 'worst case' example to address Zolberg's proposition prefacing this chapter that in the long run any foreign migrant worker will be able to transcend the role of a purely economic actor to fulfil a more stable social and political role. Has this proposition been demonstrated in the case of South Africa? Any conclusive answer still lies in the complex web of contemporary events. At the time of writing (in mid 1986), the urban townships of South Africa have exploded in violence, the scale and duration of which greatly transcends the riots in Soweto in 1976. A State of Emergency has been declared, lifted, then declared again by the South African government, while many countries have either initiated partial sanctions, or are contemplating the possibility. President Botha's first response to the sanctions threat comprised some nationalist bluster. His target?—none other than the estimated 1.5 million foreign workers. Attacking his usual *bêtes noires*, the United Nations and the Soviet Union, he suggested that those countries leading the sanctions call should provide employment for repatriated workers: 'For our part, we shall ensure that those who stand to be repatriated are properly informed that the measure is solely due to the decision of the Security Council which forced this measure on the South African government'. If the economies of the neighbouring countries collapsed, he concluded, 'I hope that they will note that the Security Council, with the Soviet Union in the lead, will have to be blamed' (*The Guardian* (London) 30 July 1985).

218

But are the foreign workers, and in particular the migrant miners, still in as weak a position that they can be kicked around like a political football? If the reaction of the Chamber of Mines to the Vaal Reefs strike in April 1985 and to the wage demands of August 1985 is taken as an indicator, the mines' management is no longer able to ignore union grievances or contemplate permanent mass expulsions without the threat of massive strike action, escalating demands by the NUM and a subsequent loss of production. Given the vulnerability of the Rand as a currency and the likelihood of an investment strike by nervous foreign venture capital, if the government or the mines decided to move to a confrontation, it seems as if Botha's threat is unlikely to be implemented, at least not in any large-scale fashion. Within the mines' management, there is grudging but definite recognition that the only path they can travel is one towards the stabilisation of at least part of their workforce. The Rand Mines group has already begun actively to encourage a settled labour force, offering married, as well as single quarters. Their industrial relations policy is to co-opt clerks and team leaders while developing the idea of a 'career' for black miners (Golding 1985: 102). Anglo-American has also issued a number of statements suggesting that at least part of their black labour force will be stabilised.

By taking as a case study the difficult position of the South African migrant miners, it has been shown how, despite the long-standing use of an exploitative migrant labour pattern and violent attempts to stop union organisation, there is convincing evidence of resistance. Miners have moved from hidden forms of protest, to open confrontation. For the first time in 40 years a powerful union has emerged to challenge the mines' managements in the mines and in the courts. The miners' industrial struggle is, moreover, linked (at least at some levels) to the general black demand for citizenship and political rights. In the long term, it seems inevitable that many of South Africa's black miners will follow a path from unfree migrants to settlers and citizens.

7 The 'new' international division of labour: *plus ça change*

> *In essence what we people of the Western Hemisphere really need is a more efficient division of labour among us. The division of labour is one of the tried and true economic principles that will be as valid in 1976 as it was in 1776 when it was first spelled out by Adam Smith ... The less developed countries would also gain. With abundant supplies of labour and wage levels well below those of the United States, they could export processed food, textiles, apparel, footwear and other light manufactures.*

(Rockefeller 1963: 102,3)

> *Capital today has two ways available to it of reconstructing the industrial army: on the one hand the intensification of capital exports and the systematic suffocation of investments at home, i.e. sending capital where there is still excess labour-power, instead of bringing labour-power to excess capital; on the other, the intensification of automation, or in other words the concentration of investments to set free as much living labour as possible.*

(Mandel 1978: 182)

When the leading living capitalist and the leading living Trotskyist agree on the best prescription for the survival of capitalism, albeit in somewhat different language, it is perhaps time for the rest of us to defer to their joint wisdom. Certainly, there is no doubt that the processes anticipated by Rockefeller and suggested by Mandel have become part of our contemporary world economy. The casual traveller to the four 'golden economies' of Asia—Hong Kong, Taiwan, Singapore and Korea—cannot fail to be impressed by the

220

sudden evidence of modernity and industrialisation. Even using the appellation 'Third World' of such places sounds absurd, particularly when one is conscious of the transformation of great sections of the old industrial boom cities— like Cleveland, Detroit, Birmingham or Liverpool—into depressed slums and economic wastelands. Clearly, an economic transformation of some magnitude is taking place, as investment patterns alter and industrial plant becomes spatially redistributed.

The global shifts in the location of manufacturing enterprises have been recognised in a number of largely discrete academic debates which still require more synoptic vision to bring them together. One line of argument has stemmed from a critique of Latin American dependency (or 'underdevelopment') theory, which, in the popularised versions offered in Frank's early works (1967, 1969), came to dominate much thinking about the non-European and non-North American countries. The model Frank suggested as characteristic of the relations between rich and poor countries was a chain of 'metropole/satellite' connections with the stronger partner being parasitic on the weaker. As Roxborough (1979: 45) notices, the image is graphically rendered by Swift's verse:

> So, naturalists observe, a flea
> Hath smaller fleas that on him prey;
> And these have smaller fleas to bite 'em,
> And so proceed *ad infinitum*.

The problem with this model is that it allowed very little room for alterations in the fleas' existing preying order. It was difficult to explain how, for example, Brazil became more powerful than Portugal, or the US than its former coloniser, Britain. Class relations within and between countries also remained obscure as the theory largely relied on aggregate trade and investment data, which intrinsically could not illuminate some of the social structural relationships that were held fundamental to the exercise. With respect to the growth of industrialisation in Third World countries, the left-wing economist, Warren (1980: 166, 193–8), denounced dependency theory as 'nationalist myth-

221

ology' arguing that, 'it may be that the greater the previous experience of imperialist penetration, the greater the subsequent ability to respond to the world market'. He showed that statistically the growth rates of many of the less developed countries compared favourably to those of the developed market economies in the period 1960 to 1973. Though Frank (1981: 96–101) has subsequently sought to derogate the extent and meaning of this development in less developed countries, the substance of Warren's critique stands—in that any student of development has to recognise a more complex picture of growth at different, and in terms of dependency theory unpredictable, points in the global economy.

Recognition of the tendencies towards the uneven distribution of global development sites in the contemporary period has also come from those working with a 'world system' perspective (Hopkins 1977, 1979; Wallerstein 1979) who allow switches in fortune between peripheral and 'semi-peripheral' states; from those who saw the multinationals as leading a new phase of capital accumulation and expanding their global reach (Barnet and Müller 1974; Hymer 1979); and from those who sought to rework the classical Marxist texts on imperialism, despite the force of Warren's (1980: 114–15) acid comment that, 'the quality of post-war literature has naturally suffered from ascribing rising significance to a phenomenon of declining importance'. (But, for exceptional accounts, see Amin 1974 and Magdoff 1978.) More recently, a thriving and self-critical group of 'urban and regional' scholars has prefigured a 'political economy of space' that attempts to contextualise the new class and economic relations arising from the redistribution of production sites (Castells 1977; Harloe 1977; Harloe and Lebas 1981). On the side of the world from which capital and jobs appear to be leaving, more alarmist and more nationalist studies talk of the 'collapse of work' or the 'deindustrialisation' of the US (Jenkins and Sherman 1979; Bluestone and Harrison 1982).

Some of the threads of these debates, though by no means all, are woven together in the work of a number of German scholars who coined the expression 'the new international

222

division of labour' [NIDL] (Fröbel *et al*. 1980; Ernst 1980). Without overt intellectual debt, the NIDL theorists basically followed the line of analysis suggested by Warren's critique of dependency theory and, to a lesser degree, the depiction of 'peripheral capitalism' suggested by Amin (1974). Taking over the vocabulary of world systems theory, they argued that industrial capital from the core was moving to the periphery as 'world-market factories' were established producing manufactured goods destined *for export*. The strategy of export-orientation from newly-industrialising countries (NICs), was also adopted as an alternative to import-substitution strategies of development, which were held to have failed Third World countries. The movement of capital away from the core industrial countries in turn was necessitated by the difficulties in securing and realising high profits—as industrial conflict, the increased reproduction costs and the growing organisation of migrant communities prevented the attainment of a high level of exploitation.

As was shown in Chapter 4, these difficulties were particularly evident in European countries, where, at the beginning of the 1970s, the initial advantages that accrued to employers by importing large numbers of migrant workers, rapidly began to erode. On the other hand, many Third World countries had large supplies of cheap, unorganised labour. The over-supply of labour-power had occurred with the commoditisation of agriculture (accelerated by technological innovations like the 'green revolution'). As the rural poor were pushed off the land, unemployment, underemployment and, for some, the process of full proletarianisation had resulted. The NIDL theorists further observed that technical and managerial developments in the labour process now allowed the effective use of peripheral labour-power. The increasingly minute division of labour permitted the reorganisation of unskilled and semi-skilled tasks. With a minimal level of training, levels of productivity soon matched or exceeded metropolitan levels. The movement of manufacturing capital to parts of the periphery was also accelerated by an investment climate made more attractive by government policies. A number of governments in the Third World passed labour laws restricting the organisation

223

and bargaining power of the unions. They provided freedom from planning and environmental controls, poor and therefore cheap health and safety standards, permission to repatriate profits without restriction, tax holidays and in some cases, like Singapore, a powerful paternal state, which seemed to guarantee political stability. At the level of transport and communications, international facilities had dramatically improved in the form of containerised shipping, cheap air cargo, and computer, telex and satellite links. Especially in the case of low-bulk, high-value goods, with a high value added at the point of production, it was often no longer necessary for the site of production to be near the end-market. Examples of goods of this kind include electrical or electronic goods, toys, shoes and clothes—virtually the same list Rockefeller had identified in the early sixties. Finally, the world market factories could be staffed predominantly by young women, who were particularly prone to exploitation given the difficulties of organising a group characteristically under patriarchal dominance and with a limited commitment to life-time wage labour (see Fröbel *et al.* 1980; Elson and Pearson 1981; Henderson and Cohen 1982a; Henderson 1985).

In short, it looks very like metropolitan employers, having been frustrated in their countries in fully exploiting imported migrant labour, had alighted on another cohort of helots in the periphery who they would now be able to deploy directly, rather than by importing their labour-power. Moreover, it was a labour force that presented few of the demands for social and political rights that even the South African government and companies are slowly having to recognise. The empirical demonstration of the thesis was supported by some convincing data (Fröbel *et al.* 1980: 275, 276–90) from Federal Germany. After 1959, when restrictions on German companies investing abroad were lifted, a steep increase in the amount of direct foreign investment began to be noticed—from DM3291 million in 1961, to DM19 932 million in 1971 to DM47 048 million in 1976. However, this investment did not, in general, represent a net expansion of German capitalist development on a world scale, but rather the integration of new sites and the reloca-

224

tion of certain manufacturing processes previously reserved for domestic manufacturing. Within Germany, this was bound to have consequences for the number of jobs available. A small rise over the period 1967 to 1973 was followed by a sudden drop of nearly a million jobs over the next three years. However, this loss of domestic jobs coincided with an *increase* in turnover and profit for key German firms. Simultaneously, an estimate for the number of jobs created abroad by German manufacturing firms by 1976 was 1.5 million. Fröbel and his colleagues (ibid: 287) are properly cautious in saying that these figures alone 'do not allow us to deduce the extent to which employment abroad has replaced employment in Germany', but the inference is nonetheless there for all to read. From the pattern of imports of manufactured goods, from the statements of the companies themselves and through an examination of the free production zones in Third World countries, one is led ineluctably to the conclusion that capital has migrated in search of its own comparative advantage, especially in respect of labour-power costs, and at the expense of domestic and imported workers, whose job chances have been correspondingly diminished.

The picture presented by the NIDL theorists seemed to confirm observable reality in the NICs and also to present a far superior explanation for industrial decline in the old centres than that currently proffered by 'monetarists' and right-wing demagogues. Consequently, part of the work undertaken by Henderson and this author (1982a) on international restructuring was a replication study using the British data. Again, the basic contours of the German experience were evident. As is shown in Table 7.1, if the rate of overseas investment by British capital is compared to the rate of investment within Britain (as measured by net domestic fixed capital formation), the former starts at three times the rate of the latter, with this already large difference rapidly accelerating towards the end of the period surveyed.

Again, although it is difficult to separate out the many factors producing unemployment (including government policy, automation, the loss of international competitiveness, under-investment, etc.), there is some evidence to suggest that in Britain, as in Germany, key firms are adding to their

225

Table 7.1
Domestic and foreign investment from Britain, 1969–80

	Domestic (£m)	Overseas (£m)
1969	4 233	13 950
1970	4 754	14 400
1971	4 911	15 180
1972	5 488	19.170
1973	6 859	19 500
1974	7 906	19 224
1975	9 603	23 415
1976	9 844	30 401
1977	9 628	30 573
1978	10 908	35 328
1979	11 483	41 024
1980	—	48 439

Source: Henderson and Cohen (1982a) citing Government Blue and Pink Books

payroll overseas and cutting their work force in Britain. Thus, an ILO report (1981: 82), surveying the operations of 118 major British firms, showed that over the period 1971 to 1975, they had added 150 000 employees to their payrolls abroad compared to only 80 000 in the UK. As the study concluded: 'employment-wise they were clearly growing much faster abroad than at home, both in absolute and relative terms'. The US also reveals a similar picture. Bluestone and Harrison (1982) found that between 1968 and 1976 there was a loss of approximately 15 million jobs as a result of plant closures. The closures partly resulted from technological changes but managers also saw the transfer of production abroad as an attractive alternative to production at home as risk was diversified, greater control over labour was achieved and they could take advantage of large international wage differentials (Nash and Fernandez-Kelly 1983: ix).

From the discussion and data so far presented, it would seem that NIDL theory provides a major key to understanding some of the processes of capital accumulation in the modern world order. While not wishing to deny its powerful explanatory value and the important contribution made by the NIDL theorists, there are nonetheless some major limitations and omissions that inhere in the theory which need explication, particularly from the point of view of someone writing on the role of migrant labour in the history of capitalist development. This critique does not, however, depend only on a switch in the focus of interest from capital export to labour deployment, but also identifies some more general weaknesses. The discussion of NIDL theory will concentrate on three issues, taking the opportunity also to develop some alternative formulations. First, *conceptual problems*—where it will be argued that the variety of meanings attaching to the phrase 'division of labour' makes it difficult to understand what precise phenomena are under investigation. This uncertainty can, in turn, lead to differing political and practical conclusions for those committed to the theory. Second, *historical gaps*—where I maintain that NIDL theorists have ignored or misconceived the historical evolution and successive phases of the international division of labour. And third, *empirical omissions*—where it will be shown that NIDL theory tends to concentrate attention exclusively on the growth of the manufacturing sector in the periphery at the expense of other growth points in the global economy, which are better reflected by measuring movements of labour, rather than movements of capital.

Conceptual problems in NIDL theory

When trying to understand the phrase, 'the new international division of labour', it is necessary first to unscramble the good deal of ambiguity arising in the prior expression, 'the division of labour'. The notion has been used very differently to explain different phenomena. In its earliest usage, it was often pressed into service to distinguish what are now described as sectoral divisions in the economy—

227

divisions, for example, between industry, agriculture and services. It was used also to define the occupational and skill structure of the labour force and the differences between skilled and unskilled labourers, masters and apprentices, craftsmen and production workers. Additionally, the division of labour referred to the organisation of tasks, characteristically dictated by the management, in the workplace. Who is on the line, who is in the office, who minds the machines and who sweeps the floors? Though related to skill and occupational structure, the detailed specification of tasks is by no means coincidental with skill, as Braverman's (1974) contribution on the process of 'de-skilling' testifies.

To these three original meanings of 'the division of labour' have been added others of more recent vintage. First, the gender or racial division of labour—indicating the new sensitivity to the ethnic composition of the labour force and to the role of women in production and reproduction (Pahl 1984: 254–76). Second, the spatial division of production and product (an aspect of the division of labour which, will be argued, is far from 'new'). And third, perhaps the latest meaning attaching to the notion, the contracting-out of some elements of the production processes to well outside the factory gates—into domestic, peasant or household units.

The changing definitions and meanings of the phrase 'division of labour' impel different discussions and have different implications of a more practical and political nature. For example, if it is argued that the putting out system has now revived on an international scale and constitutes an important new feature of capitalist production, feminists who argue for a politics of the home and of reproduction would have a strong case against those who argue for a politics of the factory—from which production would be putatively or potentially disappearing. Equally, if the manufacturing sector in Third World countries is as significant a feature of contemporary capitalism as the NIDL theorists argue, the whole structure of workers' resistance to capital will have to undergo a massive lateral shift if it is to succeed. This is particularly the case when the question of international solidarity is considered. Metropoli-

228

tan workers are confronted with two diametrically-opposed strategies. On the one hand, a more nationalist posture would argue for the preservation of jobs at home by the erection of high tariff walls and import duties designed to keep out Third World manufactures. On the other hand, an internationalist position would dictate that bonds of solidarity should be effected between metropolitan workers and workers in peripheral countries already employed in branch plants so as to restrict the manoeuvrability of multinational capital and spread the benefits of employment equally between the participant partners. For Third World workers, other dilemmas present themselves. Any significant growth of trade union activity by any one national working class in the Third World can result in footloose capital moving to another territory. Thus, the interests of Third World workers may lie in effecting labour solidarity between Third World sites rather than between themselves and metropolitan workers, where wage differentials are bound to create major divisions of interest. Even mentioning the difficulties of labour solidarity in this casual way raises complications enough. However, one can add to such dilemmas, questions such as whether organisationally it is preferable to link workers by sector (e.g. pharmaceuticals, toys, textiles) or by firm (e.g. Phillips, IBM, Shell). And this ignores the problems of transcending the major divisions within an international trade union movement currently separated on cold war lines.

In short, even only taking two possible meanings of 'the division of labour' one ends up with strongly differing pictures of the changing battle lines between the old contestants 'capital' and 'labour'. There is, of course, no need to logically admit only one meaning of the division of labour as valid, but even if one accepts that a variety of meaning has now legitimately accrued to a particular label, this raises the posterior question of the relative weight, or significance, between the different phenomena grouped under this particular label. The last question is superficially one amenable to empirical enquiry—but behind the empirical question lies a paradox which inheres in the measurements so far characteristically deployed to evaluate changes in the international division of labour. The NIDL theorists use, as their predominant data, aggregate trade and investment figures—that is, they use measures of the migration of *capital* to measure changes in the division of *labour*. This method can lead to some very misleading impressions. For example, it is possible that changes in the location of manufacturing enterprises are far less important in terms of employment (and in terms of profit) than changes between sectors (in particular the movement from industry and agriculture, to services and information) within the metropolitan economies. Thus new outlets for the deployment of subordinate and migrant sections of the metropolitan labour force in the service sector would easily be missed. There does therefore seem to be a case, on empirical as well as conceptual grounds, for using measurements of the movement of *labour* to indicate changes in the division of *labour*. Indicated in the empirical section below, are two additional sectors (in the oil rich countries and in the service and sweat-shop sectors of 'world cities') where significant employment of subordinate labour-power has taken place without these salient features being noticed in NIDL theory.

The empirical question, therefore, is linked umbilically to the prior theoretical questions of how the different conceptions of the division of labour are grouped and ranked. As Garnsey (1981) has pointed out, the first three meanings of the term division of labour (by skill, by sector and by task) were united in classical political economy which interwove economic theory with what is now called industrial and occupational sociology. This original conflation of meaning was lost in the late 19th century in what Garnsey describes as an 'intellectual *putsch*' against the division of labour by the growth of the two separate disciplines of sociology and economics. In economics, the *putsch* was effected by an increasing focus on the laws of choice in economic situations and on scarcity as the basis for value in exchange. Under such a debased notion of value, wages and profits could be analysed without reference to the social and political relations between employers, investors and wage earners. The only important issues were the aggregate transactions determined by considerations of scarcity and consumer preference. Such considerations left no place for the division of labour. In sociology, the notion was not abandoned—rather it was given more specialised meanings. In Weber, the emphasis was on the social relations that the division of labour engendered, rather than on how it created different patterns of economic and social development (Weber focused on religion as the major factor associated with these patterns). In Durkheim, on the other hand, the emphasis is on both the structurally disruptive and cohesive tendencies in the division of labour, which ultimately give rise to social integration through the process that Durkheim calls organic solidarity. Modern sociological interest in the divisions of labour by age, race and sex tend to follow the inheritance of Weber, whereas the meaning attributed to the phrase by Durkheim has largely been lost in modern sociological discourse.

Does the revival of the phrase by the NIDL theorists, though this time with an international focus, signify the possibility that the two great social-science disciplines, sociology and economics, will once again be able to unite on a common intellectual staging ground? In one sense the NIDL theorists have prefigured just such a possibility by consciously echoing back to classical 19th-century political economy. Thus they list as their progenitors the work of Adam Smith (who also gets an honourable mention from Nelson D. Rockefeller), Charles Babbage and Andrew Ure (Fröbel *et al.* 1980: 37–44). In addition to these three figures, NIDL theorists depend on another classical theory to underpin their argument—namely, Ricardo's basic law of comparative advantage. Ricardo's law can be simply stated as follows: the pattern of international trade is dependent on the principle of comparative labour costs 'which states that if two countries, A and B, entered into trade relations, each capable of producing commodities X and Y, A would sell the commodity in which its relative (rather than absolute) cost was lower and, correspondingly, B would sell the commodity in which its own comparative cost was low' (Bagchi 1982: 16). By focusing so strongly on labour costs as the primary element in the movement of capital, NIDL theory fails to take account of the important role of innovation and techno-

231

logical development in the accumulation process of modern capitalist firms (see Jenkins 1984: 33, 34).

The conceptual dependence on classical political economy raises the positive prospect of the reunification between sociology and economics, but also unfortunately brings in its baggage train the limits of the classical tradition. In the 19th century, the state was not a significant actor on the industrial scene and, again in NIDL theory, it virtually disappears— except in the Third World case, where it takes the form of a bourgeoisie *manqué* having to kotow to the overwhelming power of metropolitan capital. The <u>failure to take any account of the local dynamic</u> is also noticed by Jenkins (1984: 34), who observes: 'Policies to promote exports or attract foreign capital for instance are seen as a result of the "needs" of capital at the centre, rather than as the outcome of local class struggle'.

Just as in the 19th century, with the major exception of Marx, the rising power of the working class was ignored in economic theory, so this feature of the classical tradition reproduces itself in NIDL theory, with the social and political relations that surround the production process being almost wholly neglected in favour of discussion of aggregate trade and investment transactions, which reflect the power of capital. In such a view, all that happens can be explained by the logic of capital without seriously taking into account independent institutional forces, the contradictions between merchants, national capitalists, transnationals and governments, or, on the other hand, the political and social protests by those who fall victim to the logic of capital. In their reliance on trade and investment flows to demonstrate their thesis, NIDL theory shows an interesting correspondence with both world systems theory and dependency theory—all three exhibit the weaknesses of <u>excessive 'economism'</u>.

To summarise: NIDL theory provides only a partial answer to the need for a synoptic vision of the contemporary global capitalist world order. Except implicitly, it provides no guide through the variety of meanings attaching to the term 'division of labour', nor even if a plurality of meanings is intended, any means, empirically or conceptually, to rank one manifestation above another. Though potentially a powerful tool to reunite economic and sociological theory, the theory shows too many of the economistic features of its 19th-century origin to provide a wholly convincing and rounded picture of the workings of modern capitalism. The rather curious conceptual leap from 19th-century classical political economy to the late 20th century also reveals an odd insensitivity to the evolution of the capitalist world order— almost as if nothing of any great moment has happened over the last 100 years. This empty historical box needs some filling.

Historical gaps in NIDL theory

How new is the 'new' international division of labour? There is no way of determining this from the theory itself, as no historical comparisons with other international divisions of labour are provided. It is as if the NIDL theorists boarded a time machine in the mid-19th century to arrive at Hong Kong and Singapore late last night, without bothering to land at any of the intermediate airports—notably those marked on the historical maps as 'imperialism' and 'colonialism'. On prima facie grounds, it would seem appropriate to assume that imperialism and colonialism had something to do with the evolution of the present-day international division of labour. Indeed, I intend to make a further assertion—that the historical patterns established by prior international divisions of labour are so much part of our contemporary reality that the distinction between the 'new' and 'old' international division of labour is not a very useful one. For this reason the expression 'the *changing* international division of labour' is preferred.

How then can the successive phases in the changing international division of labour be classified and periodised? From the point of view of the form of capital hegemonic in each phase, four sequential phases can be identified—the mercantile, industrial, imperial and transnational divisions of labour. This is a convenient classification in that these labels are readily identifiable in historical writings and,

233

although not previously used to described phases in the international division of labour, do refer to readily understood historical periods. On the other hand, using labels deriving from the characteristic form of *capital* present, may spring the same trap that I accused NIDL theorists of falling into. Should, ideally, each phase be described by the characteristic form of *labour* present? Thus, should the mercantile phase be called the phase mixing free and unfree plantation labour? Should the industrial phase be signified by a label indicating the mix of free metropolitan and workers imported to the metropole? Should the imperial phase be deemed the phase mixing colonial peasant proprietorship, migrant workers in extractive industries and metropolitan wage workers? Finally, should the transnational phase be identified by its distinctive labour mix? Unfortunately, the very clumsiness of such categories inhibits their use—and I also have cognisance of the fact that the phenomenon described as capitalism equally has retained its name, even in Marx's work, from the wrong side of the contestants' ring. So, although the hegemony of particular forms of capital has been granted, it is vital to recognise that inhering in each definition is the corresponding form of labour that is intrinsic to the period and helps, in its contestation with capital, to account for the diminished significance of the prior phase.

Starting first with the _mercantile_ division of labour, the first element of conscious design on an international scale is revealed. A surplus of particular commodities can be generated simply through the accidents of geography and climate, the particular distribution of flora and fauna, or the spread of natural resources—be these commodities fur from Poland, blubber from northern Canada or coals from Newcastle. However, such surpluses only become important when they enter the sphere of circulation and when production methods and rhythms alter to try to replicate accidental patterns into permanent structures of advantage. The debate between the circulationists and the productionists therefore misses the obvious point that once a regular market develops with implied forward contracts, production methods are bound to adjust to meet anticipated demand. It is thus quite fallacious to assume that mercantilism implies pure exchange without any implication for the organisation of production. After all, it was under the aegis of *merchant* capital that labour was commoditised (turned into labour-power) and the beginnings of a global labour market organised. The plantation societies of the New World were established, lands were conquered, local populations decimated, eight million Africans trans-shipped across the Atlantic, and specialist commodities like cotton, coffee, sugar and tobacco planted, harvested and processed. Food crops like breadfruit were brought from the Pacific to the Caribbean to feed the plantation workers. There is also no doubt that institutions like the Royal Society and Kew Gardens were engaged in a systematic design in relocating such crops as is shown in a recent account of 'botanic imperialism' (Brockway 1980). For the period, the cotton ginneries, the rum distilleries and sugar mills and refineries used advanced technologies. Often small railway systems, as sophisticated as anything in the so-called metropolis, ran between the sugar canes. This division of labour was based on the spatial relocation of production, the division of product, the reorganisation of task, and also involved a specific racial division of labour.

The forms of labour characteristic of this period were, first, a combination of metropolitan free and plantation unfree labour in each regional political economy. The contrast between slave and free worker, though legally great, was often less great in practice, particularly when the exploitation of women and children in the core countries is taken into account (contemporaries often made the comparison). The second feature of the labour force in the mercantile division of labour was its increasing ethnic diversity. East Indians were forced to rub shoulders with Africans in the plantations of Natal, Trinidad and Guyana; Javanese were imported to Surinam; Italians to Brazil; Dutch burghers to South Africa—each ethnic group being incorporated into the division of labour with a different status. The present-day consequences of this division of labour are ever-visible in the numerous forms of ethnic and class conflict in former plantation societies. However, the level of plantation labour struggle against mercantile capital was severely limited, as the conditions for the trans-shipment and deployment of

235

labour were dominated by the merchants and the planters. Nonetheless, there were spectacularly successful examples of slave revolt (as in Haiti), persistent attempts to escape to the hills (as in the case of the Jamaican Maroons) and numerous instances of hidden forms of resistance, best documented for the US by Genovese (1967). The formal ending of slavery only partly reflected the strength of labour resistance on the plantation, but what also must be remembered is that the 'economic' reasons for the ending of slavery included the increased cost of supplying slaves (that is this factor reflected the withdrawal and organisation of resistance to the slavers by African communities).

The second phase previously identified was the _industrial_ division of labour. Just as the closed circuits of trade gave way to free trade, machinofacture began to replace (but never totally superseded) the production and processing of tropical commodities. It was in Europe, the _locus classicus_ of this development, that the _locus classicus_ of division of labour theory developed—particularly in the work of Smith and Ricardo, but also in the work of Babbage, Fergusson, Ure, Lemontay and Say. For these writers, the argument hinged around whether a particular division of labour could produce more machinofactured goods, lower wage costs, reduce the dependence of the employer on skilled workers and craftsmen or serve to subordinate the remaining labour force to the wishes of management. The labour forces involved were at first nearly entirely drawn from the agricultural areas surrounding the factory sites, which were in turn transformed from communal or small farmer use to large farms. Marx (1967: 895) still provides the best summary of this process for the English countryside:

> The spoilation of the Church's property, the fraudulent alienation of the state domains, the theft of the common lands, the usurpation of feudal and clan property and its transformation into modern private property under circumstances of ruthless terrorism, all these things were just so many idyllic methods of primitive accumulation. They conquered the field for capitalist agriculture, incorporated the soil into capital, and created for the urban industries the necessary supplies of free and rightless proletarians.

236

In other countries without a large agricultural population or where, as in the US, the indigenous population was virtually wiped out, industrial capitalists began to complain bitterly that the lack of labour-power inhibited the full development of their country's productive resources. Consequently, vast numbers of expropriated peasants from the decaying feudal areas in European countries (especially Poland and other eastern European countries) were sucked into the vortex of industrial production in the US through vast trans-shipments. As was noted in Chapter 1, perhaps 35 million arrived in the US alone from 1870 to 1914. This was about four times as large in scale, though done with less compulsion, than the Atlantic trade in labour-power organised under the aegis of mercantile capital. The industrial division of labour, as the name implies, is also associated with the growth in the 'mass occupations' such as those found in steel and rolling mills and related engineering activities. However, it was also a period of great infrastructural developments—the internationally-financed canals in Suez and Panama, transcontinental and local railways, inland waterways, better roads, the building of the great civic buildings in the industrial centres and the provision of working class housing. To service these infrastructural developments, labour discarded from the plantations could be redeployed—as in the use of Jamaicans to build the Panama Canal and the northern migration of blacks from the Deep South to the north-eastern cities of the US. But such was the scale of infrastructural development that Chinese had to be imported to build the Pacific Railway across the US, while perhaps two million labourers from the Celtic fringe were employed in construction works in England.

The strikes and protests of the period of rapid industrialisation have entered into the heroic annals of labour history: the Paris Commune (which Marx saw as the embryo of the coming Communist revolution); the protests by agricultural labourers and workers so vividly documented by Thompson (1963) and Hobsbawm (1964); and the 'Great Upheaval' in the US (1885/6) when union membership rose between 500 000 and 800 000 and the number of strikes more than doubled from 695 to 1886 to 1572 the next year (Dubofsky

1983: 24, 30). There are, of course, many explanations as to why such strikes and workers' upheavals failed to end the rule of the bourgeoisie in the major capitalist countries and usher in a new socialist dawn. Rising living standards, an escape to petty bourgeois activities and the life of frontiersfolk in the US, the countervailing appeals of nationalism, especially manifested in World War One. But one important reason for the failure (or perhaps the deferment?) of Marx's prediction is the successful annexation by European powers of non-European empires. The contradiction arising between capital and labour in the metropole could thereby be displaced to the colonies, which also returned sufficient resources and profits to the metropole to allow a modest increase in working class living standards.

This comment serves to usher in the third phase identified, namely, what can be called the _imperial_ division of labour. The imperial idea (be it emanating from Germany, France, Belgium or Britain) was itself a racially-based ideological version of an international division of labour. The children of Ham were permitted to grow food and dig up minerals in between drawing water and hewing wood. The fruits of such labour were exported to the patriarch and his lesser offspring in the metropole. They, in turn, were permitted to continue work in the patriarch's factories, this time sending their manufactured goods not only to regional markets but to the furthest points of the empire and beyond. If the territorial expansion of Britain is taken as an example, almost all aspects of her empire—its acquisition, governance and central direction from Whitehall—revealed a much more determined logic than is suggested in the often quoted phrase that 'Britain conquered and peopled half the world in a fit of absence of mind'. In fact this quote comes from the arch-imperialist, Sir John Seeley, who had a very clear notion of functional and product specialisation for different parts of the empire and also saw that technical developments had fundamentally altered the material basis for international association. The anticipation of the NIDL theorists is clear. Whereas _they_ point to the arrival of the telex, the telephone, cheap freight, etc., Seeley (1883) alluded to other crucial technical developments:

238

Science has given to the political organism a new circulation, which is steam and a new nervous system, which is electricity. These new conditions make it necessary to reconsider the whole colonial problem.

Unfortunately for Seeley and his supporters, who included the Imperial Federation League, the *Daily Mail* (founded by Harmsworth to proclaim 'The Power, the Supremacy and Greatness of the British Empire'), and Chamberlain (the energetic Colonial Secretary), they were never able to prevent investment leakages to outside the imperial area. If looking at the period 1905 to 1909, home investment yielded 3.61 per cent, empire investment 3.94 per cent, but foreign investment yielded 4.97 per cent. Moreover, any attempt to impose partial protectionism politically activated the colonial bourgeoisies in the white dominions (Canada, South Africa, Australia and New Zealand), just as a similar attempt in the mercantile period propelled the colonial merchant and incipient bourgeoisie of the US to revolt. Eventually, even the weak and fledgling bourgeoisies in the non-white empires heeded Adam Smith's taunt that the commercial restrictions imposed by the mother country were 'impertinent badges of slavery' and threw in their lot with the anti-colonial struggles of the peasantry and working class. Labour-power utilisation in this phase continued the prior use of metropolitan labour, but added to this group forced labour in many colonies, migrant labour in the extraction industries and in order to service the need for cheap food, turned peasant proprietors into cash-crop producers tied into the metropolitan exchange system (Williams 1983: 144–80).

Labour protests in the colonies during this phase were, for the most part, organically linked to wider anti-colonial and national struggles, but the working class in metropolitan countries was also far from dormant, especially in the wake of the First World War and the successful Bolshevik revolution—which acted as a model for some militant sections of the working class. Perhaps the most extensive protest (often forgotten because of Japan's post-war image of labour quiescence) was the uprising of some ten million people in Japan in 1918 involving slum-dwellers, peasants, dockers, industrial workers and miners (Seldon 1983: 88). But, elsewhere, revolt flamed briefly, then died, often under the impact of brutal repression. A Soviet was proclaimed in Glasgow, the American Communist and socialist parties fell apart in internal purges in 1919 to 1920, while the rising of the left in Germany was cut down, its leaders, like Rosa Luxemburg, murdered. A relative period of quiescence through the Depression years altered again with the end of the Second World War, when most European trade unions emerged as determined economic actors, even if their quest for political power had been abandoned to labour and social democratic parties acting far from perfectly in their name (Arrighi 1983: 44–8).

The final phase mentioned is the *transnational* division of labour, which is used as a category that includes the so-called NIDL but is also much wider than that. The origins of this division of labour lie in the gradually collapsing European empires which, as early as 1880, the German economist, Dietsel, claimed as insufficient for 'very basic economic reasons' because (note the phrase) 'the international division of labour in trade, in the output of raw materials and in agriculture is growing at such a pace that in the long run the isolation of individual groups is no longer possible'. (Cited in Baumgart 1982: 71). So it proved. The humiliating defeat of the European powers in Asia during the Second World War, the strength of the anti-colonial movements and the growth of competitive capital centred in the US, and later in Japan, hastened the end of the imperial order. The transnational phase left in place some neo-colonial relationships (which the French held on to notably better than the other European powers), but also led to a major restructuring of industrial production in the metropoles (allied to the importation of migrant labour), and the further internationalisation of leading fractions of capital, particularly the oil giants, the car companies, and those producing consumer durables, electrical goods and electronic components. My empirical critique of NIDL theory (see below) will include further comments on the composition of capital in the transnational phase and will refer in a more detailed way to the pattern of labour utilisation. It is therefore unnecessary to repeat a similar exercise in respect of labour as was conducted in the prior divisions of labour discussed above.

By trying to fill some of the immense historic gap left yawning by NIDL theory, I have sought to illustrate a number of major points that can be used in partial refutation of the theory. First, the supposedly novel features of the contemporary division of labour, to which the NIDL theorists draw attention, are not really so novel. Even in the mercantile period, production sites were located abroad and elements of a global labour market created and reproduced. Second, the appellation 'new' is further misleading in that it fails to recognise the indelible heritage of the past. Thus, it is more than plausible to argue that the mercantile, industrial and imperial phases have left deep scars on the face of the global population and production facilities. That there are Africans in the Caribbean and the US, Italians in Brazil and Indians in South Africa is a more salient and determinant datum informing the workings of modern capitalism than that export-processing zones have begun to employ Third World labourers. Third, there is a sense of a logical succession between the phases mentioned. Just as conventional Marxism adduces a logical end to successive modes of production as antagonistic contradictions emerge which make a prior mode obsolete, so an analogous sequence can be found in the case of the historic phases of the international division of labour. Fourth, and again the analogy with Marxist theory holds, there is a good deal of overlap between the sequential phases. This is for the obvious reason that once populations are displaced for reasons appropriate to one phase in the international division of labour, it is near-impossible to return them (like the legendary genie to the bottle) from whence they came. The forms of labour deployed in an earlier phase thus continue to operate into the next phase or phases. Fifth, it has already been hinted, and will now be demonstrated empirically that the current phase of the division of labour (i.e. the transnational phase) should be conceived as embracing a number of different forms of labour utilisation not adequately depicted in NIDL theory.

Empirical omissions in NIDL theory

It is perhaps important to emphasise, in view of my other criticisms of NIDL theory, that I do recognise that it describes an important aspect of the contemporary capitalist world order—namely the growth of export-orientated manufacturing in Third World countries. But this aspect of the transnational division of labour needs contextualisation in two senses. How significant is the growth of Third World industrialisation compared to global manufacturing output? What other changes are taking place in the global utilisation and deployment of labour-power with which the use of peripheral industrial labour may be compared?

Fröbel and his colleagues (1980: 295–391) lay great emphasis on the number of countries in the Third World constructing free production zones—36 countries in 1975, six in Africa, 15 in Latin America and 15 in Asia. This undoubtedly provides one index of the increasing scale of Third World industrialisation. However, in an oblique attempt to refute the critique of his early versions of dependency theory, Frank (1981: 96–131) seeks to deride the significance of export promotion as a strategy for the industrialisation of the Third World. Though he fails in this objective, the data he provides do allow us to gain a more balanced view of the phenomenon, neither exaggerating its extent, nor minimising it in order to ressurect an over-simplified picture of metropole-satellite relations. Between 1960 and 1975, manufacturing output increased at about 6 per cent per year in the capitalist and socialist countries, but at 7.4 per cent a year in the Third World. By 1977, the Third World's share of world manufacturing output had increased to 9 per cent from a share of 6.9 per cent 17 years later. According to a United Nations Industrial Development Organisation report, cited by Frank (ibid: 98), an extrapolation of recent trends would leave the Third World with 14 per cent of total manufacturing by the year 2000. However, the same organisation is cited in a recent ILO report (1984: 21) as estimating that the Third World already accounted for 13 per cent of the world share of manufacturing in 1979. Whatever the exact share, there is no dispute that it is highly

242

concentrated in a few countries. Hong Kong, Singapore, Mexico, South Korea and Brazil provided 54 per cent of all Third World manufacturers to the industrialised countries in 1972. With the oil crisis and the recession that was ushered in a year later, it becomes important not only to look at relative shares of output, but at the 'earning power' represented by these shares. While the terms of trade between developed and developing countries were stable for a while, since 1979 developing countries have watched their export prices shrinking rapidly, their import costs soaring and their debt and repayment position becoming critical. Two of the 'success stories' in export manufacturing, Brazil and Mexico, are also afflicted with the largest debts (ILO 1984: 5, 6). It is also unclear, as yet, to what extent the adoption of the strategy of export-led industrialisation is a zero-sum game, with each new participant cutting into the share of the older players. In East Asia there is great awareness by planners of minimum wages paid elsewhere in the region and a consequent fear that footloose capital will drift downmarket (the minimum 1985 wages varied from US$700 in Korea to US$430 in the Philippines and US$100 in Bangladesh). Certain NICs, like Singapore, where the overwhelming share of employment is generated by the multinationals, have also found themselves very vulnerable to US protectionist pressures—and both Singapore and Taiwan have recorded negative or downward growth rates in 1985, the first time for many years that this has happened.

It is time also to reassert a point made earlier—that changes in the international division of labour should not only be measured in terms of changes in the circulation of capital and the distribution of production facilities, but changes in the structure and utilisation of the labour force. According to Fröbel *et al.* (1980: 310), by 1975 about 725 000 workers were employed in world market factories and free production zones in the Third World. A wider picture can be gleaned from the ILO (1984: 20), which claims that employment generated by the multinationals— seen as the engine of growth by NIDL theorists—in *all* developing countries reached about four million people in 1980. The share of multinational employment in different

243

countries varied from a low of 2 per cent in Thailand, to a high of 70 per cent in Singapore, with employment created by multinationals accounting for 20 to 30 per cent in countries like Korea, Brazil, Kenya and Mexico. The creation of four million jobs by the multinationals in Third World countries should be contrasted with their employment of 40 million workers in industrialised countries. It is possible to argue that multinational investment will provide a positive spin-off in the creation of further ancillary industries, but this effect (which no doubt occurs) has to be set against the displacement effect multinational investment may have for local industry. I know of no attempt to quantify these contrasting tendencies in terms of job loss/creation.

To the quantitative estimate of employment must be added a more qualitative sense of who these workers in the NICs are. In this respect, the NIDL theorists provide a good general guide to the first cohort of workers (Fröbel 1980: 344). The overwhelming majority of employees in the world market factories and free production zones are women, with an age range between 16 and 25 years, unskilled or semi-skilled and employed as production workers. But a more qualitative assessment of this labour force emerges only in detailed observational studies conducted on individual workforces. Chann and her colleagues (1984: 393,399), for example, describe the paternal system of labour control in the Malaysian export-processing zone in these terms:

> Personnel policies and factory-sponsored activities direct much of their efforts to build up the notion of the factory as a family, legitimating many of the patriarchal and authoritarian relationships and features characteristic of the [Malaysian] family . . . Discipline as a form of control extends beyond work hours and the factory gates. It is regimented and controlled through management appointed houseleaders who oversee the residents' discipline and movements. Disciplinary rules and regulations or one's code of conduct and behaviour are strictly adhered to. The houseleader, who is exempt from accommodation fees, has to play the role of watchdog for the management . . . [there is] a stigma accorded to rural folks, coupled with a deep sense of being *malu* (shy, embarrassed, shamed) and *takut* (afraid) should

244

she not be able to attain her job and therefore be forced to return to the village in times of recession. This Malay attitude of *malu* and *takut* is exploited by management as a means of labour control such as when parents are informed about any infringement or belligerency on the part of the worker.

Lest we imagine that the forms of control exercised are only ideological, compare the use of traditional social sanctions in the Malaysian case with this description of the garment factories in the Philippines by Penenda-Ofreneo (1984: 355).

> In addition to the breakneck speed at which they have to work, workers in garment factories labor under oppressive conditions. In some factories, they are shouted at, forbidden to rest and to talk even during breaks, and are able to go to the toilet only at certain hours. Excessive heat and noise sap their strength, when they get sick they cannot go home, and when they stay home, they are not entitled to sick leave. Not a few are subjected to sexual harassment and other forms of intimidation. The docility of female labor is considered desirable by employers, along with youth, single status and inexperience.

Switching continents from Asia, to a small Caribbean island, does not alter the basic texture of the employment relationship. In the case of the small Dutch-speaking island of Curaçao, Texas Instruments set up a small plant assembling semi-conductors, employing 1600 workers. The government provided ten years tax-free holiday, permission to employ women to work in night-shifts (Rockwell also moved to the island from Mexico when Mexico started honouring the night-shift prohibition for women), purpose-built factories, minimum rents and permission to pay a level of wages below the industrial minimum. Abraham-Van der Mark (1983: 381) describes the labour process as follows:

> The women worked in three shifts . . . Wages were the same for the three shifts, and a major disadvantage for many of the workers was that assignment to a shift was permanent, so that women in the night shift had to remain in it for years without any hope for change. Although the work was dull, extremely fatiguing on the eyes, and poorly paid, employment was highly valued, both because of the regular income and the many social

245

contacts at work. Headaches and eye infections were not seen as a policy issue for the company but as the personal worries of the women concerned.

Given the high level of unemployment in Curaçao, it was perhaps not surprising that many women were still prepared to work at the wages paid and with the conditions on offer. But whatever the wishes of their workforce, and despite the fact the plant's productivity was second only to another branch plant in Germany, the company decided to pull out with just two years to run on its tax-free holiday. The flight of runaway transnational capital is indicative of the casual regard it has for the labour force it hires, even if the arrival of the company gives the immediate illusion that prosperity and progress has arrived.

A more recent study by Lin (1985: 76, 7) suggests that some of the features of the workforce are changing. While the majority is still young, an increasing number of female workers are getting older, becoming married while still working, are better educated and are acquiring a greater variety of work experience within and between companies. Women are increasingly 'realising that work means being valued as productive beings', ethnic particularities are breaking down and, according to Lin, there is a sense of having to 'build a new multi-cultural working class'.

The phenomenon of export-directed manufacturing is now perhaps sufficiently described both in terms of its quantitative significance and the character of the workforce deployed. But while the impact of this phenomenon on the employment available to the global labour force is not to be diminished, one must avoid not seeing the wood for the recently-sprouting trees. There are two other major sites where cheap and subordinate labour is employed, and which are equally salient aspects of the contemporary transnational division of labour.

The first site comprises the countries of the Middle East and other OPEC countries—where oil revenues, accelerated in the period after 1973 for about a decade, allowed the initiation of ambitious development plans. In Venezuela, for example, following the oil-price boom which contributed some 70 per cent of national revenue, governmental policy switched to a pro-immigration stance, which legitimised and enhanced a flow of perhaps half a million undocumented foreign migrants flowing into Caracas in addition to the vast numbers of internal migrants. The Venezuelan Council for Human Resources planned to import another half million workers during the period 1976 to 1980. The migrants arrived from Colombia, Argentina, Chile and Ecuador (amongst Latin American countries) and from Spain, Italy and Portugal, amongst European countries (Sassen-Koob 1979: 455–64). Again, the Middle Eastern oil-producing countries have shown dramatic increases in imported labour-power. Workers from India, Bangladesh, Pakistan and Afghanistan poured into the oil-rich countries of the Middle East, their Muslim religion being regarded by the authorities as an important reason for permitting their import. In the mid 1970s, an estimated 748 000 workers from these countries arrived in Saudi Arabia, with other large numbers going to the United Arab Emirates, Qatar and Kuwait (Halliday 1977; Birks and Sinclair 1980; Kidron and Segal 1981: 38). Some of this migration is between Arab countries (Egyptians in Libya; North Yemenis, Jordanians and Palestinians in Saudi Arabia, etc.). In other cases, the bulk of the labour force comes from outside the immediate area. For example, Sudan alone provides as many as 800 000 workers to the Arab OPEC countries (*Le Monde* (Paris) 3 February 1982). In some Middle Eastern countries, the proportion of foreign workers to home workers has reached almost absurd levels: 50 per cent in Saudi Arabia, 80 per cent in Kuwait and no less than 85 per cent of the total population in the United Arab Emirates (*Times Special Report* (London) 23 February 1981).

Turning next to West Africa, perhaps a million migrants from Upper Volta, Togo and other nearby countries entered Ghana during the period of its greatest prosperity in the 1950s and 1960s, though the adverse economic climate thereafter produced a strong reaction against 'the aliens' (Peil 1971). As the Ghanaian economy collapsed, workers and petty traders from that country streamed into oil-rich and development-crazy Nigeria—only, in turn, to be the subjects of mass expulsion orders in 1983 and 1985, harshly enforced by the Nigerian authorities. Despite the difficulties of aggregating figures collected by different authorities for different purposes, simply adding together the number of *foreign* labourers (alone) mentioned as migrating to oil-producing countries, yields a figure as great as the numbers employed in the export-processing zones.

Another part of the employment wood that has also been missed by the NIDL theorists is that part of the metropolitan economy marked by the switch of employment between different sectors. NIDL theory concentrates on the loss in employment in the manufacturing (or industrial) sector and the possible switch in these jobs from industrialised countries to Third World countries. However as shown earlier, even if all the jobs created by the transnationals can be said to be net losses for the industrialised countries and net gains for the NICs (a highly implausible assumption) one is only talking of perhaps four to six million jobs at stake. If, on the other hand, one looks at switches between different sectors within industrial economies, an OECD study found that, since 1950, the share of industrial country employment represented by 'information occupations' has increased by nearly 3 per cent in each five-year period. By 1975, these occupations accounted for more than one-third of the total labour force. If employment across the four sectors—agriculture, industry, services and information—is examined, one can see an anticipated shrinkage in agriculture over the period 1950 to the mid 1970s to a half or a third less people employed in France, Japan, Sweden, the United Kingdom, the United States and West Germany. With respect to industry, some shrinkage also occurs in these countries over the period mentioned (as is recognised in NIDL theory). But the most significant change is a spectacular growth in all the countries mentioned of the information sector employment, and a significant growth (with the marginal exception of the United Kingdom) in the service sector (ILO 1984: 179–80).

The growth of employment demand in the service sector is a feature of a contemporary division of labour, particularly highlighted in the work of Sassen-Koob (1983, 1984). She advances a theory, which in important respects should be

248

laid side by side with NIDL theory, arguing that the 'technological transformation of the work process, the decentralization of manufacturing and of office work, in part made possible by the technological transformation of the work process, and the transnationalization of the economy generally, have all contributed to the consolidation of a new kind of economic center from where the world is managed and serviced' (1984: 140). Her analysis is concentrated on New York City and on Los Angeles, where she shows that there has been a pronounced increase in the domestic and international demand for services—which she identifies as legal, managerial, financial, technical, engineering, accounting, consulting and 'a large array of other such services'. She argues that the expansion of these advanced services is the fastest growing sector of the US economy in terms of 'its share of GNP, employment and exports'. The employment pattern and social structure characterising Los Angeles and New York City, despite the superficial differences, are moving in a similar direction—a notable expansion in the supply of very high income jobs, a shrinking of the traditional middle income blue and white collar jobs and an *expansion* of the low wage jobs available. It is this last characteristic that provides her most surprising and important finding. Conventional wisdom and other assumptions about restructuring and industrial decline had led many observers to assume that there would be a permanent shrinkage in the number of jobs available for the more dispossessed segments of the labour force (women, blacks, migrants, etc.). In fact Sassen-Koob argues just the opposite: 'the rate of growth of various earning categories in the service industries from 1960 to 1975 show a 35 per cent increase in jobs in the highest two earnings classes, an 11.3 per cent increase in jobs in the medium earnings class, and a 54 per cent increase in jobs in the two lowest earnings classes'. As she points out, both New York and Los Angeles contain the largest concentrations of ethnic minorities— Hispanics and Asians in Los Angeles and Caribbean peoples in the case of New York City. Although migration from the Caribbean, Mexico, etc. has often been explained by push factors from the recipient countries, Sassen-Koob considers

249

that demand factors in cities like New York provide an equally salient explanation for migration.

What Sassen-Koob's data do not as yet provide is some sort of global indication of this trend and it is, therefore, only somewhat speculative to argue that one could suggest a similar tendency occurring in other 'world cities'. These, according to some of Friedman's (1985) hypotheses, are cities integrating the world economy, providing the 'base points' for production and marketing, the sites for the accumulation and concentration of capital, the points of destination for internal and international migrants, and revealing precisely the occupational profile found in Los Angeles and New York by Sassen-Koob. Such cities are arranged in a complex spatial hierarchy and include London, Paris, Rotterdam, Frankfurt, Zurich, Chicago and Tokyo, in addition to the two fortuitously (in the sense of the world city hypothesis) examined by Sassen-Koob. Though the world city hypothesis still needs much greater empirical anchorage for its validation, the notion that there are such critical nodes in the world economy has great impressionistic appeal. These cities are where the professional and manager-ial classes meet, where the Inter-Continental, Sheraton and Hilton hotels are established, where frequent connecting flights by international airlines operate. These cities contain stock exchanges, theatres, sophisticated entertainment, town houses and international schools.

If it is right to suggest that Sassen-Koob's findings for New York and London can be transposed to a world city context, a similar growth should also be found in the service industries that she describes. To generalise her argument it may be important to extend her list away from what she calls 'advanced services' into more prosaic activities which service the needs of the world's managers, professionals, financiers and consultants. She partly hints at a wider notion in her own work, but it is as well to be explicit that not only the expansion of low-wage activities directly related to advanced services is being talked about, but also the growth of ancil-lary occupations—the cleaners and porters in the world's airports, the waiters in the French restaurants, the prosti-tutes in the night-clubs, the chamber-maids in the hotels, the seamstresses manufacturing *haute couture* clothes in the back streets of Paris, New York or London.

If this picture rings true and can be empirically demonstrated in the majority of 'world cities', it could then be said that the transnational division of labour is characterised by the following features: a further shrinkage of agricultural employment in the advanced capitalist countries; a stabilisation or slight drop in manufacturing employment in these countries; an increase in information-related employment; and a growth in strategic world cities of service employment. The growth in service employment demand can be met either by transferring migrant labourers from the old manufacturing and public sector labour market or by triggering sufficient growth to encourage the development of further migrant employment—conceivably much of it illegal. Within Third World cities the accelerating pace of urbanisation indicates a further shift off the land; and some of these new urbanites will find employment in transnational companies spreading their operations abroad. Others will be forced to take employment, mainly as construction workers in the oil-rich economies. But as the price of oil drops on the world market, so this avenue of employment is declining. Illegal international migration to the industrial economies, informal activities in and around the Third World cities and, in extreme cases, the collapse into refugee status, now present the major alternatives confronting many Third World peoples.

Conclusion

In developing my critique of NIDL theory, emphasis was laid on three aspects—the lack of conceptual clarity in the German theorists, the historical gaps apparent in their neglect of a century marked by colonialism and imperialism, and some empirical omissions in the contemporary period. I have myself preferred a conceptual model concentrating on the changing division of labour in respect of the different mix of labour forms apparent in each phase identified. This conforms to the broad thesis advanced throughout this book,

251

namely that capitalism has been characterised by a combination of unfree and free labour regimes from its genesis to the present day.

While clear differences exist between each period—mercantile, industrial, imperial and transnational—in the forms of labour deployed, there is also a sense of historical continuity rather than rupture. In each phase a mix of 'free' and 'unfree' labour forms is evident. Equally, the hoary contest between capital and the labour ever takes place, with the conflict being particularly acute in relation to the freer section of the labour force. Whenever the balance of advantage tilts to the side of organised labour, capitalists move from seeking to subordinate labour to seeking subordinate labourers. This book has broadly surveyed the historical process whereby capital reaches out to neophyte cohorts of external proletarians and described the workings of the process in three major regional political economies in much more detail. Whereas for many Marxists the phenomenon was seen as unproblematic—simply the realisation of capitalism on a world scale—Luxemburg (1951) and the Austrian Marxist Bauer (discussed in Tarbuck 1972) were the first to debate the political implications of the interrupted and often partial spread of capitalism to the areas we now call the Third World. For example, Luxemburg (in Tarbuck 1972: 24) argued that:

> Since capitalist production can develop fully only with complete access to all territories and climes, it can no more confine itself to the natural resources and productive forces of the temperate zone than it can manage with white labour alone. Capital needs other races to exploit, territories where the white man cannot work. It must be able to mobilise world labour-power without restriction in order to utilise all productive forces of the globe—up to the limits imposed by a system of producing surplus value.

Despite this insight, Luxemburg laid more emphasis on the migration of European labourers to the colonies and scoffed at Bauer (and Lenin) who saw the likelihood of a movement going the other way. Again, whereas she saw the necessity for capitalism to capture non-capitalist *markets* to survive, she rather discounted the possibilities of finding

252

large cohorts of subordinate labour-power in the colonies, having been misled by the mining companies and settler cries of labour shortage. It was left to Bauer to perceive that there were huge untapped resources there for capital, once self-sustaining rural producers could be detached from the land. By failing to analyse the history and practice of imperialism the NIDL theorists have been unable to see that the phenomenon they identify is part of a much older game: one that has always had profound implications for the survival of the system itself. As Bauer (in Tarbuck 1972: 142) puts it:

> Capitalism will not collapse from the mechanical impossibility of realising surplus value. It will be defeated by the rebellion to which it drives the masses. Not until then, when the last peasant and the last petty bourgeois change into wage workers, thus no longer providing a surplus market, will capitalism disintegrate.

Theoretically, Bauer's position is still correct. There can be no socialist revolution in one country (including the countries which garland themselves with that label) because the capitalists can apparently endlessly export or displace their contradictions on to the next wave of helots they alight upon, at home or abroad. But the theory is a difficult one to sustain in the ultimate sense. We can no longer comfortably make evolutionary assumptions characteristic of pre-1945 political theory, left and right. Despite the fierce denunciations of the left, capitalism does not seem too *strong* but too *weak*—in the sense that it seems unable to produce employment for all, given the exponential population growth, the unemployment time bomb and an even more potent bomb capable of destroying the globe before capitalism can realise its immanent possibilities.

Further reading

Because this book was intended for use as a general text, I have sacrificed more elaborate theoretical exegesis in favour of descriptive and empirical material. This has meant that some scholarly debates are dealt with in a rather abbreviated manner. I have tried, nonetheless, to indicate the main lines of theoretical dispute and to take a clear position where my reading and the evidence cited warranted this. The purpose of this note on further reading is to identify the most important or most contentious authors in the field so as to permit recent students to extend their reading without having to track down too many of the obscure references cited.

On the question of the relationship between capitalism and unfree labour discussed in Chapter 1, an old but still comprehensive account is provided by Kloosterboer (1960) while a good literature survey with more up-to-date references is found in Corrigan (1977). Wallerstein's (1974) book starting his multi-volume history of capitalism, is an implicit attack on Marx's (1976) view that capitalism is only compatible with free labour. A complementary account by Wolf (1982), not discussed in my text, focuses on groups that have remained tangential to European social analysis. A forthcoming book by Miles is likely to add an important discussion to this debate.

254

Theories of migration are advanced by a wide range of demographers, geographers, sociologists and economists. Lee's (1969) article is the most concise statement of the conventional position though Ravenstein's (1885, 1889) classical papers are still worth reading. A reassessment of Ravenstein is provided by Grigg (1977). One of the most eminent post-war scholars in the field was Thomas (1973) who has also written a crisp entry on 'Migration' in the standard reference book, the *Encyclopaedia of the Social Sciences*, which students should refer to. The revival of Marxist and neo-Marxist interest in this field is shown in the work of Nikolinakos (1975), Portes and Walton (1981), and the collectively-written book of the History Task Force (1979). Though focusing on Puerto Rico, the introductory sections of the last-mentioned book provide an intelligent review of the various starting points in the study of migration, though concluding with a pro-Marxist position.

The issue of the reproduction of labour-power addressed in Chapter 4 is extensively debated in the feminist literature and a good way to approach this question is to examine back issues of the *Feminist Review*. Other useful sources include Young *et al.* (1981), Kuhn and Wolpe (1978) and Meillassoux (1981).

While Marxists and feminists have made a powerful contribution to the literature on reproduction and to the theory of migration, many writers from these schools fall into a functionalist trap in trying to locate the economic role of migrant workers. Though these writers supply a good deal of valuable material, this tendency can be observed in Castells (1979), Nikolinakos (1975), and Wolpe (1972) as well as in the work of conventional economists like Kindleberger (1967). More complex views can be obtained in Burawoy (1976) and in significant passages in Castles and Kosack (1973). Much of the US literature, which has only had a limited impact in Europe, discusses the economic role of migrants in terms of 'dual' or 'segmented' labour markets. Piore (1979) has been an important figure in this debate, as have Gordon *et al.* (1982).

On what I have called 'policing the frontiers' (Chapter 5) there is no established literature as such, though I have drawn attention to the work of a political geographer, Boggs (1940), a sociologist, Petras (1980) and two urban theorists, Harloe (1977) and Castells (1977). Though this *is* an obscure reference for somebody working in a North American or European library, if the reader is able to obtain a copy of the Riekert Commission (1978), it provides a fascinating insight into how one state (South Africa) polices its internal frontiers.

Concerning the pattern of habituation experienced and resistance undertaken by migrant workers, I found Friedland and Nelkin (1971), Galarza (1977) and Harper *et al.* (1974) instructive sources on patterns of control. Patterns of resistance are described in van Onselen (1976), Cohen (1980), Golding (1985), Sivanandan (1982), Levy (1975) and Kushner (1975), amongst many possible sources.

Finally, on the 'new international division of labour' the most powerful account is that by Fröbel *et al.* (1980), but other important references include Ernst (1980), Jenkins's (1984) critique of Fröbel, Nash and Fernandez-Kelly (1983) and Nørlund *et al.* (1984), the last containing some rich descriptive material on women workers in the export-processing zones of south Asia.

References

Abadan-Unat, N. *et al.* 1976, *Migration and development: a study of the effects of international labour migration on Bogazliyan district*, Ankara, Ajan-Turk Press.

Abraham-Van der Mark, E. E. 1983, 'The impact of industrialisation on women: a Caribbean case' in J. Nash & M. P. Fernandez-Kelly (eds) q.v.

Acuña, R. 1972, *Occupied America: the Chicanos' struggle toward liberation*, San Francisco, Canfield Press.

Adamson, A. 1972, *Sugar without slaves: the political economy of British Guyana, 1834–1964*, New Haven, Yale University Press.

African Labour News (Brussels), bi-monthly journal of the International Confederation of Free Trade Unions, Africa Information Service.

Alvarez, J. H. 1967, *Return migration to Puerto Rico*, Berkeley, University of California Press.

Amin, S. 1974, *Accumulation on a world scale*, 2 vols, New York, Monthly Review Press.

Arrighi, G. 1983, 'The labour movement in twentieth-century western Europe', in I. Wallerstein (ed) q.v.

Bach, R. L. *et al.* 1981–1982, 'The "Flotilla Entrants": latest and most controversial', *Cuban studies*, vol. 11, no. 2 and vol. 12, no. 1, July (1981)–Jan (1982), pp. 30–48.

Bagchi, A. K. 1982, *The political economy of underdevelopment*, Cambridge, Cambridge University Press.

Baird, P. & McCaughan E. 1979, *Beyond the border*, New York, North American Congress on Latin America.

Baldwin, R. (ed) 1953, *A new slavery: forced labor, the communist betrayal of human rights*, New York, Oceana Publications.

Barlett, F. P. & Howell, B. 1944, *The population problem in Puerto Rico*, San Juan, Planning, Urbanizing & Zoning Board of the Government of Puerto Rico.

Barnet, R. T. & Müller R. E. 1974, *Global reach: the powers of the multinational corporations*, New York, Simon & Schuster.

Baumgart, W. 1982, *Imperialism: the idea and reality of British & French colonial expansion*, London, Oxford University Press.

Beinart, W. 1982, *The political economy of Pondoland, 1860–1930*, Cambridge, Cambridge University Press.

Bennholdt-Thomsen, V. 1981, 'Subsistence production and extended reproduction', in K. Young *et al.* (eds) q.v.

Berger, J. & Mohr, J. 1975, *A seventh man*, Harmondsworth, Penguin Books.

Bergman, L. *et al.* 1977, *Puerto Rico, the flame of resistance*, San Francisco, Peoples Press.

Beveridge, W. H. 1944, *Full employment in a free society*, London, Allen & Unwin.

Birks, J. S. & Sinclair, C. A. 1980, *International migration and development in the Arab region*, Geneva, International Labour Organisation.

Bisharat, M. 1975, 'Yemeni farmworkers in California', *MERIP reports*, no. 34, Jan, pp. 22–6.

Bluestone, B. & Harrison, B. 1982, *The deindustrialisation of America*, New York, Basic Books.

Boggs, S. W. 1940, *International boundaries: a study of boundary functions and problems*, New York, Columbia University Press.

Bogre, M. 1979, 'Haitian refugees: (Haiti's) missing persons', *Migration today*, vol. 8, no. 4, September, pp. 9–11.

Böhning, W. R. 1972, *The migration of workers in the United Kingdom and the European Community*, London, Oxford University Press.

Böhning, W. R. (ed) 1981, *Black migration to South Africa: a*

258

selection of policy-oriented research, Geneva, International Labour Organisation.

Bonilla, F. & Campos, R. 1981, 'A wealth of poor: Puerto Ricans in the new economic order', *Daedalus*, vol. 110, no. 2, pp. 133–76.

Borkin, J. 1978, *The crime and punishment of I. G. Farben*, Glencoe, The Free Press.

Braham, P. *et al.* (eds) 1981, *Discrimination and disadvantage in employment: the experience of black workers*, London, Harper & Row.

Braverman, H. 1974, *Labor and monopoly capital*, New York, Monthly Review Press.

Briggs, V. M. jr. 1978, 'Foreign policy implications of illegal immigration from Mexico', Testimony before the Committee on International Relations, *US House of Representatives*, 24 May (mimeographed copy).

Brockway, L. H. 1980, *Science & colonial expansion: the role of the British Royal Botanic Gardens*, London, Academic Press.

Bromberger, N. 1978, 'Mining employment in South Africa, 1946–2000', *South African labour and development research unit*, Working Papers, University of Cape Town, no. 15, Aug.

Brown, B. 1983, 'The impact of male labour migration on women in Botswana', *African Affairs*, vol. 82, no. 328, July, pp. 367–88.

Buchanan, S. H. 1979, 'Haitian women in New York City', *Migration Today*, vol. 8, no. 4, pp. 19–25.

Bundy, C. 1979, *The rise and fall of the South African peasantry*, London, Heinemann Educational Books.

Burawoy, M. 1976, 'The functions and reproduction of migrant labor: comparative material from South Africa and the United States', *American Journal of Sociology*, vol. 81, no. 5, pp. 1050–87.

Burawoy, M. 1979, *Manufacturing consent: changes in the labour process under monopoly capitalism*, Chicago, University of Chicago Press.

Cadbury, W. A. 1910, *Labour in Portuguese West Africa*, London, Routledge

Callaghan, J. 1946, Speech in parliament, *Parliamentary*

debates/Commons (Hansard), series 5, vol. 424 (1945–6)
19 June, col. 3346–456.

Castells, M. 1977, *The urban question*, London, Edward
Arnold.

Castells, M. 1979, 'Immigrant workers and class struggles in
advanced capitalism: the Western European experience'
in R. Cohen *et al.* (eds) q.v.

Castles, S. 1980, 'The social time bomb: education of an
underclass in West Germany', *Race & Class*, vol. 21, no.
4, pp. 369–88.

Castles, S. 1984, 'Racism and politics in West Germany'
Race & Class, vol. 25, no. 3, pp. 39–51.

Castles, S. & Kosack, G. 1973, *Immigrant workers and class
structure in western Europe*, London, Oxford University
Press.

Castles, S. & Kosack, G. 1981, 'The function of labour
immigration in western European capitalism' in P. Braham *et al.* (eds) q.v.

Castles, S. *et al.* 1984, *Here for good: western Europe's new
ethnic minorities*, London, Pluto Press.

Chann, L. H. *et al.* 1984, 'Women workers in Malaysia
TNCs and social conditions' in I. Nørlund *et al.* (eds) q.v.

Chapman, L. F. 1976, 'Illegal aliens: time to call a halt'
Reader's Digest, no. 109, October.

Claasens, A. *et al.* 1980, 'The reserve army, legislation and
labour action in South Africa', *Africa Perspective*, no. 1,
summer, pp. 34–46.

Cock, J. *et al.* 1983, 'Women and changing relations of
control' in South African Research Service (ed) *South
African review I: same foundations, new facades*, Johannesburg, Ravan Press, pp. 278–99.

Cohen, B. G. & Jenner, P. J. 1968, 'The employment of
immigrants: a case study within the wool industry', *Race*
vol. 10, pp. 41–56.

Cohen, D. W. & Greene, J. P. (eds) 1972. *Neither slave nor
free: the freedmen of African descent in the slave societies of
the new world*, Baltimore, Johns Hopkins University
Press.

Cohen, R. 1974, *Labour and politics in Nigeria*, London,
Heinemann Educational Books.

Cohen, R. 1980, 'Resistance & hidden forms of consciousness among African workers', *Review of African political economy*, no. 19, Sept–Dec, pp. 8–22.

Cohen, R. 1983, St Helena: welfare colonialism in practice', in R. Cohen (ed) *African islands and enclaves*, Beverly Hills and London, Sage Publications.

Cohen, R. & Harris, C. 1977, 'Migration, capital and the labour process', unpublished seminar paper, Birmingham University.

Cohen, R. *et al.* (eds) 1979, *Peasants and proletarians: the struggles of Third World workers*, New York, Monthly Review Press.

Cohen, S. 1972, *Folk devils and moral panics*, London, MacGibben & Kee.

Cooper, C. 1981, 'Verdicts on South Africa's new labour act' *Africa Bureau*, Document Paper no. 27, London, African Publications Trust, November/December.

Cooper, F. 1980, *From slaves to squatters: plantation labour and agriculture in Zanzibar and coastal Kenya, 1890–1925*, New Haven, Yale University Press.

Cornelius, W. (n.d.) 'Briefing paper on illegal Mexican migration to the US', prepared for the National Security Council, Cambridge, Massachusetts Institute of Technology.

Corrigan, P. 1977, 'Feudal relics or capitalist monuments? Notes in the sociology of unfree labour', *Sociology*, vol. 11, pp. 435–63.

Craig, R. B. 1971, *The Bracero Program*, Austin, University of Texas Press.

Cross, M. 1981, 'Migrant workers in European cities: concentration, conflict and social policy', Report for the Council of Europe, *SSRC Research Unit on Ethnic Relations*.

CSE (Conference of Socialist Economists) 1977, *On the political economy of women*, London, Stage I for the CSE.

Dalla Costa, M. & James, S. 1975, *The power of women and the subversion of the community*, Bristol, Falling Wall Press.

Dallin, D. J. & Nicolaevsky, B. I. 1948, *Forced labour in Soviet Russia*, London, Hollis & Carter.

Daniel, P. 1972, *The shadow of slavery: peonage in the south, 1901–1969*, New York, Oxford University Press.

Davies, I. 1966, *African trade unions*, Harmondsworth, Penguin Books.

Davies, R. 1978, 'The 1922 strike on the road: white labor & the political economy of South Africa', in P. C. W. Gutkind *et al.* (eds) *African labor history*, Beverly Hills, Sage.

Dekker, L. D. *et al.* 1975, 'Case studies in labour action in South Africa and Namibia' in R. Sandbrook and R. Cohen (eds) *The development of an African working class: studies in class formation and action*, London, Longman.

Delius, P. 1980, 'Migrant labour and the Pedi, 1840–1880', in S. Marks & A. Atmore (eds) *Economy and society in pre-industrial South Africa*, London, Longman, pp. 293–312.

Delius, P. & Trapido, S. 1983, 'Inboekselings and oorlams: the creation and transformation of a servile class' in B. Bozzoli (ed) *Town and countryside in the Transvaal*, Johannesburg, Ravan Press.

deWind, J. 1982, 'Undocumented workers and the labour market, the impact of employers', unpublished paper presented at the 44th Congress of Americanists, University of Manchester, UK, September.

Dietz, J. 1976, 'The Puerto Rican political economy', *Latin American Perspectives*, vol. 3, no. 3, summer, pp. 3–12.

Diffie, B. W. & Diffie, J. 1931, *Puerto Rico, a broken pledge*, New York, Vanguard Press.

Dubofsky, M. 1983, 'Workers' movements in North America 1873–1970', in I. Wallerstein (ed) *Labour in the world social structure*, Beverly Hills, Sage.

Dominguez, V. M. 1982, 'Puerto Rico: colonial showcase', *Columbia report: US-Latin America and international analysis*, vol. 4, no. 1, March, pp. 6–9.

Duffield, M. R. 1981, 'Racism and counter-revolution in the era of imperialism: a critique', paper for the annual conference of the Conference of Socialist Economists, Bradford.

Dunbar, T. & Kravitz, L. 1976, *Hard travelling: migrant farm workers in America*, Cambridge (Mass), Ballinger Publishing Company.

Durkheim, E. 1970, *Suicide: a study in sociology*, London, Routledge & Kegan Paul.

Echenberg, M. 1975, 'Paying the blood tax: military conscription in French West Africa', *Canadian Journal of African Studies*, vol. 9, pp. 171–92.

Elson, D. & Pearson, R. 1981, '"Nimble fingers make cheap workers": an analysis of women's employment in Third World export manufacturing', *Feminist Review*, no. 7.

Engerman, S. 1973, 'Some considerations relating to property rights in man', *Journal of Economic History*, vol. 33.

Epstein, A. L. 1958, *Politics in an urban African community*, Manchester, Manchester University Press.

Ernst, D. 1980, *The new international division of labour: technology and underdevelopment*, Frankfurt, Campus Verlag.

Ferencz, B. B. 1979, *Less than slaves: Jewish forced labor and the quest for compensation*, Boston, Harvard University Press.

Fernandez, R. A. 1977, *The United States-Mexico border: a politico-economic profile*, Notre Dame, University of Notre Dame Press.

Finley, M. I. 1980, *Ancient slavery and modern ideology*, London, Chatto and Windus.

Finley, M.I. 1981, *Economy and society in Ancient Greece*, London, Chatto and Windus.

First, R. 1983, *Black Gold: The Mozambican miner, proletariat and peasant*, Sussex, The Harvester Press.

Foner, P. 1964, *History of the labor movement in the United States*, New York, International Publishers.

Forrest, W. G. 1966, *The emergence of Greek democracy*, London, Weidenfeld.

Fraginals, M. M. 1976, *The sugarmill: the socio-economic complex of sugar in Cuba, 1760–1860*, New York, Monthly Review Press.

Frank, A. G. 1967, *Capitalism and underdevelopment in Latin America*, New York, Monthly Review Press.

Frank, A. G. 1969, *Latin America: underdevelopment or revolution*, New York, Monthly Review Press.

Frank, A. G. 1981, *Crisis: in the Third World*, London, Heinemann Educational Books.

Fraser, P. 1981, 'The fictive peasantry: Caribbean rural groups in the nineteenth century' in S. Craig (ed) *Contemporary Caribbean: a sociological reader*, Trinidad, The Editor, pp. 319–47.

Freeman, G. P. 1979, *Immigrant labor and racial conflict in industrial societies, 1945–1975*, Princeton, Princeton University Press.

Friedland, W. H. & Nelkin, D. 1971, *Migrant agricultural workers in America's Northeast*, New York, Holt, Rinehart & Winston.

Friedlander, S. 1865, *Labor, migration and economic growth*, Cambridge (Massachusetts), Massachusetts Institute of Technology Press.

Friedman, J. 1985, 'The world city hypothesis', Unpublished paper, Conference on the International Division of Labor, Centre of Urban Studies and International Sociological Association, University of Hong Kong, August.

Fröbel, F. *et al.* 1980, *The new international division of labour*, Cambridge, Cambridge University Press.

Frost, E. C. *et al.* (eds) 1979, *El trabajo y los trabajadores en la historia de México*, México, D.F. and Tucson, El Colegio de México & University of Arizona Press,

Galarza, E. 1977, *Farm workers and agribusiness in California, 1947–1960*, Notre Dame, University of Notre Dame Press.

Garcia, J. R. 1980, *Operation wetback: the mass deportation of Mexican undocumented workers in 1954*, Westport (Cnt), Greenwood Press.

Garnsey, E. 1981, 'The rediscovery of the division of labour', *Theory & Society*, vol. 10, no. 2.

Genovese, E. D. 1967, *The political economy of slavery*, New York, Pantheon Press.

Glazer, N. & Moynihan, D. P. 1963, *Beyond the melting pot: the Negroes, Puerto Ricans, Jews, Italians and Irish of New York City*, Cambridge (Mass), Massachusetts Institute of Technology Press.

Godfrey, M. 1977. 'Surplus population and underdevelopment: reserve army or marginal mass', *Manpower and unemployment research*, vol. 10, no. 1, pp. 63–71.

264

Golding, M. 1985, 'Mass struggles on the mines', *South African Labour Bulletin*, vol. 10, no. 6, May, pp. 101–22.

Golding, M. 1985a, 'Mass dismissals on the mines: the workers' story', *South African Labour Bulletin*, vol. 10, no. 7, June, pp. 97–113.

Gonsalez, R. A. 1977, 'The Chicana in south-west labour history, 1900–1975: a preliminary bibliographic analysis', mimeographed Paper, Program in Comparative Culture, University of California, Irvine.

Goodman, D. & Redclift, M. 1981, *From peasant to proletarian: capitalist development and agrarian transitions*, Oxford, Basil Blackwell.

Gordon, D. M. *et al.* 1982, *Segmented work, divided workers: the historical transformation of labor in the United States*, Cambridge, Cambridge University Press.

Gordon, R. J. 1977, *Mines, masters and migrants: life in a Namibian mine compound*, Johannesburg, Ravan Press.

Gorz, A. 1971, 'Avant-propos-le colloque de Tarquinia', *Partisans*, no. 61.

Granotier, B. 1973, *Les travailleurs immigrés en France*, Paris, Maspero.

Green, W. 1976, *British slave emancipation: the sugar colonies and the great experiment*, Oxford, Clarendon Press.

Grigg, D. B. 1977, 'E. G. Ravenstein and the "laws of migration"', *Journal of Historical Geography*, vol. 3, pp. 41–54.

Gutiérrez, C. M. 1972, *The Dominican Republic: rebellions and repression*, New York, Monthly Review Press.

Guzman, R. 1978, 'La repatriación forzosa como solución política concluyente al problema de la immigración ilegal: una perspectiva histórica', *Foro Internacional*, vol. 18, no. 3, pp. 496–508.

Hall, S. *et al.* 1978, *Policing the crisis: mugging, the state and law and order*, London, Macmillan.

Halliday, F. 1977, 'Labour migration in the Middle East', *MERIP Reports*, no. 59, pp. 1–17.

Handlin, O. 1953, *The uprooted*, London, Watts & Co.

Handman, M. S. 1930, 'Economic reasons for the coming of the Mexican immigrant', *American Journal of Sociology*, vol. 35, no. 4, pp. 601–11.

Hammer, T. 1982, 'Swedish immigration policy: a country report', paper for the *Swedish Commission on Immigration Research*, Stockholm. A version of this paper is published in T. Hammer (ed), 1985, *European immigration policy*, Cambridge, Cambridge University Press.

Harloe, M. (ed) 1977, *Captive cities: studies in the political economy of cities and regions*, London, John Wiley.

Harloe, M. and Lebas, E. (eds) 1981, *City, class and capital*, London, Edward Arnold.

Harper, D., Mills, B. & Parris, R. 1974, 'Exploitation in migrant labour camps', *British Journal of Sociology*, vol. 25, pp. 183–211.

Harris, M. 1959, 1960, 'Labour emigration among the Mozambique Thonga: cultural and political factors', *Africa*, vol. 29, pp. 50–56, and vol. 30, pp. 243–50.

Harris, N. 1980, 'The new untouchables: the international migration of labour', *International Socialism*, vol. 2, no. 8, pp. 37–63.

Head, J. 1980, *State, capital and migrant labour in Zambezia, Mozambique: study of the labour force of Sena Sugar Estates Limited*, Durham University, PhD thesis.

Heine, J. 1981, 'Puerto Rico, from bad to worse', *Guardian Weekly*, 13 December.

Henderson, J. 1985, 'The new international division of labour and urban development in the contemporary world-system' in D. Drakakis-Smith (ed), *Urbanisation in the developing world*, London, Croom Helm.

Henderson, J. & Cohen, R. 1982, 'On the reproduction of the relations of production', in R. Forrest *et al.* (eds), *Urban political economy and social theory*, Aldershot, Gower, pp. 112–43.

Henderson, J. & Cohen, R. 1982a, 'The international restructuring of capital and labour: Britain and Hong Kong', unpublished paper, World Congress of Sociology, *International Sociological Association*, Mexico City, August.

Hendricks, G. 1974, *The Dominican diaspora*, New York, New Teachers College Press.

Hennessy, A. 1978, *The frontier in Latin American history*, London, Edward Arnold.

266

Hindess, B. & Hirst, P. Q. 1975, *Pre-capitalist modes of production*, London, Routledge & Kegan Paul.

Hindess, B. & Hirst, P. Q. 1977, *Modes of production and social formation*, London, Macmillan.

Hirson, B. 1979, *Year of fire, year of ash: the Soweto revolt, roots of a revolution?* London, Zed Press.

History Task Force, Centro de Estudios Puertorriqueños, 1979, *Labour migration under capitalism: the Puerto Rican experience*, New York, Monthly Review Press.

Hobsbawm, E. 1964, *Labouring men*, London, Weidenfeld & Nicolson.

Hoffman-Nowotny, H. J. 1982, 'Immigration policy in Switzerland', draft report for the study of Swedish and European immigration policy, Soziologisches Institut, University of Zurich.

Homse, E. L. 1967, *Foreign labor in Nazi Germany*, Princeton, Princeton University Press.

Hopkins, T. K. 1977, 'Patterns of development of the modern world-system', *Review*, vol. 1, no. 2, pp. 111–45.

Hopkins, T. K. 1979, 'The study of the capitalist world-economy: some introductory considerations', in W. L. Goldfrank (ed), *The world-system of capitalism: past and present*, Beverly Hills, Sage.

Hymer, S. 1979, *The multinational corporation: a radical approach*, Cambridge, Cambridge University Press.

Innes, D. 1984, *Anglo American & the rise of modern South Africa*, London, Heinemann Educational Books.

Innes, D. & O'Meara, D. 1976, 'Class formation and ideology: the Transkei region', *Review of African Political Economy*, no. 7, pp. 69–86.

Institute for Industrial Education, 1979, 'The Durban strikes: South Africa 1973', in R. Cohen *et al.* (eds) *Peasants and proletarians: the struggle of Third World workers*, London, Hutchinson.

International Labour Office 1981, *Employment effects of multinational enterprises in industrialised countries*, Geneva, ILO.

International Labour Organisation 1984, *World labour report I: employment incomes, social protection, new information technology*, Geneva: ILO.

267

Jackson, J. A. 1963, *The Irish in Britain*, London, Routledge & Kegan Paul.

Jackson, J. A. (ed) 1969, *Migration*, London, Cambridge University Press.

Jenkins, C. & Sherman, B. 1979, *The collapse of work*, London, Eyre Methuen.

Jenkins, R. 1984, 'Divisions over the international division of labour', *Capital & Class*, no. 22, spring, pp. 28–57.

Joshi, S. & Carter, B. 1984, 'The role of Labour in the creation of a racist Britain', *Race and class*, vol. 25, no. 3, pp. 53–70.

Kalecki, M. 1971, 'The political aspects of full employment' in his *Selected essays on the dynamics of the capitalist economy*, Cambridge, Cambridge University Press.

Kidron, M. & Segal, R. 1981, *The state of the world atlas*, London, Heinemann Educational Books.

Kindleberger, C. P. 1967, *Europe's post-war growth: the role of labor supply*, Cambridge, Harvard University Press.

Kiser, G. C. and Kiser, H. W. (eds) 1979, *Mexican workers in the United States: historical and political perspectives*, Albuquerque, University of New Mexico Press.

Kloosterboer, W. 1960, *Involuntary labour since the abolition of slavery: a survey of compulsory labour throughout the world*, Leiden, E. J. Brill.

Korman, G. 1967, *Industrialisation, immigrants and Americanisers*, Madison, State Historical Society of Wisconsin.

Korte, H. 1985, 'The established German and their foreign migrant outsiders', Paper for the Annual Conference of the *Association for the Study of German Politics*, University of Surrey, April 11–13.

Kritz, M. M. 1981, 'International migration patterns in the Caribbean basin: an overview' in M. M. Kritz *et al.* (eds) q.v.

Kritz, M. M. *et al.* (eds) 1981. *Global trends in migration: theory and research on international population movements*, New York, Center for Migration Studies.

Kuhn, A. 1978, 'Structures of patriarchy and capital in the family', in A. Kuhn and A. Wolpe (eds), q.v.

Kuhn, A. & Wolpe, A. (eds) 1978, *Feminism and materialism:*

women and modes of production, London, Routledge & Kegan Paul.

Kushner, S. 1975, *Long road to Delano: a century of farm-workers' struggle*, New York, International Publishers.

Lacey, T. 1977, *Violence and politics in Jamaica, 1960–1970: internal security in a developing country*, Manchester, Manchester University Press.

Laclau, E. 1971, 'Feudalism and capitalism in Latin America', *New Left Review*, no. 67.

Layton-Henry, Z. 1982, 'British immigration policy since 1945', mimeographed paper, Dept of Politics, University of Warwick.

Lee, E. S. 1969, 'A theory of migration', in J. A. Jackson (ed) q.v.

Lefebvre, H. 1976, *The survival of capitalism*, London, Allison & Busby.

Legassick, M. and de Clerq, F. 1984, 'Capitalism and migrant labour in southern Africa: the origins and nature of the system', in S. Marks & P. Richardson (eds) q.v.

Lever, J. 1981, 'Capital & labor in South Africa: the passage of the Industrial Conciliation Act, 1924', in E. Webster (ed) q.v.

Levy. J. E. 1975, *Cesar Chavez: autobiography of La Causa*, New York, W.W. Norton & Co.

Levy, N. 1982, *The foundations of the South African cheap labour system*, London, Routledge & Kegan Paul.

Lewis, G. 1974, *Notes on the Puerto Rican revolution*, New York, Monthly Review Press.

Lewis, G. A. 1974a, *Puerto Rico: freedom and power in the Caribbean*, New York, Monthly Review Press.

Lewis, W. A. 1954, 'Economic development with unlimited supplies of labour, *The Manchester School of Economics & Social Studies*, vol. 23, May.

Lin, V. 1985, 'Health, women's work and industrialisation: women workers in the semi-conductor industry in Singapore and Malaysia'. Unpublished paper, Conference on the International Division of Labour, Centre of Urban Studies and International Sociological Association, University of Hong Kong, August.

Lincoln Letter: X-ray on South Africa, periodic newsletter issued by the Lincoln Trust (London and New York).

Lipton, M. 1980, 'Men of two worlds, migrant labour in South Africa', *Optima*, no. 29.

Lipton, M. 1985, *Capitalism and Apartheid*, Aldershot, Temple Smith/Gower.

Lodge, T. 1983, *Black politics in South Africa since 1945*, Johannesburg, Ravan Press.

Lopez, A. & Petras, J. (eds) 1974, *Puerto Rico and Puerto Ricans*, New York, John Wiley & Sons.

Louis, W. R. & Stengers, J. 1968, *E. D. Morel's history of the Congo movement*, Oxford, Clarendon Press.

Luxemburg, R. 1951, *The accumulation of capital*, London, Routledge & Kegan Paul.

Maciel, D. R. 1977, *La otra cara de México: el pueblo chicano la raza unida*, Los Angeles, Tlaquilo Publications.

MacShane, D. *et al.* 1984, *Power! Black workers, their unions & the struggle for freedom in South Africa*, Nottingham, Spokesman.

Magdoff, H. 1978, *Imperialism: from the colonial age to the present*, New York, Monthly Review Press.

Magubane, B. 1979, *The political economy of race and class in South Africa*, New York, Monthly Review Press.

Majka, T. 1980, 'Poor people's movements & farm labor insurgency', *Contemporary Crisis*, vol. 4, no. 3, July.

Maldonaldo-Denis, M. 1972, *Puerto Rico: a socio-historical interpretation*, New York, Vintage Books.

Maldonaldo-Denis, M. 1976, *Puerto Rico y estados unidos: emigración y colonialism*, Mexico, Siglo Veintiuno.

Mandel, E. 1978, *Late capitalism*, London, Verso.

Maré, G. 1983, 'Africans under apartheid in the 1980's in South African Research Service (ed), *South African Review I: same foundations, new facades?* Johannesburg, Ravan Press, pp. 72–81.

Marshall, A. 1973, *The import of labour*, Rotterdam, Rotterdam University Press.

Marshall, R. 1974, *Rural workers in rural labor markets*, Salt Lake City, Olympus Publishing Company.

Martin, P. L. 1981, 'Immigration 1981: the US Debate'. Unpublished paper.

Martin, W. G. 1983, 'Cycles, trends or transformations? black labour migration to the South African gold mines in the long twentieth century', paper for the seventh annual political economy of the world system conference, Centre for International Studies, Duke University, 30 March–1 April, p. 28.

Marx, K. 1976, *Capital: a critique of political economy, Vol. one*, Harmondsworth, Penguin Books.

Marx, K. & Engels, F. 1971, *Ireland and the Irish question*, Moscow, Progress Publishers.

Massey, D. 1984, *Spatial divisions of labour: social structures and the geography of production*, London, Macmillan.

McDonough, R. & Harrison, R. 1978, 'Patriarchy and relations of production' in A. Kuhn & A. Wolpe (eds) q.v.

McWilliams, C. 1971, *Factories in the fields: the story of migratory farm labor in California*, Santa Barbara, Peregrine Smith Inc.

Meer, Y. S. 1980, *Documents of indentured labour: Natal 1851–1917*, Durban, Institute of Black Research.

Meillassoux, C. 1981, *Maidens, meal and money: capitalism and the domestic economy*, Cambridge, Cambridge University Press.

Mikes, G. 1946, *How to be an alien: a handbook for beginners and more advanced pupils*, London, Deutsch.

Miles, R. 1982, *Racism and migrant labour*, London, Routledge & Kegan Paul.

Miles, R. forthcoming, *Anomaly or necessity? capitalism and unfree labour*, London, Tavistock.

Miller, S. C. 1974, *The unwelcome immigrant: the American image of the Chinese, 1785–1882*, Berkeley, University of California Press.

Mills, C. W. *et al.* 1950, *The Puerto Rican journey*, New York, Harper & Brothers.

Mintz, S. 1974, *Caribbean transformations*, Chicago, Aldine.

Misham, E. J. 1970, 'Does immigration confer economic benefits on the host country', in Institute of Economic Affairs, *Economic issues in immigration*, London, IEA.

Misham, E. J. & Needleman, L. 1968, 'Immigration: long-run effects', *Lloyds Bank Review*, January.

Mitchell, C. 1959, 'Labour migration in Africa south of the

Sahara: the causes of labour migration', *Bulletin of the Inter-African Labour Institute*, vol. 6, no. 1, pp. 12–46.

Moore, B. 1966, *Social origins of dictatorship and democracy: lord and peasant in the making of the modern world*, Harmondsworth, Penguin University Books.

Moore, R. 1977, 'Migrants and the class structure of western Europe', in R. Scase (ed) *Industrial society: class, cleavage and control*, London, Allen & Unwin.

Morokvasic, M. 1983, 'Women in migration: beyond the reductionist outlook', in A. Phizacklea (ed) q.v.

Morony, S. 1981, 'Mine worker protest on the Witwatersrand, 1901–1912', in E. Webster (ed) q.v.

Mueller, C. F. 1981, *The economics of labour migration: a behavioural analysis*, New York, Academic Press.

Murray, C. 1979, 'Explaining migration: the tradition in eastern and southern Africa'. Unpublished paper, Institute of Commonwealth Studies, University of London.

Murray, C. 1981, *Families divided: the impact of migrant labour in Lesotho*, Cambridge, Cambridge University Press.

NACLA (North American Congress on Latin America) 1975, 'Hit and run: US runaway shops on the Mexican border', *NACLA's Latin American and Empire Report*, vol. 9, no. 5, July–Aug.

NACLA 1977, 'Immigration: facts and fallacies' (pamphlet).

NACLA 1977a, 'Caribbean immigration: contract labor in US agriculture', *NACLA's Report on the America's* vol. 10, no. 8, Nov–Dec.

Nash, J. & Fernandez-Kelly, M. P. (eds) 1983, *Women, men and the international division of labour*, Albany, State University of New York Press.

Nelson, E. 1975, *Pablo Cruz and the American dream*, Santa Barbara, Peregrine Smith Inc.

Nevinson, H. W. 1906, *A modern slavery*, London, Harper.

Nicholls, D. 1986, *Ethnicity, economy and revolt in Haiti*, London, Macmillan.

Nieboer, H. B. 1910, *Slavery as an industrial system*, The Hague, M. Nijhoff.

Nikolinakos, M. 1975, 'Notes towards a general theory of migration', *Race and Class*, vol. 17, no. 1, summer.

Noakes, T. D. 1980, Review of Ferencz q.v., *Times Higher Educational Supplement*, 18 April.

Nørlund, I. *et al.* (eds) 1984, *Industrialisation & the labour process in South-East Asia*, Rosenborg-gade, Institute of Cultural Sociology, University of Copenhagen.

Nzula, A. *et al.* 1979, *Forced labour in colonial Africa*, London, Zed Press.

Orde-Browne, G. St. J. 1967, *The African labourer*, London, Frank Cass & Co.

Pahl, R. E. 1984, *Divisions of labour*, Oxford, Basil Blackwell.

Palmer, R. & Parsons, N. (eds) 1977, *The roots of rural poverty in central and southern Africa*, London, Heinemann Educational Books.

Pandya, A. & Schey, P. A. 1981, 'Analysis of the Reagan immigration/refugee plan', *Immigration Law Bulletin*, vol. 2, no. 3, July–Aug.

Peil, M. 1971, 'The expulsion of West African aliens', *Journal of Modern African Studies*, vol. 9, no. 2, pp. 205–29.

Penenda-Ofreneo, R. 1984, 'Sub-contracting in export-oriented industries: impact on Filippino working women' in I. Nørlund *et al.* (eds) q.v.

Petras, E. 1980, 'The role of national boundaries in a cross-national labour market', *International Journal of Urban and Regional Research*, vol. 4, no. 2, pp. 157–95.

Philpott, S. B. 1973, *West Indian migration: the Montserrat case*, London, Athlone Press.

Phimister, I. & van Onselen, C. 1978, *Studies in the history of African mine labour in colonial Zimbabwe*, Gwelo, Mambo Press.

Phizacklea, A. (ed) 1983, *One way ticket: migration and female labour*, London, Routledge & Kegan Paul.

Phizacklea, A. & Miles, R. 1980, *Labour and racism*, London, Routledge & Kegan Paul.

Piore, M. 1975, 'The illegals: restrictions aren't the answer', *The New Republic*, vol. 172, February.

Piore, M. J. 1979, *Birds of passage: migrant labour and industrial societies*, Cambridge, Cambridge University Press.

273

Portes, A. & Walton, J. 1981, *Labor, class and the international system*, New York, Academic Press.

Power, J. 1979, *Migrant workers in western Europe and the United States*, Oxford, Pergamon Press.

Power, J. & Hardman, A. 1978, 'Western Europe's migrant workers', *Minority Rights Group*, Report No. 28, London, MRG.

Prescott, J. R. V. 1965, *The geography of frontiers and boundaries*, London, Hutchinson.

Pryce, K. 1979, *Endless pressure*, Harmondsworth, Penguin Books.

Puerto Rican Socialist Party 1975, *Political thesis of the Puerto Rican socialist party: the socialist alternative*, New York, published for the PRSP by the North American Congress on Latin America.

Puerto Rico, Government of, 1944, *A development plan for Puerto Rico*, San Juan, Planning. Urbanizing and Zoning Board.

Quintero Rivera, A. G. 1973, 'Background to the emergence of imperialist capitalism in Puerto Rico', *Caribbean Studies*, vol. 13, no. 3, October, pp. 31–63.

Ravenstein, E. G. 1885, 'The laws of migration', *Journal of the Statistical Society*, vol. 48, pp. 167–235.

Ravenstein, E. G. 1889, 'The laws of migration', *Journal of the Statistical Society*, vol. 52, pp. 214–301.

Rex, J. & Tomlinson, S. 1979, *Colonial immigrants in a British city*, London, Routledge & Kegan Paul.

Richardson, P. 1976, 'Coolies and landlords, the North Randfontein Chinese miners' strike of 1905', *Journal of Southern African Studies*, vol. 2, no. 2, pp. 151–77.

Richardson, P. 1984, 'Coolies, peasants and proletarians: the origins of Chinese indentured labour in South Africa, 1904–1907', in S. Marks and P. Richardson (eds), *International labour migration: historical perspectives*, London, Maurice Temple Smith for the Institute of Commonwealth Studies.

Richardson, P. & van Helten, J. J. 1983, 'Labour in the South African gold mining industry, 1886–1914' in S. Marks & R. Rathbone (eds) *Industrialisation & social change in South Africa*, London, Longman.

274

Riekert Commission 1978, *Commission of inquiry into legislation affecting the utilisation of manpower (excluding the legislation administered by the Departments of Labour and Mines)*, (Chairman P. J. Riekert), Pretoria, Government Printer.

Rockefeller, N. 1963, *The Rockefeller report on the Americas*, Chicago, Quadrangle Books.

Rosberg, G. 1978, 'Legal regulation of the migration process: the "crises" of illegal immigration' in W. H. McNeill & R. S. Adams (eds) *Human migration: patterns and policies*, Bloomington, Indiana University Press.

Roxborough, I. 1979, *Theories of underdevelopment*, London, Macmillan.

Russell, P. 1977, *Mexico in transition*, Austin, Colorado River Press.

Safa, H. I. 1974, *The urban poor of Puerto Rico, a study in development and inequality*, New York, Holt, Rinehart & Winston.

Salt, K. 1981, 'International labour migration in western Europe: a geographical review', in M. M. Kritz, *et al.* (eds), q.v. pp. 133–157.

Samora, J. 1971, *Los mojados: the wetback story*, Notre Dame, University of Notre Dame Press.

Samora, J. & Simon, P. V. 1977, *A history of the Mexican-American people*, Notre Dame, University of Notre Dame Press.

Santana, A. D. 1976, 'The role of Haitian braceros in Dominican sugar production', *Latin American Perspectives*, vol. 3, no. 1, winter, pp. 120–36.

Sassen-Koob, S. 1979, 'Economic growth and immigration in Venezuela', *International Migration Review*, vol. 13, no. 3, pp. 455–71.

Sassen-Koob, S. 1979a, 'Formal and informal associations: Dominicans and Colombians in New York', *International Migration Review*, vol. 13, no. 2, pp. 314–31.

Sassen-Koob, S. 1983, 'Capital mobility and labour migration: their expression in core cities' in R. Timberlake (ed), *Urbanisation in the world economy*, New York, Academic Press.

Sassen-Koob, S. 1984, 'The new labour demand in global

cities' in M. P. Smith (ed), *Cities in transformation*, Beverly Hill, Sage, pp. 139–71.

Saxton, A. 1971, *The indispensable enemy: labour and the anti-Chinese movement in California*, Berkeley, University of California Press.

Scarman, Lord, 1982, *The Scarman report: the Brixton disorders 10–12 April 1981*, Harmondsworth, Pelican Books.

Schapera, I. 1935, 'The social structure of a Tswana ward', *Bantu Studies*, vol. 9, pp. 203–24.

Schapera, I. 1947, *Migrant labour and tribal life*, London, Oxford University Press.

Schapera, I. & Roberts, S. 1975, 'Rampedi revisited: another look at a Tswana ward', *Africa*, vol. 45, no. 3, pp. 258–79.

Seccombe, W. 1974, 'The housewife and her labour under capitalism, *New Left Review*, no. 83.

Seeley, J. R. 1883, *The expansion of England*, London.

Seldon, M. 1983, 'The proletariat, revolutionary change, and the state in China and Japan, 1850–1950', in I. Wallerstein (ed), *Labour in the world social structure*, Beverly Hills, Sage.

Senior, C. 1961, *The Puerto Ricans, strangers then neighbours*, Chicago, Quadrangle Books.

Servin, M. P. 1974, *An awakened minority: the Mexican Americans*, Beverly Hills, Glencoe Press.

Short, J. R. 1982, *An introduction to political geography*, London, Routledge & Kegan Paul.

Simons, H. J. & Simons, R. E. 1969, *Class & colour in South Africa: 1850–1950*, Harmondsworth, Penguin Books.

Sivanandan, A. 1982, *A different hunger: writings on black resistance*, London, Pluto Press.

Slater, M. 1982, 'Migration, labour markets and social conflict in western Europe: some empirical and theoretical conclusions', paper for European Consortium of Political Research, Workshop, Aarhus, Denmark, 30 March–3 April.

Smith, P. 1978, 'Domestic labour and Marx's theory of value' in A. Kuhn & A. Wolpe (eds) q.v.

Solzhenitsyn, A. 1979, *The Gulag Archipelago: 1918–1956*, London, Fontana.

South African Newsletter (London), periodic handouts from the South African Embassy in London.

Southall, R. 1982, *South Africa's Transkei: the political economy of an 'independent' bantustan*, London, Heinemann Educational Books.

Speer, A. 1981, *The slave state*, London, Weidenfeld & Nicolson.

Stahl, C. W. 1981, 'Migrant labour supplies, past, present and future: with special reference to the gold mining industry' in W. R. Böhning (ed) q.v.

Starobin, R. 1970, *Industrial slavery in the Old South*, New York, Oxford University Press.

Steinbeck, J. 1975, *The grapes of wrath*, London, Pan Books.

Steiner, S. 1974, *The islands: the worlds of the Puerto Ricans*, New York, Harper & Row.

Steiner, S. 1979, *The Mexican Americans*, London, Minority Rights Group, Report No. 39.

Streek, B. & Wicksteed, R. 1981, *Render unto Kaiser: a Transkei dossier*, Johannesburg, Ravan Press.

Swianiewicz, S. 1965, *Forced labour & economic development*, London.

Tarbuck, K.J. 1972, *Imperialism and the accumulation of capital*, Harmondsworth, Allen Lane.

Taylor, J. G. 1979, *From modernisation to modes of production: a critique of the sociologies of development and underdevelopment*, London, Macmillan.

Thomas, B. 1973, *Migration and economic growth: a study of Great Britain and the Atlantic community*, Cambridge, Cambridge University Press.

Thompson, E. 1963, *The making of the English working class*, Harmondsworth, Penguin Books.

Tinker, H. 1974, *A new system of slavery: the export of Indian labour overseas: 1830–1920*, London, Oxford University Press.

Trapido, S. 1971, 'South Africa in a comparative study of industrialisation', *Journal of Development Studies*, vol. 7, no. 3, pp. 309–20.

Tugwell, R. H. 1947, *The stricken land*, Garden City (New York), Doubleday & Company.

Turner, F. J. 1920, *The frontier in American history*, New York, Holt.

Turner, J. K. 1911, *Barbarous Mexico*, London.

United Kingdom Government 1977, *The role of immigrants in the labour market*, Project report for the Unit of Manpower Studies, Department of Employment, London.

United States Department of Justice 1980, *Prevention and control of urban disorders: issues for the 1980's*, Washington DC, Government Printing Office.

United States Department of Labor 1930, 'Unemployment in Puerto Rico, 1928–1929, *Monthly Labor Review*, vol. 31, no. 5, May.

United States Department of Labour 1959, *Farm labor fact book*, Washington, Government Printing Office.

Valdez, L. & Steiner, S. (eds) 1972, *Aztlan: an anthology of Mexican American literature*, New York, Alfred Knopf.

Valentine, C. A. 1968, *Culture and poverty: critique and counter proposals*, Chicago, Chicago University Press.

van der Horst, S. 1971, *Native labour in South Africa*, London, Frank Cass & Co.

van Onselen, C. 1974, 'The 1912 Wankie colliery strike', *Journal of African History*, vol. 15, no. 2, pp. 275–89.

van Onselen, C. 1976, *Chibaro: African mine labour in Southern Rhodesia, 1900–1933*, London, Pluto Press.

van Velsen, J. 1959, 'Labour migration as a positive factor in the continuity of Tonga tribal society', *Economic Development and Cultural Change*, vol. 8, no. 2.

Verbunt, G. 1985, 'France' in T. Hammer (ed), *European immigration policy*, Cambridge, Cambridge University Press.

Vicioso, C. 1976, 'Dominican migration to the US', *Migration Today*, (Geneva), no. 20, pp. 59–72.

von Welhof, C. 1980, 'Notes on the relation between sexuality and economy', *Review*, vol. 4, no. 1.

Wachter, M. L. 1978, 'Second thoughts about illegal immigrants', *Fortune*, 22 May, pp. 78–86.

Wages Commission (n.d.), *Riekert: don't worry, everything's okay*, mimeographed pamphlet, Students Representative Council, University of Cape Town.

Wallerstein, I. 1974, *The modern world system: capitalist agriculture and the origins of the European world economy in the sixteenth century*, New York, Academic Press.

Wallerstein, I. 1979, *The capitalist world-economy*, Cambridge, Cambridge University Press.

Warren, B. 1980, *Imperialism: pioneer of capitalism*, London, Verso.

Warwick, P. 1981, 'Black industrial protest on the Witwatersrand, 1901–1902', in E. Webster (ed) *Essays in South African labour history*, Johannesburg, Ravan Press, pp. 20–31.

Watson, W. 1958, *Tribal cohesion in a money economy*, Manchester, Manchester University Press.

Webster, D. J. 1977, 'The origins of migrant labour, colonialism and the underdevelopment of Mozambique' in P. L. Bonner (ed) *Working papers in southern Africa*, Johannesburg, African Studies Institute, University of the Witwatersrand, pp. 236–79.

Webster, D. J. 1978, 'Migrant labour, social formation and the proletarianisation of the Chopi of southern Africa', *African Perspectives*, vol. 1, pp. 157–74.

Williams, G. 1985, 'Taking the part of peasants: rural development in Nigeria and Tanzania', in P. C. W. Gutkind & I. Wallerstein (eds) *Political economy of contemporary Africa*, Beverly Hills, Sage, pp. 144–80.

Wilson, F. 1972, *Labour in the South African gold mines, 1911–1969*, London, Cambridge University Press.

Wilson, F. 1981, Talk on 'Changes in South Africa' at Warwick University, 29 April 1983.

Wilson, G. 1941–1942, 'An essay on the economics of detribalisation in Northern Rhodesia', Parts 1 and 2, *Rhodes-Livingstone Papers*, no. 5 and no. 6.

Wilson, M. *et al.* 1952, *Social structure: the Keiskammahok rural survey vol. III*, Pietermaritzburg, Shuter & Schuter.

Wolf, E. R. 1982, *Europe and the people without history*, Berkeley, University of California Press.

Wolpe, H. 1972, 'Capitalism and cheap labour–power in South Africa: from segregation to apartheid', *Economy and Society*, vol. 1, no. 4, November, pp. 425–56.

Womack, J. 1979, 'The historiography of Mexican labour' in E. C. Frost *et al.* (eds) q.v.

Worsley, P. 1973, *The Third World*, London, Weidenfeld & Nicolson.

Young, K. *et al.* (eds) 1981, *Of marriage and the market: women's subordination in international perspective*, London, CSE Books.

Zolberg, A. 1981, 'International migrations in political perspective' in M. M. Kritz *et al.* (eds) q.v.

Index

281

282

Kuwait 247